THE
MYTH
OF LAZINESS

Mel Levine, M.D.

SIMON & SCHUSTER

NEW YORK   LONDON   TORONTO   SYDNEY   SINGAPORE

SIMON & SCHUSTER
Rockefeller Center
1230 Avenue of the Americas
New York, NY 10020

For information regarding special discounts for bulk purchases,
please contact Simon & Schuster Special Sales at 1-800-456-6798 or
business@simonandschuster.com

Designed by Karolina Harris

Manufactured in the United States of America

1   3   5   7   9   10   8   6   4   2

Library of Congress Cataloging-in-Publication Data is available.

ISBN 0-7432-1367-X

To Leonard, Eileen, and Keith—they were mentors and an abiding cheering squad whose interest in my output enabled me to discover that effort was worth the effort while I was growing up. And to Pamela, who could herself write the definitive book on the art of raising a challenging child.

ACKNOWLEDGMENTS

Many individuals contributed to the output of *The Myth of Laziness*. My wife, Bambi, as usual, was patiently tolerant when I seemed wedded to the keyboard. She also offered her wise advice, much aided by her possession of the world's most richly wired prefrontal lobes!

I thank the board and the many generous donors to All Kinds of Minds, our nonprofit institute for the understanding of differences in learning, which continues its intelligent and fervent crusade to help children and adolescents who contend with vexing learning but have minds that are worth redeeming and celebrating. I am very appreciative of the support and leadership of Mark Grayson and Mike Florio, both of whom have guided our institute with brilliance and zeal. Their work and mine has been so ably brought to fruition by Dr. Craig Pohlman, Mary Dean Baringer, Stacy Fisher Parker, Ann Hobgood, and Donna Yerby. We all have benefited from the technical genius and managerial output of Jeff Lowe. I am always appreciative, too, of the unwavering leadership of my boss, Dean Jeffrey Houpt.

I also want to acknowledge my numerous heroic patients who, over the decades, have taught me most of what I know about the ways of learning and producing and about the obstacles all of us have to face in living with our own wiring.

My assistant, Pam McBane, has played her usual valiant role in the creation of this book. I also am grateful to Janet Furman for her talented assistance with the illustrations.

Much credit is due Bob Bender, my brilliant editor at Simon & Schuster. I think he's as good as they get—most likely better. He has taught me that criticism is a form of dialogue. I am also indebted to Lane Zachary, who is more than a top literary agent; her judgment and advice are indispensable. I feel grateful to David Rosenthal, publisher of Simon & Schuster, and to Ruth Fecych for their lucid vision and affable leadership—and for ensuring that some goose silhouettes were granted safe passage into the pages of this volume.

Meanwhile, back on the farm, a critically important mode of output in my eccentric life, I thank Mr. David Taylor, who is so skilled and dependable at looking after our too many animals when I am on the road (i.e., almost every week) and at compensating for my own complete absence of any mechanical aptitude (a potentially paralyzing dysfunction on a farm). Finally, I want to thank those loving creatures who contribute so much deep meaning to my own existence, including Rose the mule; Rescue Fantasy, the twenty-year-old Appaloosa; Susanna, the loving and loyal jenny whose father abused her as a baby; and the more than two hundred geese, fifteen mammoth donkeys, fourteen swans, forty-five pheasants, twelve peacocks, six dogs, and six Maine coon cats who make up our high-output, highly vocal animal extended family on Sanctuary Farm.

CONTENTS

PROLOGUE:
THE MYTH OF SISYPHUS

Sisyphus, who founded the city of Corinth . . . witnessed the abduction of young Aegina, daughter of Asopus, at the hand of Zeus and revealed the name of the abductor to the girl's father. . . . When at last he died at a great age, the gods made haste to give him a task that would hold him prisoner. He had to roll an enormous rock up a mountain and, when it reached the top, the rock rolled down to the bottom and Sisyphus' task began at the beginning again.

—Pierre Grimal, "Greece: Myth and Logic" in
Larousse World Mythology

In Greek mythology, King Sisyphus of Corinth witnessed Zeus's abduction of Aegina and told her father, the river god Asopus, who was searching for his lost daughter. Although Sisyphus was merely a bystander, his disclosure angered the other gods, who unjustly condemned him to spend eternity using his hands and his head to roll a mammoth boulder up a mountain in the underworld, repeating the arduous task over and over again.

Countless desperate children and adults are the modern-day versions of Sisyphus as they toil with their hands and their heads but fail to reach the hoped-for summits of performance in school and in the workplace. And so often they, too, are unjustly accused, in their case, of laziness. They, like Sisyphus, are innocent victims who deserve our sympathy and understanding, for they possess minds that learn and think better than they work. They may radiate brilliance when it comes to logical thinking, humor, and the social skills. But what they produce or the effort they put forth falls short of expectations—the expectations of their parents, their teachers, their bosses. For them, work doesn't work. Like Sisyphus, they feel as if they are getting nowhere as they toil. Their low or nonexistent productivity is not their fault, not in the least intentional. Yet, like Sisyphus, they are often blamed and even punished for crimes they never committed.

THE
MYTH
OF LAZINESS

1

GETTING A MIND TO WORK

Lily O'Grady,
Silly and shady,
Longing to be
A lazy lady, . . .
—Edith Sitwell, "Popular Song," *Façades* (1922)

Laziness is not an innate trait. We all are born with a drive to produce, and like saplings growing in an orchard, we have within us the resources to bear fruit, to be and to feel useful and effective. Most of our own success and that of our children is experienced and demonstrated through accomplishments, the attainments of our heads and our hands, the sum total of our school, family, and career contributions. From early in childhood on through our adult years, we want to show what we can do. We gain energy and feel good about ourselves whenever our personal output wins the approval, the acceptance, the respect of our friends, our families, our bosses (or teachers), and, most of all, our own self-critical selves. To feel fulfilled in life, it helps immeasurably if you can take pride in your work.

Some individuals somehow, somewhere lose momentum; in the pursuit of accomplishment they fail to produce; they stall out. And often they face accusations of laziness. In truth, through no fault of their own, they suffer from hidden handicaps that disrupt and interrupt their output. They are not lazy; they have output failure.

The power and the vulnerability of the drive to be productive are frequently neglected. I believe that adults and children alike feel that a large part of who they are comes from what they do, particularly what they have produced or are producing, and what they aspire to achieve in the future. Casualties result when individuals have output failure and come to believe that their work is worthless and perhaps never will be worthy. Our society pays an exorbitant price to restore their mental health, to punish them within our justice system, to deal with their underemployment, and to cope with the many other negative effects of their thwarted drives toward success.

WHEN WORK IS WORKING

On the positive side, there are countless diverse ways to savor recognition and personal satisfaction from high-quality output. Garnering rave reviews for your leading role in a musical comedy, scoring a hat trick in hockey, getting mostly A's on your term papers in religious studies, raising a well-adjusted child, and successfully replacing the gasket in a car engine are among the varied instances of output success. No one can emerge productive in all fields of endeavor, any more than any single piece of high-tech apparatus can accomplish all of the chores around the house. Each of us is destined to exhibit one or more personal forms of productivity. What matters is whether the necessary mind and body assembly lines are operating the way they should. Are you doing what must get done? Are the resulting products of sufficiently high quality? Are you generating *enough* output or are you putting forth a feeble trickle of inadequate stuff? In other words, is your work working?

THE EASILY AND OFTEN MISUNDERSTOOD BREAKDOWNS: OUTPUT VIRUSES

Thanks to progress in the neurosciences and related fields, we have learned a great deal about brain wiring, including how, when, and where it operates. As a developmental-behavioral pediatrician specializing in learning differences, I have spent three decades concentrating on the varied and often subtle breakdowns within a developing brain that trip up basically bright children during their school years. In particular, I have studied the wide spectrum of dysfunctions, the very numerous discrete weaknesses that deprive so many students of success. Kids afflicted with these difficulties are the innocent victims of their own wiring. They have specific shortcomings in areas of the mind that control essential aspects of memory, language, attention, motor function, and other processes required for mastery of school subjects. The gaps in these areas are called neurodevelopmental dysfunctions. Some are inborn, some acquired. Some are mainly genetically caused; some stem principally from environmental conditions. But most dysfunctions are mysterious, of unknown origin. I have described the wide array of these heartbreaking limitations in my book *A Mind at a Time*.

Many students wrestle with learning problems that are totally transparent. They manifest obvious trouble becoming good readers, mastering computations in mathematics, succeeding on scholastic aptitude tests, or surviving the social demands of the school day. But there is a substantial group with hidden miswiring, and they have been woefully neglected and misunderstood. These are individuals who struggle with output failure, a phenomenon that can decimate their productivity in school and cause some to fail in the workplace as adults.

At first glance, kids and grown-ups with output failure may seem entirely competent—so much so that they tantalize us with their abundant intellectual promise. But then that promise isn't kept. Often these individuals absorb and process information well; they learn, but they don't produce. They keep promising and intending to do things, but they seldom come through. In most instances, they can read far better than they can write, and they can interpret information but somehow can't put what they learn to productive use. It seems as if they have working disabilities; they are unable to get their minds to work! So their intake greatly exceeds their output, and they disappoint themselves even more than they disappoint others. People say glibly that they are not "living up to their potential."

THE ORIGIN OF THE TERM "OUTPUT FAILURE"

In the early years of my clinical practice, I was struck by the sizable number of children referred to me who learned more effectively than they worked. I saw a particular concentration of such students cropping up during their middle school years—when there often is a dramatic upsurge in the demands for high output of high quality (particularly in the form of writing). These students had in common their inability to meet the intensified production demands. They became less and less successful as students. As I got to know them, I kept having flashbacks to my medical school days when we learned about "cardiac high-output failure." The following quotation from the sixteenth edition of Nelson's *Textbook of Pediatrics* captures the common phenomenon: "The condition, high-output failure, produces the signs and symptoms of heart failure . . . when the demand for cardiac output exceeds the ability of the heart to respond. Chronic severe high-output failure may ultimately result in a decrease in myocardial [i.e., heart muscle] performance." Perhaps because of hardening of the arteries or high blood pressure, the heart is forced to work too hard. Eventually the organ weakens. The failing heart becomes dilated, its beats increasingly feeble, so it is unable to fulfill adequately its blood-pumping role, its output job. The same cycle can pertain to a mind, one that has become ineffective— when the demands upon it keep on exceeding its output capacities. When a mind is forced to strain excessively to meet production demands, academic output failure may ensue. Incidentally, we don't call a failing heart lazy.

In 1981 I and two of my colleagues wrote an article entitled "Developmental Output Failure in School-Aged Children" for the medical journal *Pediatrics*. We described a group of students with various forms of output failure. Since then I have continued to study this too often neglected or misunderstood phenomenon.

OUTPUT FAILURE AS A WIDESPREAD PHENOMENON

Output failure is not a distinct syndrome, nor should it be understood as any sort of label or category. It is a result, not a cause. Low output occurs when one or more neurodevelopmental dysfunctions interfere with productivity. This is a very common phenomenon, examples of which include trouble writing a report or difficulty completing a project. Students who manifest output failure are a heterogeneous group. They have a mixed bag of neurodevelopmental dysfunctions and strengths. Some have serious problems getting organized. Others find it too hard to put their thoughts into words. There are those who can't deploy their muscles in a coordinated, efficient manner. Still others lack the mental energy, the stamina needed for output. Some may experience problems remembering. But all of them face one or more high hurdles stubbornly obstructing their pathways to successful output. For the most part, their actual output barriers are seldom identified and dealt with. Instead, too many of these students stand unjustly accused of laziness or charged with some other form of moral turpitude. And they unfairly assume the blame for their reduced output.

Output failure is by no means confined to the first twenty-one years of life. The condition plagues numerous adults as well and very commonly leads to chronic career underachievement and gnawing discontent. We all know of individuals who seem competent and well meaning but whose productivity in the workplace is inadequate, perhaps even unacceptable. It may be the plumber who took forever and did a shoddy job fixing your bathtub drain, or the accountant who had to keep applying for extensions because he couldn't get to your taxes, or a coworker who triggered bitter resentment because she never accomplished her fair share of the workload. It may be the person who comes up with great ideas but never carries any of them out. A traditional military adage applies here; as the commanding officer says to his platoon, "The people who rise out of the ranks are the ones who can get the job done." Like students with output failure, the countless adults who cannot seem to get the job done deserve our understanding and our compassion. They are not intentionally turning off their spigots of output. Branding them as lazy accomplishes nothing.

The Myth of Laziness is intended to shed much-needed light on the phenomenon of output failure. As it explores the dysfunctions that result in output failure, this book will uncover some of the principal ingredients of successful output. Because I am a pediatrician and the bulk of my clinical experience has been confined to the five- to eighteen-year-old age group, most of what I have to say will concern productivity in school. However, I will also devote attention to some adult mechanisms and manifestations of output failure. Often the identical neurodevelopmental dysfunctions that thwart output in children can lethally affect adult productivity, too. A child may fail to do homework because she lacks mental energy. An adult with low mental energy may often be late to or absent from work because she has agonizing difficulty getting out of bed in the morning. An adolescent exhibiting problems with time management in school may be the equivalent of an adult who is always late for appointments and often running behind— perhaps without even realizing it.

Over a lifetime, the course of output failure may vary. Some individuals seem condemned to lifelong frustration with productivity. The problems they endured in school return to haunt them throughout their careers. In other cases, children with output failure become successful and remarkably productive adults in their chosen niches. Still others may develop signs of output failure as adolescents or as adults despite having created their share of praiseworthy products at an earlier time of life. As the demands on them change, as people themselves change, as their environments change, their output can change—for better or for worse.

CHILDHOOD VERSUS ADULTHOOD

As we try to comprehend output success and failure through someone's life, we need to reckon with a fundamental difference between childhood and adulthood. When you're a child, you are expected to be competent in many basic fields. You're commanded to be a good writer, a decent artist, a competent athlete, and an astute mathematician. You are evaluated daily on the quality and quantity and even the speed of your output across these diverse territories. Luckily, once your education is completed, you are unshackled and permitted to pick your own output pathways, to choose and work on those you prefer. And, not at all coincidentally, you are likely to opt for what works best for you. What a relief! That's one reason I tell my pediatric patients with learning differences that it's going to be ten times easier to be an adult than a kid!

Unfortunately, some people who chose their careers contend with unexpected barriers to productivity. That's often because most young adults don't fully grasp their own strengths and weaknesses, nor do they have a lucid picture of the demands that lie ahead in their chosen fields. In my work I pay a great deal of attention to a person's neurodevelopmental profile, that individual's spreadsheet of neurodevelopmental strengths and weaknesses. Unfortunately, a person with weak social skills may be lured into a career pathway that is highly political, such as a government job. A medical student with subtle motor problems affecting his dexterity may become infatuated with the specialty of surgery. Someone who has always had trouble expressing herself may opt to become a trial lawyer. These poor fits occur all the time, revealing a potentially lethal hidden discrepancy between a person's interests and his or her abilities. The result may be output failure.

WHAT'S RIDING ON WRITING

Through my years of research and clinical work, I have found that difficulty with writing is far and away the most telling sign of output failure during the childhood and teenage years. The majority of my patients with output failure have serious difficulty getting their thoughts down on paper. Many also have other signs of low output, such as trouble doing projects, completing homework in general, or making oral presentations, but almost all of them falter and fail when it comes to writing. For that reason, *The Myth of Laziness* will emphasize difficulty with writing as a conspicuous reflection of deficient productivity among students.

In contrast, many adult careers require a minimum of writing. In many fields, the writing burden consists only of such elementary challenges as filling out forms, producing brief memoranda, or making lists. Not many adults regularly write lengthy reports, probing essays, or creative stories. Yet I have seen many instances across a broad range of careers where people with writing difficulties during childhood ultimately had trouble completing very different demanding challenges on the job.

Why is writing such a stringent test of output capacity during the school years? I suspect it's because there's no other requirement that demands the coordination and integration of so many different neurodevelopmental functions and academic subskills. Just think about it: writing requires you to generate good ideas, organize your thoughts, encode your ideas into clear language, remember many things at once (such as spelling, rules of punctuation, facts, and instructions), coordinate your fingers so they can keyboard or form letters, plan and monitor the quality of your work, and marshal the materials you need (pencils, reference books, or computer equipment) and your time. Writing also requires a great deal of concentration and mental effort. It takes energy and fortitude to complete a term paper. Intense focus is called for in answering an essay question well. All of those simultaneous demands must then be smoothly integrated and synchronized to achieve writing success.

Writing is the largest orchestra a kid's mind has to conduct. So it shouldn't surprise us that if one or more of the instruments are lacking, their absence will seriously undermine that student's papers. For the most part, kids with output failure hate to write, but in truth, they are fearful of writing.

Since writing plays such a trivial role in most careers, why should we fret over it during youth? Perhaps some kids simply should be granted writing waivers! No, I don't really believe that, although it's not an absurd notion. I think that the very fact that writing is so complex justifies its leading role in a curriculum. By writing, a kid learns how to mesh multiple brain functions, and ultimately that's something you need to do well whatever you do to earn a living. In a sense, the act of writing helps build and maintain the brain pathways that connect diverse functions, such as language, memory, and motor control. In other words, writing is a great way for a kid to practice getting his act together.

Writing also serves as a platform for systematic thinking and a means of problem solving, two more abilities needed in any career. There's an old adage: "How can I know what I think until I read what I write?" Writing forces a student to think out loud and to communicate that thinking in a way others can grasp.

Although I'm certain it is the largest, writing is by no means the only big orchestra a kid gets to conduct. Playing soccer, participating in a marching band, and building a model rocket ship also require getting numerous brain functions to work together. Yet students whose teachers demand minimal writing, as well as those whose written output is a trickle at best, are educationally deprived. They may be less prepared to produce as adults.

THE ABUNDANT SOURCES OF GRATIFICATION

I am not arguing that productivity in school or at work is the sole source of gratification and happiness in life. Nor am I saying that people with low levels of output are condemned to lives of abject misery. There are other ways to be a happy person. Having positive relationships, being altruistic, living a rich spiritual life, enjoying one's family, excelling at partying, and loving to read are but a few of the limitless potential sources of gratification in life. Nevertheless, feeling productive, showing off a product line in which you can take pride, and reaping recognition for your output are major sources of satisfaction and meaning in your life. I have seen way too many adolescents and young adults get into serious trouble as a result of chronic success deprivation. They are the ones who after years of having nothing to show for their efforts have decided to cancel all effort or to commit themselves to self-destructive or perhaps even illegal activities. Individuals with output failure all too often are tragedies in the making. They need our compassion, help, and understanding.

THE MYTH OF LAZINESS

When we call someone lazy, we condemn a human being. I am convinced that laziness is nothing more than a myth—hence the title of this book. Everybody yearns to be productive. Every kid would prefer to do his homework and be praised for its quality. Every grown-up would like to generate output that merits a raise or a promotion. It's all part of a natural search for both recognition and self-satisfaction. As I've said, it's a basic drive. Therefore, when someone's output is too low, we shouldn't accuse or blame that individual. Instead, we should wonder what could be thwarting that person's output, obstructing his or her natural inborn inclination to produce.

There are constructive ways to help children and grown-ups with output failure. There's even more we can do to prevent output failure. But to be most effective, we have to both understand what it takes to be productive and identify the specific weaknesses that trip up so many people. Over the course of these pages, I will delve into the lives of eight individuals whose output has been inadequate. Each will illustrate a different underlying mechanism for low productivity. Many academicians equate learning difficulty with reading problems, but the individuals described in this book were all basically good readers throughout their elementary school years. Yet they underachieved dramatically when it came to output.

I will explore the roles of such neurodevelopmental areas as motor function, memory, language, and organization as they either contribute richly to output or fall short and result in output failure. The stories are drawn from the experiences of real individuals I have met during the more than thirty years I have devoted to understanding human development and repairing its glitches. Names and other identifying details have been substantially modified to preserve these persons' privacy. In some cases I have combined individuals with the same neurodevelopmental dysfunction into a composite character.

As you can tell, *The Myth of Laziness* is based largely on my own career as a passionate clinician who has specialized in children's learning and students' valiant quests for success. The book also reflects my extensive experience working with schools all over the world. I have been influenced heavily by research in the neurosciences, in education, and in other fields related to learning and differences in learning. However, I have benefited most of all from what the children and their parents have taught me. So this volume is not a review of the scientific litera-ture; it is primarily a close examination and interpretation of what I have heard and seen. *The Myth of Laziness* is intended to offer help and hope to those with output failure and to provide some practical ways to im-munize all individuals against it.

2
RUSSELL STRINBERG:

A Case of Low Motor Turnout

I get the ideas going. Then I write down, I copy out of any books that stimulate me at the time many quotations and I keep it. And I put down the source. Then when it comes to the actual work, I keep a complete record of the steps. I keep every note of every dance I have . . . I just put it down and know what the words mean, or what the movements mean.

—MARTHA GRAHAM, QUOTED IN HOWARD GARDNER, *CREATING MINDS*

Enough, if something from our hands have power
To live, and act, and serve the future hour.

—WILLIAM WORDSWORTH, "AFTER-THOUGHT"

On that mid-October evening, Russell's parents sensed that some flames were burning out of control within his mind. His usual gluttonous appetite at the dinner table and habitual talkativeness were absent. Dr. and Mrs. Strinberg had commented a few nights earlier that Russell seemed "out of sorts." Over a period of weeks, they had observed their eleven-year-old son shrinking into an increasingly quiet and lethargic state. He seemed to be spending too much of his time passively immersed in one or another totally immobile calorie-conserving activity— not at all good for a boy who was already overweight. He had even lost interest in his video games. But at this particular meal, Russell, their only child, seemed to be clouded in a dense vapor, unresponsive to their conversational initiatives and standard inquiries about the day's events in school. This was truly odd, since if nothing else Russell was a world-class conversationalist and an avid narrator of personal experiences.

Suddenly, Russell looked up from his glass bowl of boysenberry sherbet and announced in a slow monotone, "I've been thinking about killing myself. I don't want to live anymore. I don't have any reasons to live. I hate school. I hate the other kids. I even hate myself. I love you both." His parents, of course, were stunned and horrified. Russell got up and fled to his bedroom, pursued by two frantic grown-ups. For more than an hour they sat at his bedside, soothing their son without knowing what they were consoling him about, expressing their love and respect for him while intermittently interrogating the boy in an effort to uncover the source of his sadness. Not a clue; Russell was not forthcoming and instead kept requesting solitude ("Please leave me alone"), a demand the Strinbergs were not about to grant. Actually, they took turns sleeping in Russell's room for the next seven or eight nights.

The morning after the confession, his father requested an emergency psychiatric evaluation at the community hospital where he was the chief of cardiology. The boy saw a child psychiatrist, Dr. Joe Pinkham, late that morning. Russell communicated nothing during this fifty-minute interview; he wouldn't even make eye contact with the soft-spoken therapist. He mumbled his responses and was noncommittal—the child was "in denial." Dr. Pinkham diagnosed depression and put Russell on two different psychoactive medications. He cautioned the parents to monitor him closely and called Russell's school to request their vigilance, as well as any diagnostic observations they might be able to offer. Russell's teacher and the school psychologist were plainly surprised; they had been aware of no difficulty, except that Russell was having chronic problems achieving in certain subjects and had not been turning in his homework with any regularity. Actually, this was news to no one; the Strinbergs had been told about his unreliability regularly in recent years. Grace Murphy, his fifth-grade teacher, noting the apparent paradox, described Russell as "no doubt one of the smartest students in our school."

Dr. Pinkham continued to see Russell, who seemed to be less agitated on the medication and no longer talked about suicide. The boy consistently appeared preoccupied yet reticent to divulge much of anything. It was actually the school psychologist, Dr. Tom Williams, who seemed to unplug the emotional dike when he was called to see Russell because of his strident refusal to suit up for his gym class.

Russell was noticeably agitated as he steadfastly refused to go to physical education. Tom Williams virtually pleaded with Russell to reveal why he was so unwilling. Russell kept saying, "I don't know. I'm just not going." But after nearly fifteen minutes of defiant denial, Russell admitted, "It's embarrassing. They all make fun of me because I'm fat and because I can't catch and throw a ball as well as they can. And I can't run as fast either. I look stupid when I run. And I make tons of dumb mistakes when we play sports. They call me real bad names a lot, too." Then Russell put his face in his hands. "I don't feel like talking about it anymore." Dr. Williams tried to reassure Russell, saying that there were many great kids who had trouble playing sports and that when you grow up no one cares how fabulously you catch and throw a ball. The psychologist even confessed his own chronic athletic ineptitude. But all this professional reassurance appeared to make no impression whatsoever on Russell.

Dr. Williams communicated his finding to Russell's therapist, Dr. Pinkham, who discussed Russell's athletic shortcomings with the boy on several occasions. It was evident that the recurring humiliation in gym had carved a hefty wedge out of Russell's self-esteem. But that was not the whole story.

As Russell became more candid, he talked about an incident that had occurred the previous August during his summer vacation. His cousins had invited Russell to come with them and a few of their friends to the town swimming pool to have some fun and defeat the ninety-degree heat. The boys went to change in the locker room. When Russell disrobed to put on his bathing suit, the three other kids started laughing at the very small size of his genitals. Sporting my pediatrician's cap, I can say that it is not at all unusual for obese boys like Russell to appear to have a seemingly small penis because the organ is buried in what is called a prepubic fat pad. The phenomenon is quite normal, but it understandably engenders some anxiety. That certainly occurred in Russell's case when the other boys started laughing in derision, and one remarkably insensitive juvenile commented, "Look how small Russell's thing is. It's tiny; you can't hardly see it. He'll never be able to make a baby with that. He's, like, almost a girl." Laughter and giggling further saturated the humid atmosphere, but soon all was forgotten—that is, forgotten by everyone except poor Russell. Combined with his poor athletic performance and his conspicuously pudgy figure, this low blow really made him wonder if he was a "real man."

Russell's self-doubt was heavily fortified by the fact that for years he'd been awakening each morning in a puddle of urine; he was a chronic bed wetter. He felt terribly ashamed of his enuresis. In other words,

Russell's body image was about as diminished as it gets. This was occurring at a time when most kids are starting to become heavily self-conscious about their body development. Russell was able to talk about all of this only scantily with Dr. Pinkham; it was exceedingly painful for him to discuss it at all. At one point he sobbed and asked, "Why did God give me such an awful body to live in?" The experience in the locker room also reminded Russell of the many times in school he had been called "fatty" and "blimp," as well as a catalog of other cruel, physically derisive labels. Recently some kids had been taunting him and threatening to "get him after school." Russell had begun to live in terror of his peers.

The evening when Russell told his parents he was contemplating ending his life was the culmination of many months of simmering anxiety and gnawing feelings of worthlessness. Yes, Russell was depressed, but with good reason in the world of eleven-year-old values and life experiences.

To make matters worse, Russell was not achieving up to par in school. And that is how I got to know this boy. Dr. Pinkham asked me to evaluate Russell to see if he had "some kind of learning difference" that might be causing him to earn poor grades in school.

I and other members of a multidisciplinary team at our Center for Development and Learning in Chapel Hill evaluated Russell. We harvested useful information about this boy from a careful review of his history. Currently, early in the fifth grade, Russell was reported to be reading at the level of a late sixth grader and was equally advanced in all areas of mathematics. However, he appeared guilty of negligence when it came to completing any written assignments, including math homework. He hated to write and often would falsely deny that he had homework to do. Typically, he would say, "No, I did it all in school." When he was forced to write in class, it was evident that getting thoughts down on paper was a traumatic ordeal for this kid. He wrote slowly, and his legibility was a challenge for any reader to decrypt. Even Russell sometimes had problems reading his handwriting. His letters were formed laboriously; nothing seemed automatic when it came to the motor aspects of writing. His brain dissipated all its resources on forming the individual letters, leaving nothing for spacing, punctuation, or other such details. A typical sample of his writing can be seen in Figure 2-1. At his age, most kids can make letters unconsciously and rapidly—not Russell. At least this year, his teacher had been letting him print. Last year, when he had been forced to write in cursive, he'd felt trounced at school and drained of all motivation.

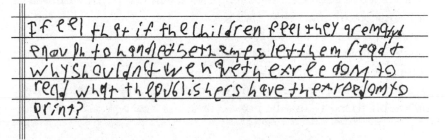

Figure 2-1.   This example of Russell's written output reveals his awkward letter formation and spacing. Although at this point he had mastered individual printed letters, his symbols are inconsistent in their style, and he has trouble staying on the lines, spelling, and punctuating while writing. Incidentally, when instructed to do so, Russell could insert the proper capitalization and punctuation, showing that he knew the rules but could not apply them at the same time that he was struggling to remember how to make the letters. The sample above took Russell more than eight minutes to write.

Complicating matters was the fact that Russell was never at a loss for words and ideas, thoughts that made him sound like an assistant professor skyrocketing up a tenure track. His bubbly mind was like a hot spring. In science class Russell was the leader at synthesizing all kinds of original ideas and cogent insights. For example, he became fascinated with the study of gravity and was attempting to design a car whose engine worked by converting gravitational pull into energy (sounds good to me). His parents described how Russell had created his own science laboratory in their basement, where he would spend hours on end tinkering with such items as electronic components, the disassembled innards of an old toaster, and rusty parts of a long-deceased sewing machine. He loved making fanciful animals and cars out of these remnants.

It seemed that whatever he did was strikingly creative. But it was close to impossible for Russell to convey all this magnificent thinking on paper. There was a paralyzing disparity between the speed and richness with which this boy could generate ideas and encode them into language, on the one hand, and the inefficiency of his efforts to get his fingers to form written words, on the other. As a result, he had to labor so hard on the motor aspects of writing, devoting a massive share of his attention to letter formation, that he would forget, unconsciously cut short, or simplify his thinking and his sentence structure. His teachers commented regularly on the incredible difference between Russell's brilliant ideas during a class discussion and the very skimpy, primitive, "immature" content of his written reports. For a long time they blamed this on simple laziness, a diagnosis with which, for several years, his parents reluctantly concurred. Thus, Russell kept hearing the shaming put-down "You can do better, and you could certainly do better if you'd only apply yourself." But the poor kid was not lazy; he was battling output failure.

THE POSSIBLE MOTOR OBSTACLES— FIGURING OUT RUSSELL

Whenever I encounter a kid with low output, like Russell, I work much as a detective does to solve a perplexing mystery. In my Sherlock Holmes role, I am called in to figure out where the breakdown is occurring when a person has low levels of output. The detective role can then lead to effective treatment. If you can identify the problem precisely, it's a lot easier to fix it. That was my assignment in Russell's case. I went about my work, keeping in mind the potential neurodevelopmental obstacles to output and trying to find which of these affected this boy.

Our educational tests confirmed that Russell was an outstanding reader and a very capable mathematician. I was impressed that he had a remarkably active, inquisitive, exploring mind. He was awesome at conceptualizing not only in science but also in the humanities. I asked him to talk about a book he had just read, *The War of the Worlds.* I was taken by his clever interpretation and his ability to put himself into a book and actively elaborate on its content. I thought this was strong evidence that Russell's verbal abilities and his capacity to organize his thoughts were pretty much intact. According to his teachers and his parents, he also showed strong memory function. Additionally, there were no signs that Russell was experiencing breakdowns in his attention. So I was pretty sure we had ruled out several common causes of apparent laziness.

I performed a neurodevelopmental examination on Russell. The findings were generally consistent with his history. He turned out to have excellent language abilities both in the understanding of linguistic inputs and in his own oral communication. Russell also displayed strengths in his visual memory for designs as well as many other operations calling for filing and retrieving information. Throughout our testing he came up with all kinds of excellent strategies. For example, he often whispered under his breath to help himself remember things that were said to him. He seemed to be highly effective at planning his work and monitoring the quality of his output. On several tasks he discovered his own errors and corrected them without being told to do so. He revealed no difficulty whatsoever with his attention. So Russell obviously was endowed with a good many important strengths.

Several areas of dysfunction became apparent during my assessment. First and foremost, Russell exhibited some very specific motor dysfunction. He was frustrated repeatedly by tasks that involved moving his fingers rapidly and in a particular sequence. Such movements were slow and effortful. Additionally, he could never seem to remember the order, which finger to move when. When I went over a motor pattern several times with him, Russell was able to remember it, but his movements still were slow and labored. Thus, I concluded that he was having trouble not only remembering motor patterns but also actually implementing them smoothly—two barriers thwarting Russell's written output. At one point I asked him to bend his index and ring fingers while keeping the other three digits straight. After several futile attempts, he used his other hand to pull down his index and ring fingers.

When I watched Russell write, it was clear that he could not rapidly and dependably recall the sequences of muscle movements required for letter formation. Therefore his writing was hesitant, the letters poorly formed. As if to compensate for his lack of control over its unruly wanderings on the page, he held the pencil much too tightly and too far down near its point. He told me he often got "writer's cramp," and I could see why.

One very interesting but not unusual finding emerged during Russell's testing. I gave him a very complicated design to study and then asked him simply to copy it. His reproduction of the image was good— as you can see in Figure 2-2. The lines were reasonably straight, the intersections precise, and his proportions within the complex pattern were nearly perfect.

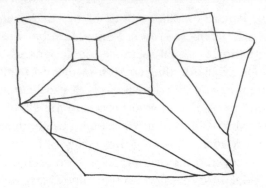

Figure 2-2.   Russell's reproduction of a complex design reveals generally good pencil control and an appreciation of the spatial relationships within the overall design.

So Russell's fingers worked far more obediently when drawing than when writing. He was showing us a discrepancy between his fine motor function, which was effective, and his graphomotor function (the aggregation of motor abilities needed for letter formation), which wasn't at all good. I'll account for that difference later in this chapter. (By the way, Dr. and Mrs. Strinberg had mentioned to me that Russell was their "Mr. Fixit" around the house. Several months previously, they'd had their broken vacuum cleaner repaired, but it had stopped functioning again after only two days. On his own, Russell had taken it apart, diagnosed the problem, and reassembled the appliance. It has been operating dependably ever since his intervention. That pair of hands seemed to have good mechanical aptitude as well.)

When I tested Russell's gross motor abilities, I could see right off why sports were such an embarrassment for him. He had serious trouble using spatial information to direct a gross motor act, which is what you need to do in order to catch or deflect a ball in flight. He mentioned to me as an aside that he'd always had trouble understanding directions from his gym teacher. I later realized that Russell could understand verbal information from all of his teachers except the coach. I could sympathize with the confusion and pained humiliation he must have endured in physical education classes because I'd faced the same plight as a kid. Russell and I, both good linguists, had trouble tying a verbal input to a motor output. I've encountered this phenomenon in many children with effective language functioning but inept athletic performance.

Also, Russell could not recall on demand the motor sequences for specific parts of gross motor performance. You have to move certain muscles in the right order to dribble a basketball, serve a volleyball, putt a golf ball, or swim a backstroke. Motor sequences were allocated no space in Russell's brain. He had trouble perceiving them, observing movements in a particular order and really appreciating that order. So if a coach demonstrated a multistep motor activity, it made no impression on Russell. In contrast, this boy did not have problems dealing with sequencing that spared his muscles. He could recall a long series of numbers in the right order and had no difficulty retelling a story in a logical narrative sequence. He also had readily mastered the steps in mathematical procedures such as long division. This kid simply could not select and direct the right large and small muscles to move in a particular sequential order to fulfill many motor requirements. He could not tie his sequencing abilities to a motor action. As a younger child, not surprisingly, it had taken a lot of practice for him to learn to tie his shoelaces. Incidentally, although Russell and I shared the same liabilities when it came to sports, unlike him, I was inept with fine motor tasks but had no serious trouble with graphomotor function. There are so many ways minds can vary in their output.

As a result of my testing I was certain that Russell was engaged in a losing battle with some noncompliant muscles! But I still needed to know more, since there are a number of different ways in which motor dysfunctions can impede output. To think through this boy's specific muscular blockades, I applied a scheme that depicts the steps in a motor act such as catching a football or forming the letter *y*. I used this method to determine which step or steps were problematic for Russell, as I've done with other kids who have coordination problems thwarting output.

HOW WE PINPOINT A MOTOR BREAKDOWN

Thanks to the brain-controlled activity of muscles, we implement an extraordinary range of intentional acts as we display our remarkably diverse product lines. Regrettably, as in Russell's case, those same muscles may reveal some heartbreaking inadequacies.

Our motor output is delivered in a variety of attractive and effective packages, or so we hope. Three of these merit close examination in children. First, there is *gross motor function,* featuring mainly the large muscles of the trunk, arms, and legs (pectorals, triceps, quadriceps, and the like) and consisting of the muscular agility needed to play a sport, rake a garden, or take out the trash. Second, *fine motor function* mainly recruits the fingers to manage such enterprises as artwork and sewing, construction of model rocket ships, the use of chopsticks, origami, or tying knots. Much of fine motor function is strategically navigated by our eyes, the so-called eye-hand coordination. Interestingly, Russell did not suffer any such fine motor gaps. Third, there is *graphomotor function,* Russell's most costly liability, the deeply mysterious and too often elusive form of motor ability needed for writing. Take note: graphomotor effectiveness is quite separate from fine motor ability, even though your fingers do the walking in both instances. There are countless children and adults, like Russell, who are excellent with their hands (for crafts and for fixing things around the house) yet make illegible letter formations or produce script that makes a mess of the page. Graphomotor function takes place over very different neural pathways from the ones that carry out fine motor function. Russell's fine motor circuits were in good shape, while his gross and graphomotor wiring were clearly deficient.

FINDING THE WEAK LINKS IN RUSSELL'S MOTOR CHAINS

When I try to decipher the plight of a kid like Russell and understand why his muscles are not cooperative during writing and, in his case, sports, I have to keep in mind how motor function is supposed to work when it's working right. All our intentional motor exploits (as opposed to the involuntary ones that make your eyes blink and your stomach gurgle when you're hungry) can be thought of as a chain containing seven crucial links leading to effective muscle activity. We can summarize these links as follows: 1) setting up a specific motor goal (planning); 2) gathering and sizing up (processing) outside information to help guide the motor action; 3) using motor logic (a kind of muscular intelligence); 4) accessing and applying stored procedures (motor memory); 5) activating the right muscles in the right order with enough speed and stamina to do the job (motor implementation); 6) monitoring movements as you go and making needed adjustments; and 7) learning from motor experience. So when I see a kid who's having motor difficulties, I examine closely how she or he performs at each of these seven links in the motor chains. Invariably, I find that one or more links are problematic and thus impeding gross motor, fine motor, or graphomotor function (or any combination of these). I will now explore the motor chain, commenting, in particular, about our findings in Russell's case. (The reader may know other individuals who reveal weak links that differ from those that thwarted Russell's output.)

Setting Up a Specific Motor Goal (Planning)

The first link in all voluntary motor output is deciding to act, determining what it is you would like your muscles to accomplish. If Russell were a right wing in hockey, he might decide to attempt a slap shot twelve feet from the goal. A golfer takes aim at the seventeenth hole. A writer decides to form the letter *f.* These are sharply focused motor goals. The person about to undertake such a voluntary activity previews a specific end point and gets ready to meet it. Often this involves a nearly instantaneous process of picturing the outcome: visualizing the puck gliding through the upper-right-hand corner of the goal, imagining the golf ball dropping into the cup, foreseeing the shape of the letter *f* before inscribing it. Knowing specifically what you're aiming for or at will help to tighten the subsequent links toward a motor achievement.

This critical blueprinting step has been christened with the readily forgettable term *ideomotor praxis.* In other words, an idea or intention starts to get converted into a motor action. To accomplish this, you're supposed to pause long enough to envision the intended results, much like an architect's rendering of what she hopes to see constructed. Many children with weak attention controls tend to omit this step. They are described as "impulsive" because all too often they do not sufficiently think about their motor goals in advance; consequently, they keep doing things they don't particularly intend to do—without previewing. Did Russell manifest a gap at this step in motor functioning? No, that was never a problem for him. We could rule out a motor planning problem.

Gathering and Sizing Up Outside Information
to Help Guide the Motor Action

Much of our motor output is guided by information from one or another form of input, such as language, objects moving in space, touch sensations. The challenge is to plug the input into the proper output.

That way, when the baseball coach explains the deft act of sliding into second or third base, you can translate his verbal instructions into an obedient motor response. When a child copies from the board, her graphomotor output is guided reliably by her interpretation or perception of the visual data on the board; hopefully her motor actions will accurately reproduce that material on paper. A trumpeter is expected to read a musical score and respond with the corresponding finger and mouth movements. The processes of input guiding output are recruited into active service when you cut your toenails (safely), open your combination lock (on the first try), or slice bagels (evenly).

How effectively you are able to link various kinds of input to various forms of output is a key determinant in establishing motor mastery. Not surprisingly, there's a lot of variation among us. Many children have motor problems because they cannot respond motorically to a visual or verbal input. Those who have a disconnection when attempting to integrate visual information with motor outputs are sometimes described as having visual-motor or visual-perceptual motor dysfunctions. In psychological testing, this breakdown is often confirmed by having a child simply copy a design. Those who perform poorly—for example, who write illegibly—may have trouble forming letters in large part because they have not perceived the letters very accurately; they are using distorted mental stencils to create the letters.

In some cases a child is able to visualize the letter only somewhat vaguely, and that image seems to flash onto and off the child's preview screen. The result is writing that is painfully hesitant, labored, and inconsistent. The same letter may be formed in different ways in different sentences. The overall impression is that there is no clear and stable visual guidance for letter formation. That same student is likely to have spelling problems; not only can he not visualize the individual letters clearly but he also has trouble picturing the words in his mind. So he relies excessively on phonetics and can't make use of the visual appearance of words to guide spelling. The child spells *fight* as *fite* and *thought* as *thawt*.

As you might guess, many children with visual-perceptual motor deficiencies also run into problems creating acceptable work in art class. Their drawings may reflect confusion regarding perspective, three-dimensionality, relative size and position of objects, and other features of the spatial realm. Being keen at interpreting spatial data also affects performance in many sports. Judging the speed of a hockey puck gliding toward you so you can skate to the right place at the right time is an example of the use of spatial inputs.

What about Russell? You may recall that he was skillful at copying designs. But when it came to his large muscles, he was unable to launch a well-timed and -executed gross motor response to a visual input—that is, those pesky trajectories (baseballs, volleyballs, and other such objects arcing toward or away from him). Russell could make use of visual information for fine motor purposes but not to program his big muscles. We thus uncovered one weak link in his motor chain.

Using Motor Logic (a Kind of Muscular Intelligence)

Although at first it may sound far-fetched to you, there's no doubt that the motor system has some intelligence of its own. And some people's muscles are much smarter than others'. Motor intelligence can take many forms, enabling you to navigate your car sensibly, so that you can make a U-turn without getting a summons. A star football player applies motor logic to maneuver his body through both expected and unanticipated obstacles as he cradles the ball on his run down the field. The fingers of a surgeon are solving problems as they probe relevant internal organs and safely tie off the proper blood vessels. A landscape artist is employing calculated techniques when he makes brush strokes with varying degrees of pressure and distance to capture the motion of leaves in a squall. A car mechanic uses motor logic in deciding which tool to use for each repair chore or subchore. I remember being told by a surgeon during my third year in medical school that if a task seems too difficult, you're using the wrong instrument.

Problems with motor logic are unlikely to compromise someone's writing. That's because the motor aspects of writing are not a problem-solving task. (Other parts of writing, such as picking a topic and deciding how best to express an idea, do require some logical thinking.) But motor-logical gaps certainly erode your mechanical aptitude—the ability to repair your bicycle, construct a model missile, or mend a broken zipper. I myself candidly confess to severely limited motor logic. I have trouble figuring out how to hammer a nail in straight (I've never done so despite thousands of well-motivated unsuccessful attempts), how to engage in strategic combat with a resistant zipper, how to reload a stapler without hemorrhaging (I consider purchasing a new one whenever the implement is empty), and how to fold a piece of stationery in three equal segments so it will evenly fit in an envelope. The evidence for recurrent motor-logical failure is undeniable. I have seen modest self-improvement over the decades. Nevertheless, I would have been described as having output failure had I chosen a career pathway demanding this element of motor proficiency. Thank goodness there are well-paid and gratified adults out there who are brilliant when it comes to fixing garage doors and building doghouses. Some of them didn't do very well in school, since most of our educational institutions tend not to nurture and celebrate motor thinking (except possibly as it plays out on the basketball court).

I have to mention that I am encountering more and more children who possess awesome motor-logical talent. That's because they are being reared on computer games. These seductive pastimes are like aerobic exercises for motor problem solving, but in some cases they have replaced the strengthening of any other forms of thinking, such as the ability to reason verbally! Russell was a computer-game fanatic, and in this pursuit he demonstrated that he had real ability when it came to motor-logical thinking. I also discovered that despite Russell's success deprivation in sports, he was an avid baseball and football fan and was often astute in pinpointing mistakes made by players and coaches. This was a budding young Monday morning quarterback. So I doubted that motor logic was his weak link.

Accessing and Applying Stored Procedures (Motor Memory)

In pinpointing Russell's motor problems, I had to check out the transmission lines connecting his muscles with his memory. When we decide to make a particular organized move with our body or our fingers, we have to remember how to do it. To accomplish this, our brains store thousands of motor maps that guide our actions in an endless array of circumstances. Your procedural memory stores ways of doing things successfully. It works in partnership with declarative, or factual, memory. Whereas procedural memory stores information about how you do things, declarative memory is the ability to express facts, things you can talk about. How you remember to ride a bicycle draws from a different brain warehouse (procedural memory) than the one you access in reciting the Pledge of Allegiance (declarative memory).

The renowned early-twentieth-century Russian neuropsychologist Alexander Luria aptly described what he called "kinetic melodies," what motor specialists, such as physical and occupational therapists, call *motor engrams*. These are the stored sequential plans for the complex motor activities that we have to keep engaging in as we go through our lives. Included are techniques for how to form specific letters when writing. For students with writing problems, a key question to ask is, How accessible are these plans? For Russell they were inaccessible.

When I tested Russell I showed him some sequences with my fingers and then asked him to imitate the order in which I'd moved my fingers. He was unable to do this with accuracy. He could not even answer questions about my finger movements (such as "Which finger did I move last?"). Even on a short-term basis, he could not store motor sequences. I see many students like him who, while trying to write, have trouble remembering how to move the pencil or pen to form the letters. It is hard for them to recall quickly and accurately enough the motor sequences for making each letter. Most of them much prefer printing to cursive writing. I think that's because printing requires you to remember only twenty-six kinetic melodies, whereas in cursive, every single word is a unique series of muscle movements—far too heavy a memory burden for some kids to store and later retrieve from their motor-procedural files. Thus motor-procedural memory is a vital transistor in our writing circuitry.

Many students like Russell simply can't readily access the kinetic melodies they need for writing. This breakdown results in some of the most illegible handwriting we encounter. Russell's writing sample is typical. By the time they reach fifth grade, affected students might be characterized as having poorly "automatized" letter formation. That simply means that they can remember how to make the letters, but it takes them too long and requires too much conscious effort to do so. Letter formation needs to be instantaneous and automatic. After all, if you have to stop and think about how to make a *j*, you're probably not going to be able to spell accurately and synthesize commendable ideas at the same time. That's what happened when Russell tried to write. His excessive motor effort undermined the other aspects of his writing. As a result, he could spell most words accurately in a spelling bee, but he'd misspell the very same words during a writing assignment. That's enough to make you hate writing, as Russell did. And it can lead people to accuse you of being careless and lazy. Russell withstood such accusations regularly.

Motor-procedural memory isn't confined to the act of writing. It dominates athletic prowess, talent with a musical instrument, automobile driving, computer keyboarding, and limitless routine and special capacities. In Russell's case, his weak motor-procedural memory pretty much obliterated his athletic aspirations as well as his written output, while creating the very false impression that he was a lazy kid.

The recall of motor procedures is highly responsive to plain old practice; the more you use a recipe, the more automatic it becomes. But repetition doesn't always do the trick. Practice dribbling a basketball didn't help Russell much.

Activating the Right Muscles in the Right Order with Enough Speed and Stamina to Do the Job (Motor Implementation)

This was another of Russell's breakdowns, although at times it was hard to know whether he just had trouble remembering the steps or whether he also had trouble recalling and implementing them with the right muscles. Ordinarily, once we have all our information and plans assembled, we can initiate motor activity. Nearly simultaneously, your brain is deciding precisely which muscles to push and pull to accomplish action. For example, during the graphomotor performance of writing, brain signals have to be dispatched to certain tiny muscles in the ends of a child's fingers, which are then assigned to vertical movements, rotary movements, and/or horizontal movements. In addition, some muscles are going to have to stabilize the pen or pencil during letter formation (we don't want it slipping or falling to the floor in the middle of a short story). The process is often termed *praxis,* and when it's not operating as it should, we say an individual reveals *dyspraxia.*

Many kids have trouble with this process of actual implementation. They can't seem to transmit multiple signals from their brains to different teams of small muscles all at the same time. Remember that these minuscule muscles are very remote from the brain (like a long-distance call). Very young students who have trouble with implementation appear to neglect stabilization responsibilities; all of their muscles try to get into the act of letter formation, so they keep dropping their pencil or reveal a very inconsistent, unstable pencil grasp. After many months of having to pick up the pencil, they seem to overcompensate. That is, all of their muscles are assigned to stabilize their pencil, and there are none left for letter formation.

Russell typified this with his fistlike, clenching, perpendicular grip. Watching how hard it was for him to write smoothly, I decided that he was having trouble with both memory and implementation—two weak motor links. Some students with his problem contort their fingers and wrists into a hook when they try to write. In all such instances, the child then starts writing with his elbow! That's what Russell was doing. Regrettably, his large two-way elbow joint, although a lot bigger and closer to the brain than the finger joints, was not designed mechanically to handle writing, so letter formation became tedious, effortful, and much too slow to synchronize with the steady flow of ideas and language—output failure in the making.

It is not unusual for kids who have trouble assigning muscle groups to form letters to also have problems with their speech articulation. Interestingly, I found out that Russell had been in speech therapy when he was four years old because he'd had problems pronouncing multisyllabic words. The same difficulty he eventually experienced in deciding which muscles should do what in which order during writing had sabotaged his ability to activate the right muscles in his mouth and cheeks to form words while talking. I come across many an elementary school kid like Russell who hates to write and has received speech therapy. We call this a combined oro-motor-graphomotor dysfunction (an oral and written mouthful and handful).

The highly selective mobilization of the correct muscles to accomplish discrete tasks is not limited to writing. It is, in fact, common to all complex motor activities. Russell himself once complained to me, "You know, when the coach tells about how to pass a football, I think I understand a lot of what he is saying. I bet I could probably describe to the other kids how to do it. It's just that my muscles won't do it. Or maybe they can't." What an illuminating description of a breakdown at the implementation stage of motor output!

Motor implementation also takes in three additional capacities. One is the ability to move muscles fast enough to keep pace with demands. The second involves synchronization with other functions, such as moving your fingers at a pace that matches the flow of ideas and language during writing. The third, a combination of motor strength and motor stamina, provides the power to complete demanding motor tasks. When he wrote or played sports, Russell revealed sufficient strength and stamina, but his output was slow, mainly due to his difficulty activating the right muscles quickly and in the correct sequence.

Monitoring Movements as You Go and Making Needed Adjustments

An important issue for kids like Russell is their awareness of where they are in space at any one instant during a motor activity. This is a form of self-monitoring. The challenge differs according to the kind of muscular venture you're on. Two kinds of motor performance are often cited, namely, static and dynamic. In static motor output, a consistent motor map is followed under all conditions. Thus, a bowler unleashes the bowling ball aimed at ten standing pins in a particular manner, using a preset kinetic melody that needs to be implemented as exactly as possible. A soccer forward, on the other hand, needs to keep continuously monitoring his position and making modifications depending on changing conditions. That's dynamic motor action. In both scenarios the athlete must receive consistent ongoing feedback from those peripheral muscle groups in the arms, legs, or fingers. The bowler needs to know how closely his moment-to-moment actions are approximating his motor plan. He might then make fine-tuned adjustments while releasing the ball.

Even greater monitoring and regulating are required for dynamic motor actions; that soccer player might need to slow down, speed up, alter direction, pursue the ball, or make other modifications as the play proceeds. Some aspiring athletes are far ahead of others when it comes to self-monitoring and regulation, the quality-control link in motor output. The production controls, a set of important components of attention (see table, page 84), govern self-monitoring. Some children with signs of attentional dysfunction have serious problems watching what they're doing with their muscles, just as they have difficulty watching what they're doing in most other parts of their lives. In other cases, problems with feedback and regulation are strictly confined to motor pursuits. One example of this is a condition called finger agnosia, which can seriously impair writing fluency.

Finger agnosia is seen in kids who have trouble keeping track of where their pen or pencil is during writing. When someone is forming letters, tiny nerve endings in the fingers send messages back to the brain reporting on the current location of the pen or pencil within a letter. That is called proprioceptive-kinesthetic feedback (*proprio* refers to position, *ceptive* to receptor, and *kinesthetic* to the sense of movement). Feedback information is relayed to a network within the brain called the motor analyzer. This analyzer operates much like an air-traffic controller. The fingers report, "We are just about at the top of a *g*," and the motor analyzer sends off the instant message, "You'd better turn right and start your descent." That feedback, as well as the response to it, operates nonstop during writing. But if your brain isn't provided with the feedback information or has some trouble interpreting and responding to it, then you suffer finger agnosia. It's fairly simple: you are forced to use your eyes to track the writing utensil. So your six-year-old plants his chin on the desk and watches carefully to see where the pencil point is from instant to instant. But there's a serious problem with that: visual feedback is too slow, and it consumes too much of his limited effort and attention.

Proprioceptive-kinesthetic feedback is instantaneous and automatic, a freebie during writing. Otherwise you have to concentrate with your eyes to survey your pencil movements, and it will be nearly impossible to do that and spell and think and punctuate at the same time. This is a familiar problem in output failure; it's hard to combine something that's taking too much effort with other needed processes. Over the years I've observed that many of the students with this problem try to rectify the situation by clamping their thumb over their index and middle fingers, thereby preventing their fingers from meaningful participation in the act of writing. If you watch closely, you'll notice they write with their wrists instead of their fingers. This has some advantages, since wrists move through larger excursions, so the feedback might be more detectable. But, alas, while writing with your wrist can yield reasonably legible symbols, you are likely to experience a horrible case of writer's cramp. So affected kids are likely to write as little as they can possibly get away with.

I needed to determine whether or not motor feedback was a weak link for Russell, so I tested him for finger agnosia by having him imitate the movements of my fingers without looking at his own fingers. This way he had to know at all times where his fingers were in space with no help from his eyes. I also asked him to write some letters with his eyes closed. Since Russell had no trouble at all with either task, I concluded that the accurate monitoring of his finger movements was not one of Russell's weak motor links.

Learning from Motor Experience
Practice makes perfect—or so they say. It turns out that individuals vary considerably in how much practice they will require to master a motor procedure or activity. Once attained, a motor skill becomes part of one's repertoire. Some people have conspicuously weak motor learning. They lack skills, and repetition helps them only minimally. I've mentioned Russell's relative lack of dramatic writing improvement in the

face of repeated training. Ironically, the best-coordinated people are the ones who improve the most with practice—it doesn't seem fair.

Teachers and parents should be aware that when it comes to sports, writing, or other motor challenges, some children require far more practice than others. And in some cases practice has realistic limitations. Even with drills comparable to the routines of a precision marching band, some individuals will never boast elegant handwriting; there seems to be a ceiling to their writing ability. Practice may help but only to a point. It might be cruel and unfair to push an individual beyond this level.

The links in many motor actions occur with impressive speed and, over time, they generally become so automatic that they operate without our conscious involvement—unless you're striving toward a totally new skill or one that is especially taxing for you, in which case the process can be slow and burdensome, a motor drag. As we have seen in Russell's case, an individual's output could break down due to a weakness at any of several links in the motor chain.

The links in the motor chain are summarized in Figure 2-3.

Through my testing and discussions with Russell and his parents, I could understand the effectiveness of his motor chain (see the table below). As with so many other individuals, there were discernible differences between these links as they were applied to gross motor function (sports), fine motor ability (arts and crafts), and graphomotor function (writing).

THE STATUS OF RUSSELL'S MOTOR LINKS

Motor Link	Sports	Arts/Crafts/Repair Work	Writing
Planning	not a problem	not a problem	not a problem
Processing outside information*	a problem	not a problem	not a problem
Motor logic	not a problem	not a problem	not needed
Motor memory	a problem	not a problem	a problem
Muscle implementation	a problem	not a problem	a problem
Monitoring/regulation	not a problem	not a problem	not a problem
Learning from experience	a problem	not a problem	a problem

*Mainly the use of verbal directions and/or visual imitation to guide motor output.

THE MOTOR CHAIN

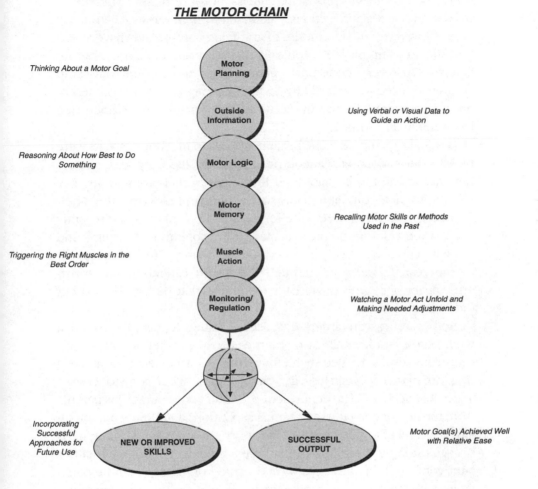

Thinking About a Motor Goal — Motor Planning

Outside Information — *Using Verbal or Visual Data to Guide an Action*

Reasoning About How Best to Do Something — Motor Logic

Motor Memory — *Recalling Motor Skills or Methods Used in the Past*

Triggering the Right Muscles in the Best Order — Muscle Action

Monitoring/ Regulation — *Watching a Motor Act Unfold and Making Needed Adjustments*

Incorporating Successful Approaches for Future Use — **NEW OR IMPROVED SKILLS**

SUCCESSFUL OUTPUT — *Motor Goal(s) Achieved Well with Relative Ease*

Figure 2-3.   The specific links in a motor chain. Any of these may be a weak link that deters motor performance and efficiency.

RUSSELL'S COMPLICATIONS

I often find that students with motor difficulties acquire various complications that can make their problems tricky to manage properly. Russell was no exception. I have pointed out Russell's weak links: his trouble recalling motor sequences for gross and graphomotor output, his trouble getting his muscles to cooperate in implementing specific motor ac-

tions, and his difficulty producing a gross motor response to outer spatial data and verbal instructions. The result for him was too many weak
links, allowing for too few modes of gratifying output. And I have to add
that the adults in his life chronically misinterpreted this boy's output
failures. On several occasions a gym teacher and a young day-camp
counselor called Russell a "klutz," while several of his classroom teachers and sometimes his parents accused him of first-degree laziness due
to his minimalist writing.

Gradually the home scene became clearer to me. Both parents were
highly educated, socially adept, productive adults. They seemed hap-
pily married and well established in the life of their community. The
telephone rang out abundant social opportunities for the adult
Strinbergs, but there were none for Russell. Dr. Strinberg had recently
been voted chief of the medical staff at his community hospital, and
Russell's mom had been honored as the county's real estate agent
of the year. Russell had attended the award ceremony and apparently never once smiled. He later recounted that he had felt sad but
didn't know why.

Both parents were ardent and accomplished tennis players. For a
while, Russell took tennis lessons at the Glen Maples Tennis Club—with
disastrous results. He fled shamefully from the last of five lessons like a
dog with his tail between his legs. Russell looked awful trying to serve or
learn the backhand. The benevolent pro tried to discourage his parents
from further kindling Russell's tennis aspirations. Quitting tennis, actually, was a relief for him. He said the sport was stupid and boring. Kids
his age often put down things that make them feel inferior. His father
later confessed that he had always dreamed of having a son he could
volley with. That wasn't meant to be. In a real sense, Russell was a disappointing child.

Russell's motor humiliation was no doubt exacerbated by his obesity, and you can be sure that his obesity was worsened by his self-
protective motor inactivity! Understandably, he had no motivation to
risk embarrassment on the playing fields, so he opted for a safe,
sedentary lifestyle. Then the combination of being overweight, wet-
ting his bed, and appearing clumsy compared to other boys made Russell feel he was living in a defective body. The blow to his masculinity
in the locker room had reinforced his negative body image and depressed him. His bed-wetting further convinced him that he had little
control over his own body. He came to feel that he wasn't a real man.

Further, Russell loved and admired his parents but felt that he had let them down, that he had been a disappointment to them. After all, they were thin, attractive people who were good at sports, were highly productive, and had been successful in school when they were kids. Russell was haunted by the belief that he might not be living up to their expectations. His guilt clung to him despite constant reassurance from his mother and father. It's hard to grow up feeling that you are disappointing those whom you love. Russell's story was an all too familiar clinical script—namely, high-output parents raising a currently unsuccessful, low-output, seemingly lazy kid.

All of this boy's cumulative stress was taking place at a time (late elementary into middle school) when kids are often obsessively preoccupied with appearances and blatantly cruel to those whose bodies fail to make the grade. No wonder Russell was condemned to live with the terror of imminent public humiliation. That further caused him to flee from threatening social contact with peers. He would engage in mostly solitary entertainment or else converse mainly with adults, while losing out on much-needed social experience and opportunities for learning from peers. He was living the life of an outcast. Add to that the fact that he faced daily criticism and accusations of laziness for his low output in school, and it is no wonder that this boy with an excellent mind felt worthless.

HELPING RUSSELL

I believe that a key component to helping a kid is to enable him or her to understand and be able to talk about the dysfunctions that are getting in the way of success. I call this crucial process *demystification*. A person can't work on a weakness that is causing trouble if he doesn't even know what it's called. So after evaluating Russell, I spent a good bit of time demystifying him, explaining his strengths and weaknesses in words he could understand. I started by discussing all the things Russell was good at: reading, understanding language, learning science and math, drawing, and fixing things.

It was easy to enumerate his strengths; they were many. Yet Russell seemed surprised; somehow he had gotten out of the habit of perceiving his strengths as strengths, instead taking them for granted and underestimating their value. That's something I see all the time in kids with output failure. They just write off their assets. I talked to Russell about all the fantastic careers that he could someday select based on his strengths. I also pointed out that many adults find it easier being a grown-up than it was to be a kid. Russell perked up when he heard this optimistic observation.

I then helped Russell understand his dysfunctions and their impact on his productivity in school and elsewhere. I actually taught him about the motor chain (Figure 2-3). He seemed riveted as we explored the various links together. I explained how problems with motor memory were getting in the way of his writing in school. I described the problem he had getting the right muscles to play their various roles quickly and accurately while forming letters. I also explained how his motor-memory and muscle-coordination problems were limiting his abilities in sports. Russell appeared to be thoroughly digesting everything I said, and in fact he became more animated than I had seen previously, even providing examples of the phenomena I was describing to him.

I reassured Russell that his output problems did not signify that he was dumb or that he had an inferior mind. I told him I would like to help him improve his output in school and find some ways to deal with his athletic suffering. After I performed a physical examination on him, I also had a chance to talk to Russell privately about his obesity. I reassured him about his masculinity concerns and emphasized that he needed to work on losing weight. Additionally, I started him on some medication for his enuresis; that helped from the first night. I was surprised that no one had treated this problem in the past. His parents had been told that Russell would outgrow it, which is most likely true. But we couldn't wait any longer, as Russell's self-esteem was continuing to plummet.

I advised Russell to avoid getting undressed in front of other kids for the time being, so they wouldn't have a chance to humiliate him; he had already adopted that policy on his own. I explained that when he reached puberty, he wouldn't look that different from other kids. I told him I would set up an appointment with a dietitian. He seemed eager for this help.

We also needed to assist Russell with his writing problems. I urged him to try a wide variety of pens to find one that felt as if it had the right thickness and gave him the best feedback and was most comfortable to handle so that he wouldn't have to bear down too hard. I find that many kids with graphomotor dysfunction benefit from greater traction between the writing instrument and the page. Second, I stressed how important it was for him to use a computer for much of his important writing activities. He would need to become skilled at keyboarding. I warned Russell this would not be easy, since kids with motor-memory dysfunctions for writing may endure the same problems with a keyboard, but that his trouble implementing motor patterns would be less severe with a keyboard than with a pen. I explained that finger movements are less complex (mainly up and down) during typing. He reported that he had already tried to master the keyboard several times—unsuccessfully. I emphasized that he shouldn't give up on computer writing, because at some point he would experience a fantastic breakthrough and be able to produce writing that took less effort and was more attractive looking. I suggested he start with just two-finger keyboarding and then progress to ten fingers. He seemed reluctant to try. Kids like him are understandably loath to risk any new form of motor failure. They've failed too often. I suggested to his parents and wrote to his teachers that Russell needed to be encouraged (more accurately, required) to work on keyboarding.

At the same time, we sought accommodations in school, so that Russell would have more time on written tests, other kids wouldn't be checking his work, and no one would be taking off points for handwriting problems. I also suggested that Russell work with an occupational therapist and go back to practicing basic letter formation to make this process automatic. I told him to stick with printing. Further, I suggested that every evening he practice copying word lists for several minutes just before bedtime, since what you drill on right before sleep tends to replay in your mind during the night. I also asked him to practice using a normal tripod pencil grasp, which would be more efficient than his present awkward and tight manner of holding the utensil.

It was essential to make physical education less traumatic for Russell. His compassionate gym teacher worked on ways of protecting him from athletic exposure that made him look foolish, emphasizing instead personal fitness. I later found out that Russell became highly enthusiastic about muscle-building activities, an interest he has kept up with good results after six months. His physical education teacher was helping Russell learn to become a shot-putter. Russell also was being groomed to try out wrestling (no outer spatial trajectories there).

We had to develop some overall strategies to deal with the realization that Russell really had no form of output that was rewarding for him, that could generate personal gratification as well as praise from the outside world, especially the ruthlessly judgmental peer community. Everybody has a need to be creating laudable products; when that need goes unfulfilled, it's nearly impossible to feel good about oneself. Russell felt adamant that sports were not the way to go for him. We talked about art, and Russell volunteered that he'd love to learn how to be a cartoonist. I suggested that he keep working on the cars and animals he was creating out of spare parts in his basement laboratory; he had never thought of these as worthy products.

We talked about musical instruments. His mother wanted Russell to take piano lessons, and his father suggested the viola (yes, the viola). I thought the piano might be a reach because of Russell's problems remembering motor sequences. Also, I wanted him to pick an instrument that would help with his social life, one he could play in a marching band, a rock group, an orchestra, or a jazz ensemble. I suggested something macho, such as the trombone or drums. When Russell heard the word "drums," he literally leapt like a bullfrog from his chair. Drummers use sequencing, but often the kinetic melodies are guided by prevailing rhythms and entail the use of larger muscles than those demanded for piano playing and for writing. In fact, one could speculate that playing the drums could actually serve to enhance motor sequential memory functions. I sometimes recommend instruments like the trombone or double bass to kids with motor-implementation problems because these instruments involve the use of larger upper-limb muscles that are closer to the brain and therefore generally easier for them to command. Down deep in his heart, Russell longed to be cool, and the drums represented a sure route to this social destination.

Russell was also praised and encouraged for his love of reading, math, and science. We worked out ways for him to do some special projects, acquire expertise, and strengthen his abilities in these areas. He expressed a very strong interest in meteorology. I urged his parents to make this a priority. They actually went out and set up a home weather station, subscribed to two weather magazines, and got him some relevant books. His teacher cooperated, and each Friday morning, Russell presented his weekend weather forecast, laced with impressive technical data. His classmates were floored.

I saw Russell twice after his evaluation at our center—most recently about a year after that initial assessment. At that point he was making great strides. He was following his diet fairly well, having lost some weight, abetted by some weight lifting and a growth spurt in height. We stopped his anxiety medication, but he was continuing to see Dr. Pinkham occasionally. The drum lessons were going well, although his parents are paying an auditory price. Russell was animated as he talked to me about starting a high school rock group and seeking gigs around town. Computer keyboarding was still arduous, but there had been improvement, and Russell was doing reports on his laptop, although with some difficulty. He had become intrigued with computer graphics and loved using illustrations in his stories and reports. Russell was taking art lessons once a week, and his teacher was displaying his satirical output prominently in the classroom. His father was learning to praise his son, which was tremendously important to Russell. No one was pressuring the boy to become an athlete. Russell seemed happy with himself and with his life (and with his output). Importantly, his parents had all but broken their habit of bringing up the "L word"— that is, *lazy.*

3
CLINT WALKER
Forgetting How to Remember

Mr. John Pringle's memory was restored in a great degree by leaving off the use of snuff. . . . Mr. Pope commends a trotting horse above all things in order to excite dormant ideas. . . . The cold bath, Milton's memory was always improved by that. . . . It is from the motion excited in the brain, by means of fever that persons often recollect ideas and speak languages, which appeared to have perished in their memories.

—BENJAMIN RUSH, "OF DERANGEMENT IN THE MEMORY,"
MEDICAL INQUIRIES AND OBSERVATIONS, UPON THE
DISEASES OF THE MIND (1812)

Clint looked as if he slept through every night in his maroon-and-tan cowboy boots. And his ten-gallon hat appeared to be sutured to his scalp with only a modest fringe of his ruby red hair sneaking out beneath the brim. His red leather boots with their rattlesnake-patterned inlays were a pesky distraction to an eastern dude like me. This handsome ten-year-old cowhand from a rural town not far from Fort Worth, Texas, was lean and lanky and tall for his age, his suntanned face liberally peppered with freckles. He was the consummate outdoors person, and if you gave in to your stereotyping impulses, you could easily visualize Clint out there rounding up cattle. His brain should have been stamped with the caution "For Outdoor Use Only." He spent every millisecond of his spare time on his grandfather's ranch a hundred miles from his home.

Clint was a skillful horseman, and his dream was to compete one day at the Fort Worth Stock Show rodeo. On the ranch he affectionately tended to the populous herd of elephantine Brahman steer as if he were kin to them, and he looked forward to grooming some of the handsomest bulls for showing each January at the stock show.

Clint had always maintained that he wanted to be a large-animal vet-erinarian like his uncle Mike someday. He took pains to communicate this stubborn intention at least twice a day. His fervent aspiration broke his mother's heart because, as she put it, "Clint's no student." Earlier that year Mrs. Walker had quit her job as a hairdresser to home-school Clint. Mr. Walker was the local postmaster.

Mrs. Walker told anyone who would listen that her boy Clint was her whole life; there was nothing she wouldn't do to help him succeed and feel good about himself. But eight-year-old Jan was leaving her big brother behind in numerous skill areas. She was far ahead of him in math, spelling, and writing. She earned straight A's and had won a trove of awards in school. Clint had been adopted as an infant. Jan was the Walkers' biological daughter.

Clint's parents knew the boy's biological mother. He had been born out of wedlock to a sixteen-year-old girl who'd been a chronic disgrace to her parents. She had dropped out of school following eighth grade, after which she'd compiled a terrible reputation for sexual promiscuity and drug use; her vices were amply publicized by word of mouth in her small town. There was speculation regarding several of the commu-nity's young male ne'er-do-wells, but no one was sure about Clint's bio-logical father. The Walkers lived in fear that their son would find out about his mother and be devastated. He had actually heard some of the racy gossip about her. He knew he had been adopted, but he had never asked for more details. His parents sometimes felt as if they were living in an earthquake zone; the truth could erupt at any time and cause heavy damage to their son's already frail self-esteem. They tried not to think about it much, yet on many occasions after he had gone to sleep crying, they'd discussed whether Clint's school problems were inher-ited and whether he was destined to be a dropout like his biological mom. Many parents I have seen over the years have lived with a gnaw-ing dread of what their naive and innocent son would be like when he turned sixteen.

After months of deliberation, the parents had decided on home schooling, largely because Clint's teacher and the guidance counselor had started talking about keeping him back in the fourth grade. Mrs. Walker didn't feel that retention would accomplish anything other than making Clint feel "dumber than ever." By the way, I have to agree with her: grade retention accomplishes nothing. It just serves to destroy any remaining self-esteem in a struggling kid. The practice should be abolished. Imagine punishing a kid because the school doesn't understand his learning breakdowns! On numerous occasions, the Walkers had been informed that their son could do the work if he made up his mind to do it. There were overt and covert accusations of laziness. It should come as no surprise that Mr. and Mrs. Walker had concluded that the school personnel had no grasp of their son's difficulties. Nor were school officials the least bit sympathetic. The principal asserted on several occasions that Clint required no special services, that he could be managed entirely in a regular classroom, while his teachers confessed that they didn't know what to do with him in class, since he was so far behind his classmates. His teachers had received no training whatsoever in dealing with kids who have differences in learning.

Mrs. Walker objected to what she described as the school's total insensitivity to Clint's plight, an alarming callousness that manifested itself in multiple hurtful ways. For instance, other kids were allowed to correct and poke fun at Clint's terrible spelling and "babyish" handwriting. In front of the whole class, one boy described Clint's paragraph on insects as "retard writing." He was called on in class on numerous occasions when his teacher understood full well that Clint wouldn't know the answer. To make matters worse, despite realizing that Clint didn't comprehend math, his teacher regularly asked him to solve problems at the blackboard. Each time, his peers would watch him fumble; then they'd vie to grab Clint's chalk and show him up in public. His teacher earnestly believed that knowing he would have to do problems in front of his classmates would motivate Clint to study harder—a misguided strategy.

Kids have very little insulation to shield them from public humiliation. (Neither do adults, but they're in a better position to avoid it.) It wasn't that the other students disliked Clint; when they derided his work at the board, they were just being competitive and typically insensitive fourth graders.

So poor Clint kept having to lick his inflamed ego wounds. When his mother complained about her son's nearly daily humiliation, she was reminded sternly, "We treat everyone exactly the same around here. It's the only fair way. Clint has to learn to do what everyone else does." Mrs. Walker resented this rigid "one size fits all" approach and commented to her husband that she might have been able to get decent sympathy and help for Clint if he had serious discipline problems or if he couldn't read at all. In fact, reading was the least troubling skill for Clint.

Clint's life at school felt about as comfortable to him as having a permanent case of the flu. His academic aches and pains seldom abated. He consistently tried very hard, but he enjoyed precious little success. Through it all, miraculously, this boy maintained a cheerful, upbeat, and motivated demeanor. Many children start to misbehave when they've been made to feel inferior. But not Clint; he was never a behavior problem. He was all smiles, forever eager to please—a tribute to his resilient temperament and, as well, to his phenomenal parents and grandparents. Nevertheless, beneath the surface he had to be hurting. Clint was just too nice a kid to trouble anyone else with his troubles—hence the upbeat veneer.

But some subtle signs of emotional turmoil were starting to erupt. Clint was beginning to complain of acute abdominal pains several times a week, and he was having very disturbing dreams. They seemed to alternate between nightmares of public humiliation (showing up at school without his clothes on, everyone laughing at him as if he were at the board doing math problems) and of being trapped inside the school when the building caught fire (feeling hopelessly engulfed and destroyed by his academic predicaments). Meanwhile, he had also developed some nervous facial twitches, especially when he felt under duress, which was all too frequently.

On many weekday mornings Clint complained of headaches, no doubt indicating that this boy was putting up a very good front for the outside world. His body, however, wasn't as deft at keeping secrets, a pattern I encounter among lots of kids with school problems.

After three months of home schooling, Mrs. Walker noticed definite progress, although Clint was still dreadfully far behind, and she was aware that he might not pass the end-of-grade testing required every May. But at least her son was being shielded from daily embarrassment. Mrs. Walker was concerned that Clint had very little understanding of his own learning problems, by which she meant that he didn't exactly know where the gaps in his mind were, which weaknesses were making it so hard for him to succeed in school. She had read somewhere that when kids don't understand their specific dysfunctions, they tend to think of themselves as hopelessly "stupid," a perspective that could make them give up on themselves. At the local library she had borrowed a book I wrote called *Educational Care* and she decided to fly to North Carolina so Clint could undergo an evaluation at our center in Chapel Hill, where we work with children and adolescents with learning and output problems. Mrs. Walker told us that she wanted to know how best to help Clint, and she felt that both she and he needed to be demystified about his specific dysfunctions and strengths.

CLINT'S EVALUATION

In the process of assessing Clint's educational needs, we sifted through the questionnaires sent in by his parents and the school. We examined previous achievement-test data and some typical samples of Clint's work. Then we interviewed his mother and father. Our child psychologist commented that Calvin Walker was especially perceptive and well informed regarding his son's learning difficulties. Mr. Walker choked up as he described his son lovingly: "Clint's a people person, an animal person, a hard worker, a terrific outdoorsman. He's good at art and sports. And I've never known anyone to love animals the way Clint does. Few weeks back, my father-in-law had a stallion with a real mean infected wound on his leg. He was in serious pain and running a fever; the vet didn't know if he'd make it or not. Well, Clint insisted on sleeping all night in the next stall in the barn. Darned if he didn't get up every hour to check on that Morgan and make him keep drinking liquids. When his grandma went after Clint to come in for breakfast in the morning, she found him with his arms around the stallion's neck, telling him stories and trying to make him forget about his pain. That's Clint for you. By the way, that horse is okay now, and Clint may have had something to do with that. In my opinion this kid has it all, everything he needs to be a success when he grows up. I just gotta figure how to get him there without him being wiped out. Right now he's hurting bad inside, real bad." In one form or another, I keep hearing this despairing tale about a kid contending with his failure to fit into childhood. And it makes me want to cry in sadness and protest when I know a patient of mine has all it takes to attain fulfillment in adult life but is destined to suffer so needlessly on the way there.

Mr. Walker further related how close he and Clint were. "We're best friends, the two of us. Clint's got plenty of friends his own age, but every Saturday morning first thing he asks me, 'What are we doin' today?' Imagine that, a boy who'd rather be with his dad than his friends. You know, I feel the same way about him. And we do things together all the time. One more thing: Clint likes to sit there and listen while I talk to my friends down at the store; we talk about the huntin' season, pickup trucks, and how damned mad we are at folks in Washington, and Clint, he just sits there and listens. That boy, he loves to be with grown-ups— and to learn from them all he can."

When I spent time talking to Clint, I was taken with his colorful charm. Although he showed no telltale signs of being depressed or overly anxious, this appealing boy was earnestly crying out for help. At one point he stared intently at the rug and softly mentioned that other kids and his sister were a whole lot smarter than he was. He went on to confess that he worried sometimes about being adopted and thought maybe his adoptive parents were disappointed in him and were sorry they'd taken him in. But then he made firm eye contact and asserted that he was sure his mom and dad loved him and that he loved them more than any other people in the world. He hastened to point out that he loved his little sister too.

Our educational testing documented that Clint was at grade level in all aspects of his reading. On the other hand, there were very serious spelling problems. Most of his errors didn't even come close to accuracy. In math Clint was significantly delayed. He had slow recall of his basic facts and often couldn't remember how to do procedures such as basic division. The educational diagnostician found a revealing discrepancy in that Clint seemed to be able to understand and explain concepts in math, even tough ones like the concept of a fraction and the concept of place value, but he just couldn't remember how to do things in math.

Clint's most calamitous area of academic blight was his written output. It was a mess. There were profuse mistakes in spelling, punctuation, capitalization, and even letter formation, accompanied by a serious shortage of facts and ideas. His handwriting's legibility was poor, and if you watched Clint while he was writing, you could see how slow and arduous the task was for him. Also, there was an extreme difference between Clint's oral language production, which was colorful and fluent, and his written language output, which was strikingly simplistic, dry, and vague. I learned that Clint was a child star orator during spontaneous class discussions and presentations (as opposed to answering highly specific questions in class), but you'd never know it from his writing. Moreover, he was able to copy samples of Chinese calligra-

phy with pinpoint accuracy and speed but found it hard to form the letters of his own culture while writing. And, not surprisingly, Clint had
begun to hate and resist writing assignments. A sample of his writing
can be seen in Figure 3-1.

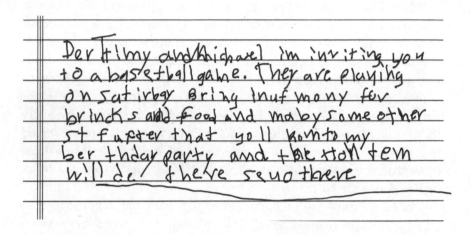

Figure 3-1.   Clint was asked to write a letter inviting his friends to his birthday celebration.
With great effort he produced this communiqué. It is clear that he had trouble recalling spelling
and rules of punctuation and that he reversed some letters, which is common in kids whose memories are overwhelmed when they write.

One common theme pervaded all of Clint's weak scholastic domains.
That was output. He could take in and interpret information accurately
while listening or reading, but he could not convert the knowledge that
he seemed to have into a written format. In math he could easily grasp
the never-ending onslaught of new concepts and procedures, but
somehow he couldn't apply them readily when completing a work
sheet. He would seem to absorb material while reading but had trouble
answering direct questions about a text. I was pretty certain that Clint
was manifesting one common form of output failure, a pattern of difficulty with the memory feed into output, something that I will explain
later.

The neurodevelopmental testing I performed on Clint uncovered
many strengths. He was found to have advanced fine and gross motor
coordination. When asked to run his pencil through a maze, he did
so with remarkable precision and speed. But when he wrote the alpha-

bet for me in cursive lowercase letters, his rendition was painfully awkward and slow and many of the letters were poorly formed. He would hesitate in midstream as if suddenly forgetting how to form a symbol.

Clint was successful on most tasks dealing with receptive and expressive language. He was a proficient verbalist. Even more highly developed were Clint's spatial capacities. He was excellent at copying complex designs, telling left from right, and manipulating shapes in his mind. He achieved a perfect score on a nonverbal problem-solving task, parts of which are illustrated in Figure 3-2.

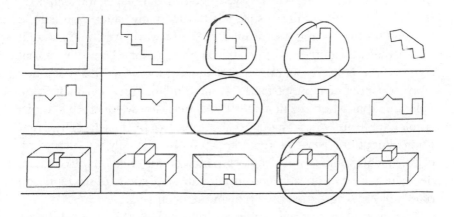

Figure 3-2.   Part of our neurodevelopmental examination PEERAMID-2, this exercise requires a student to identify which shapes on the right in each row could be rotated to fit with the one in the first column to form a perfect square. This is a test of spatial perception and the ability to reason nonverbally. Clint achieved a highly unusual (for his age) perfect score on this activity.

Clint's excellence in spatial tasks fit snugly with his parents' observations regarding Clint's fabulous mechanical aptitude. His grandfather boasted that he saved a lot of money on tractor repairs by having Clint check out malfunctioning implements.

Throughout the neurodevelopmental testing, Clint was cooperative and invested in his performance. However, he constantly required reassurance. He incessantly asked how he was doing. It was as if he had been so immersed in failure that he had little confidence in his personal performance on anything—even in areas where he did exceptionally well. I did not detect any sign whatsoever of attentional dysfunction. In fact, Clint's attention controls were an area of substantial strength for him; he was constantly alert to little details and noticeably systematic in his approach to tasks. Another positive feature was that he utilized a good many clever strategies when he worked. For example, before copying a design he would trace it with his finger and whisper some of its features under his breath.

In light of all of this stellar cognitive functioning, what was holding Clint back? What was clogging his output pipes? Whenever we evaluate a child, we seek recurring themes. These are patterns of performance that keep coming back in different years and in different ways to reveal the secrets of a person's wiring. By integrating our diagnostic team's direct observations during testing with the many clues that shone through his history and the samples of Clint's work, we could see that he was having trouble with the full range of demands in school that required the efficient operation of long-term memory. This was a boy who was far better at understanding than remembering. What's so compelling is that when we first met Clint, he acknowledged this shortcoming up front! When I inquired about his trouble in school, the first thing Clint uttered was, "I forget lotsa stuff." Incidentally, too often clinicians, teachers, and parents neglect to include the child on the diagnostic team. With a little gentle prompting and reassurance, students can often tell you where their breakdowns are occurring.

Further evidence of retrieval memory gaps were found on the neurodevelopmental examination. Clint had trouble recalling the months of the year in the right order. He was shown a drawing of a piece of furniture and asked to name parts as rapidly as possible. It took him a long time to name many of them, and sometimes he couldn't locate the item in his long-term memory. Clint listened carefully as a brief story was read to him, and then he was asked to summarize it in his own words. While he captured the general drift or plot of the narrative, he entirely forgot the names of the two children it was about and also forgot some other salient details. That is to say, he understood the passage better than he remembered it. So, again, all signs pointed to Clint suffering from memory breakdowns.

ABOUT CLINT'S MEMORY AND OUTPUT

At first glance it may seem odd, but much of efficient output in school depends upon a brisk, even flow of knowledge and skill emanating from the storage vats of long-term memory. Students have to file and later retrieve vast quantities of information, a steady infusion of new skills, and a flood of directions and explanations from their teachers. The memory demands imposed on kids in school far exceed those faced by adults in careers. Once you've grown up, you're pretty much opening the same kinds of memory files every morning at work, in many cases year after year. If you're an accountant you open the auditing files, if you're a plumber you download your well-worn knowledge of fittings, and when you're a dermatologist you log on to your brain's rash directory. But when you're Clint's age or an adolescent, entirely new and often unfamiliar material must be instantly sorted out, stored away in memory, and located on demand in a flash. When called on in class, Clint and his classmates have three seconds to recall the right answer. Looking ahead to secondary school, every fifty minutes or so Clint will have to keep on opening entirely new memory folders as he ambulates from Spanish to math to history to science. It turns out that some students are much better endowed than others when it comes to shouldering the cumbersome memory burdens of school.

Writing inflicts one of school's heaviest drains on memory resources, and some kids lack the memory capacity to support writing. Clint was a prime example. Like others with this shortfall, he could invent original thoughts and insights, but he couldn't get them down on paper without having to "dumb them down." He could deploy sophisticated sentence structure when he spoke in class, but his language on paper was too simplistic, more like that of a much younger child. Clint displayed great pencil control in a maze, but he couldn't form letters legibly. Why? Because drawing a line through a maze takes no memory, while letter formation requires you to rapidly recall the motor steps, the kinetic melodies (page 24) needed to form the letters. You may recall this was also a problem for Russell in chapter 2, our boy with motor dysfunctions, but his problems were limited to motor memory, the sequences of movements required to form letters. Clint had trouble with all varieties of memory retrieval (including memory for spelling, punctuation, and specific words).

It seemed that nothing was automatic for Clint during writing. He could remember punctuation and letter formation, but he had to stop and think about them too much, which slowed him down and disrupted the synchrony of his writing. Russell had to learn to make letter formation automatic, while Clint lacked a smooth and rapid flow from multiple memory reservoirs.

Spelling was a source of unending shame for Clint. Kids at his age take spelling very seriously and become painfully self-conscious when they commit too many errors. Spelling is conspicuous, nonnegotiable, and rigidly intolerant of deviation. If you can't spell, there must be something seriously defective in your brain—at least that's how many young delayed spellers think about their deficiency. And they dread the ever-lurking prospect of their peers seeing and ridiculing their spelling errors.

Students can manifest any number of forms of spelling difficulty. It is possible in many cases to uncover the breakdown that is the basis of a child's spelling difficulty by analyzing the kinds of spelling errors he makes. That was done during Clint's evaluation. Some children have trouble with the language sounds (i.e., they show weak phonological awareness). Their spelling reveals this confusion as they assemble letter combinations that fail to represent language sounds accurately. Often their spelling of a word bears a pretty good visual resemblance to the word but fails to approximate it phonetically. An example would be *mahgt* for *might*. These children seem to rely overly on visual memory. Because of their struggles with phonology, they are likely to have reading problems in addition to their spelling delays. Clint, however, was a very strong reader. Some inaccurate spellers have trouble with visual memory. This makes it hard for them to visualize words, so they work off the clues from how a word sounds. Such a misspeller is apt to substitute *enuff* for *enough* (it sounds right but bears little resemblance to the correct spelling). Our team had given Clint some designs to reproduce from memory, and he had done well on these. His parents had informed the team that Clint always remembered best the things that he had seen, suggesting strengths in his visual memory. Besides, his spelling errors were not all that phonetically accurate.

Some students spell inaccurately because they lack a sense of the recurring patterns or letter combinations within words; consequently, they keep making use of letter combinations we don't have in English. This was definitely true in Clint's case (see Figure 3-3). Some students

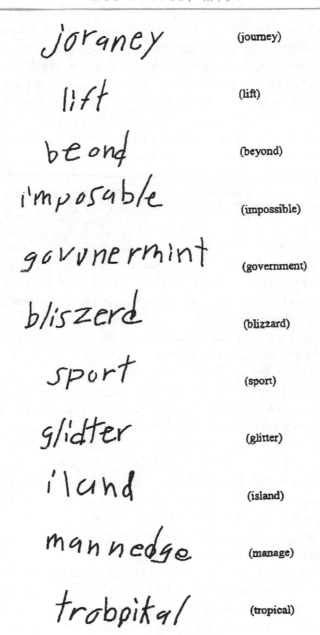

joraney (journey)

lift (lift)

beond (beyond)

imposable (impossible)

govvnermint (government)

bliszerd (blizzard)

sport (sport)

glidter (glitter)

iland (island)

mannedge (manage)

trobpikal (tropical)

Figure 3-3.   Clint's patterns of spelling are shown in this sample from a quiz he took in school. Many of his errors are phonetically accurate (such as "bliszerd" for *blizzard*), but they reflect trouble recalling fine details in the midsections of long words. He also makes use of letter patterns that are rare or nonexistent in English (e.g., "sz" and "dt"). These findings are common in students with memory-based writing difficulty.

can't recall conventional spelling rules or have diminished memory for the parts of words that recur regularly in our language. These meaning-ful fragments are called morphemes (such as *pre-, auto-, -tion*). The spelling errors of kids who have trouble with rules and regularity are sometimes described as "illegal." They defy our accepted spelling rules and patterns. Of course, English contains its share of irregular spellings, but it's hard for a kid to be aware of exceptions to the rules when he has only a tenuous grip on the rules themselves.

Sometimes children with weak attention controls show highly incon-sistent spelling, depicting a particular word correctly in one sentence and misspelling the same word farther down the page. But this was not true in Clint's case.

In addition to Clint's trouble recalling spelling rules and regulari-ties, his spelling, seen in Figure 3-3 and in his writing sample (Figure 3-1), contains mixed error types. There are phonetic mistakes, visual mistakes, and flagrant violations of spelling rules. Unfortunately, it has been shown that children who commit such a mixed bag of miscues have the gloomiest spelling outlook. Theirs are the hardest break-downs to repair. In perusing Clint's spelling quiz, you might notice a pattern that I come across very frequently in students with memory problems like Clint's. Observe that most often he is accurate with the first couple of letters in a word and also the last one or two letters, but he consistently gets in trouble in the midsections of words. It's as if he can't retrieve an entire string of letters intact, so he is able to preserve only a word's most conspicuous highlights, which for him are the first and final letters. The inside is a bit of a blur. I encounter this kind of spelling very often among students, like Clint, who are having long-term memory difficulties across the board in school. Their spelling in-accuracy is just one manifestation of a more basic problem with the precise recall of information.

Clint's long-term memory frustration sabotaged his work in mathe-matics. Whenever I encounter a child of his age who reads well but is having trouble in math and writing, I am prompted to take a close look at memory. In Clint's case there was a gap between his understanding of mathematical concepts, which was strong, and his computational skill, which was lacking. That's because he had trouble remember-ing his math facts and procedures. From what I learned, Mr. and Mrs. Walker regularly worked with him on his times tables after dinner on school nights, but he had serious trouble excavating those facts when he needed them for a quiz or a work sheet. His teacher noted that often Clint would come to a type of problem he had solved successfully on a previous occasion and comment, "I can't remember how to do that kind anymore."

HELPING CLINT

Clint was at a receptive age when we evaluated him. Ideally we want to see kids as young as possible. At age ten, Clint had not yet developed a host of typically adolescent complications (such as depression, delinquent tendencies, or a loss of motivation and ambition). At the same time he was old enough to understand the exact nature of his difficulty if it was explained to him with care and sensitivity. So I took on the responsibility for demystifying Clint. First of all, I destigmatized the problem by explaining that all kids have strengths and weaknesses and that sooner or later everybody's weaknesses are apt to trip them up from time to time. I wanted Clint to know that he was not unique in his troubles, not a special case, not a weird kid, and that the discussion we were having was one any student could benefit from. I pointed out that everybody in the world succeeds best in life when he understands his specific strengths and weaknesses.

I next described to Clint his impressive collection of strengths, including his athletic skill, his ability to express himself, his mechanical aptitude, his spatial capacities, his social assets, his talent riding horses, and even his good looks. The boy blushed but consumed what he was hearing like cotton candy. It's important to celebrate kids' strengths, especially when they're having a hard time with their schoolwork.

Then it was time to help Clint grasp his dysfunctions, his areas of weakness. This included giving him the terms or words for what he needed to be working on. After all, how can you try to improve on something if you don't even know what it's called? I have discovered that there's real magic in giving kids the words. It empowers them. Also, a kid then doesn't feel as if he's "retarded," pervasively and hopelessly defective. Instead, he is able to say, "So I'm real smart. I just have some problems getting stuff out of my long-term-memory storage tanks." Clint could grasp readily that he was struggling with memory weaknesses, and I tried to help him see the connection between these gaps and his problems in writing, in math, and in answering factual questions in class or on a test.

The final elements in Clint's demystification included what I call the induction of optimism and alliance formation. I wanted Clint to feel upbeat about his future and to know that we were his allies, his partners in the effort to succeed in school and beyond. I explored different careers in which Clint could combine his love of the outdoors with his great skill at fixing things and his devotion to animals. As we talked about various exciting agricultural careers Clint became so exuberantly bouncy and wriggly that I asked him if he needed to go to the bathroom. We discussed how exciting it would be to work as a ranger in the National Park Service, or become an athletic coach (Clint loved basketball), or maybe own his own ranch, or become a vet curing sick animals. To strengthen our alliance, I told Clint I would like very much to stay in touch with him and I would be available to help him achieve his goals in the years ahead. He nodded with enthusiasm and got up and quietly put his left arm around my shoulders.

Our diagnostic team compiled an extended list of recommendations to help Clint. His mother wanted to get him back into a regular school despite his recent progress during home schooling. Clint deeply missed his classmates and the sports program. So we were asked to prepare suggestions the school might (hopefully) follow through on. The recommendations are reproduced in the list below. They include accommodations (ways of working around the boy's memory problems) and what we call interventions at the breakdown points (suggestions aimed at strengthening Clint's memory).

RECOMMENDATIONS FOR CLINT

Accommodations:

• In view of his memory problems, upon his return to school it would be best to call on Clint in class for questions that can be answered "yes" or "no" rather than those requiring detailed responses. Alternatively, he could be warned a day in advance of a question he would be asked during class.

• When he returns to a regular school, other children should not correct Clint's papers. Also, he should not be required to solve math problems on the board in front of his classmates.

• When he writes something, Clint should be given separate grades for content and mechanics. He should not be penalized for poor spelling and handwriting problems.

• Clint should be allowed to use a laptop computer for at least some of his writing.

• Sometimes Clint might be allowed to give an oral report or submit a cassette recording rather than write a report.

• If he prefers, Clint should be permitted to print instead of having to use cursive writing, since for most students printing is less of a drain on memory.

• Clint will need extra time on tests in math and whenever extended writing is required. Alternatively, he might be given fewer problems to solve or allowed to write shorter answers. He could complete any unfinished portions at home.

• To bypass his memory gaps and allow Clint to keep progressing in his skills, he should be permitted to use a calculator during math quizzes or tests. Once his math facts become automatic, his use of the calculator can be discontinued.

Interventions at the Breakdown Points:

• Clint needs to do his writing in stages: first, he should brainstorm his ideas on blank paper or on his computer. Then he should arrange these ideas in a good order. Then he should write a rough draft without attending to neatness or accurate spelling. Then he should go back and find any errors. Finally, he should make one or more revised versions. Whenever possible, each of these steps should take place at different times—ideally no more than one stage on any given day.

• It will be important to give Clint plenty of opportunities to engage in highly motivational writing, creating written reports within his area of passion and expertise. He should be encouraged to write horse stories, descriptions of rodeos, and reports about animals.

• Whenever Clint writes, he should be asked to go back and review the "middle parts" of long words to see if he thinks he spelled them accurately. When he is stumped, his teacher should provide alternative spellings (including the correct version) for a misspelled word, allowing Clint to pick the best one. This will enable him to use recognition in place of retrieval memory. The former often works better for kids like him.

• Clint would benefit from being taught spelling rules. He should maintain his own personal spelling rule book. He should also practice defining morphemes, that is, identifying the meanings of parts of words such as *pre-, hyper-,* and *mega-*. Additionally, Clint could be shown lists of letter clusters and asked to circle the ones that occur in English and cross out the ones that don't. Then he could be asked to provide a real-word example for each of the sets of letters that are found in English.

• Clint will need continuing drills on his math facts, on common spelling words, and on rapid letter formation, so he can attain an efficient level of automatization. Such practice might be made into a game with suitable scoring and rewards (appealing to Clint's competitive spirit). These activities should take place at home immediately before Clint goes to sleep, since it is known that this is a time when information best consolidates in long-term memory.

• Clint is a highly effective strategist. Therefore, he is likely to respond to being taught various memory-strengthening techniques. For example, he should be helped to understand that it is easiest to remember information by doing something to it rather than just trying to remember it by rote. If it's verbal, make it visual (e.g., draw a diagram). If it's visual (like a parallelogram), describe it in your own words. He should use his good verbal skills to keep talking about what he is learning, to elaborate on information he needs to remember.

• It will be very important for Clint to learn more about memory and how it's supposed to work. It is suggested that he read Dr. Mel Levine's book *Keeping a Head in School* for some more suggestions he could grasp with his very good reading skills. Whenever he studies, Clint needs to pose to himself the question "How am I going to remember this?"

Other Suggestions:

• We do not recommend that Clint be retained in his current grade. Grade retention at this point would deal a serious blow to his self-esteem, and scientific studies have shown that it simply doesn't help kids his age academically. It is also known that many people in their forties and fifties are still losing sleep over having been left back! We feel this could have seriously adverse effects on Clint's mental health. There is no reason to believe that grade retention will improve his memory.

• It will be very important to strengthen Clint's strengths. He needs abundant opportunities to keep on perfecting his verbal assets. Making oral presentations, making announcements over the P.A. system, acting a role in a school play, or running for political office could bolster Clint's self-esteem while polishing his strong communication skills. He also would benefit from opportunities to take care of animals and to further develop his mechanical aptitude. For example, he could assist a farrier with shoeing horses or gain experience with the maintenance of ranch equipment.

• Clint's equestrian interests should be cultivated and celebrated in school and at home. He should develop expertise in this area of passion. It would help him if he became an authority on horses, on ranches, or on cowboy history. He is most likely to enhance his memory function and written output within his area of affinity and expertise. He might then extend it to other domains.

• Clint's parents need to keep reassuring him that he is smart. From time to time they should discuss his memory issues with him.

CLINT'S PROSPECTS

Although Clint lived too far from North Carolina for any follow-up visits, I received and responded to several letters. One was from Clint himself, about a month after his visit. It included a great passage that went something like this (I've corrected the spelling): "Doc, I used to think when you're messin' up in school there's only two reasons—you're either dumb or else you're just plain lazy. I knew I wasn't dumb, so I thought I was lazy. Now I know I have a lot of trouble with my remembering. So now I'm completely sure I'm not dumb and I'm not lazy either." Clint reported that he felt great after his evaluation. A note from his mom confirmed this. Clint thought the evaluation had helped him a lot, mostly by letting him know that he had a problem he could work on and that he had plenty of strengths to build on as well.

When he arrived home Clint called his grandparents with the official announcement that he was not lazy or stupid. He described to them the evaluation process step by step, but he couldn't recall my name.

Somehow Clint's well-meaning teachers had convinced him that laziness was his moral crime in school. Our center had found him innocent. In my opinion a good assessment should always be a form of treatment and redemption. Kids should come away from an assessment feeling uplifted, seeing positive possibilities for themselves, the proverbial light at the end of the tunnel. At the same time, they should feel that they are accountable for continuing to expend effort (with help) to improve their output.

Several months later a letter from his mother indicated that Clint was back in the public school "on a trial basis." She was hoping our report would sensitize the school to Clint's legitimate needs, and later she reported that his teacher had been very open and receptive when she had read the recommendations.

4

GINNY CALDWELL

Repeated Energy Crises

A pen is certainly an excellent instrument to fix a man's attention.
—JOHN ADAMS, *LETTERS* (1760)

When children or adults are distracted they are paying attention to something else. Whether it's soap falling into the bathtub, an apple falling from a tree, or the peculiar way an insect walks across the floor, small attractions may lead to bigger ideas. Being distracted, in other words, means otherwise attracted.
—ELLEN J. LANGER, *THE POWER OF MINDFUL LEARNING* (1997)

Ginny is most definitely her own worst enemy. She shows streaks of brilliance, true talent in so many areas—but only once in a while. There are countless hours and days during which she accomplishes absolutely nothing. That is, nothing except fooling around with her friends during class. I never know if she will hand in a homework assignment, finish a test, or make any progress whatsoever on a science or art project. She's downright unpredictable. And when you come right down to it, she's just plain lazy. It's as simple as that. But I've seen her shine often enough to know that when Ginny really makes up her mind to do her work, she can do it and she can do it commendably. Unfortunately, all too often she has a negative attitude, and pure and simple laziness takes over. That's why she is getting failing grades. She will continue to fail until she gets herself motivated and decides to start putting forth consistent effort. I know she can do it." These comments were communicated on the midterm report card of sixth grader Virginia ("Ginny") Caldwell. Such comments are commonly aimed at children with misunderstood output failure.

I first encountered Ginny when her pediatrician in North Carolina referred her to our center for an evaluation. She had copper-blond hair tied back in an eight-inch ponytail and a perfectly sculpted face with a dusting of fine freckles on each cheek. She was wearing blue denim shorts cut short with a scalloped edge and a golden yellow ruffled tank top that nicely clashed with her shocking pink mother-of-pearl toenail polish. She was a beautiful and flamboyant twelve-year-old awkwardly striving to be mistaken for sixteen. She spoke with a deep southern rural accent that was both disarming and charming, a cultural amalgam of Tennessee Williams syntax and country-music lyricism. I kept wanting to mimic her speech. She talked with a rapid drawl—that sounds contradictory, but that's how the flow of her words came across.

When Ginny entered my office, she appeared fiercely angry with her mom for bringing her to see me. I'm quite accustomed to that frosty cold demeanor in my patients between ages twelve and sixteen. They so fervently yearn to be perceived by the adolescent throng as the picture of normalcy (i.e., "coolness") that a visit to Dr. Mel Levine is like a painful wound to one's reputation. Ginny therefore made no eye contact with me, and instead stared through the window as if she were a botanist intently investigating Chapel Hill flora.

Mrs. Caldwell, in her daughter's presence, described Ginny's school and home problems. She reported that Ginny was very popular with other kids of both genders, that she was "from the tips of her toes to the top of her head a true people person." She was never a behavior problem at home or in school, but her troubles were attributed to the fact that she was "just plain lazy." It seemed that this girl was a workaphobic (my invented facetious word, not her mother's). So she produced virtually no homework, mostly refused to study for tests, and seldom accomplished any assigned reading. Instead she filibustered on the phone much of every evening. Mrs. Caldwell lamented, "I have never met anybody who was as good at wastin' time as my Ginny."

Ginny's mother related that her daughter was a night owl. She often read plays and would stay up late drawing costume designs or sketching scenery. She loved theater and design, two deep interests that were often activated during her hours of nocturnal creativity. She would remain awake night after night until one or two A.M., sometimes even later, and the next morning her mother and father would almost have to pry her out of bed in time to catch the school bus. The girl seldom had time for breakfast. On average she seemed to be getting about five or six hours of sleep on school nights. On weekends Ginny would often hibernate until noon. She insisted adamantly that she could never fall asleep at a decent hour; while trying to doze off, she would fold and unfold her body in bed like a hyperactive inchworm. Besides, she maintained, she did her best thinking late at night.

Ginny's teachers completed a school questionnaire to provide our diagnostic team with comprehensive information about her day-to-day behavior and performance. Again, there were no indications of serious behavior problems, but Ginny was described as "socially distractible," far too intrigued and preoccupied with her peers during class. One teacher wrote at the bottom of one page, "I have never seen anyone as interested in everyone around her as this child seems to be. She listens in on three conversations at once and tries to get her two cents into each of them! She is so tuned in to the other children that she can't seem to think about much else."

Ginny's academic skills were inconsistent. She was a very competent reader and speller, at least one year above her grade level. This was a tribute to her innate language talent. Mathematics was nothing short of torture for Ginny; she was still struggling with long division, couldn't grasp fractions, and made profuse calculation errors on tests and work sheets. Often the quality of Ginny's math work would fluctuate within a single assignment. She might miss an easy problem only to succeed on a more difficult challenge farther down the work sheet.

Her teachers had a hard time commenting on Ginny's writing abilities because they were so inexplicably erratic. From time to time, this girl would write a poignant story or skit worthy of publication as the lead article in the middle school literary magazine. At other times her written output was either nonexistent or reminiscent of the naive scrawl of a second grader. Such performance inconsistency baffled her parents and teachers.

In the classroom Ginny acted as if she were allergic to whatever the janitors cleaned the chairs with. You would think that some toxic substance was causing a chronic itch of her back and buttocks, as she would writhe, fidget, gyrate, and modify her posture in endless cycles of restlessness. She alternated among sitting on one foot, on the other foot, on both feet, and on no feet. She would maneuver her weight deftly in rhythmless rocking so that the chair was a fulcrum balanced precariously on two of its legs, or three of its legs, but rarely all four. One teacher wrote that although Ginny was exceedingly fidgety, she wasn't actually "hyperactive." She didn't race around. She also didn't get into fights or do impulsive things that might land her in trouble.

When I spoke alone with the beguiling Ginny, she revealed her hand with the greatest of caution—typical of kids who have been numbed with criticism. At first she denied having any problems in school. She said she liked school, especially lunch and phys ed. She reported that she couldn't stand either of her two teachers and reassuringly chanted the classic early-adolescent comforting refrain "And none of my friends like them either." She pointed out she could do well only when she liked the teacher (another common middle school excuse—especially since you may like only teachers whose class you do well in). Ginny admitted that most of school was boring and commented that what they taught kids in her school was "less than useless" (a tough description to quantify). She added, "I'm never gonna use any of it" (yet another traditional middle school rationalization). She then confessed her dread of mathematics, presumably the most useless subject to her way of thinking. The denigration of anything you're not good at is one more overutilized defensive ploy in this age group. Of course, there are some adults who also employ this self-protective adolescent tactic!

Ginny mentioned to me that she had a lot of trouble sleeping and often felt tired during the day. She added vividly, "In school I only feel totally awake when I'm on the go, when I'm walking around, having lunch, or talking to my friends. The rest of the time I mostly zone out."

I really felt for what she was enduring. Under her veneer of self-assured charm and indifference, she was hurting badly. She was disappointed in herself and uneasy about her future, about where her ways were leading her.

I did a complete physical and neurological examination on Ginny. She turned out to be a pretty normal early adolescent, and there were no disturbing neurological findings. Then I performed a neurodevelopmental examination, throughout which Ginny was cooperative and pleasant, but I could see that she was struggling valiantly to maintain her focus. She yawned, stretched, and fidgeted pretty much nonstop. I felt as if I were pushing her up a steep slope. As the examination proceeded, Ginny's mental fatigue became increasingly disabling. Reflecting on her history as told by her mother and the school, and adding my own direct observations, I concluded that Ginny was having significant trouble mobilizing and maintaining a steady flow of mental energy. She lacked the stamina needed to sustain her concentration and put forth dependable effort. She was running on empty. A lack of mental energy is often misconstrued as laziness. Nevertheless, Ginny revealed a nice stockpile of usable strengths. She exhibited, in particular, strong language functioning, excellent motor coordination, and keen spatial perception.

Only two forms of neurodevelopmental dysfunction surfaced during my evaluation of Ginny. First, there were her obvious problems with attention in the form of a difficulty marshaling and sustaining the needed supply of mental energy, but, as well, Ginny's active working memory was also weak. The latter consists of the ability to hold or juggle several things in your mind at once. Active working memory lets you stop and think about the right punctuation for a sentence without forgetting what you intended to say in the next sentence. It also allows you to hold in your head the various parts of a math problem while solving it; that way you don't lose track or forget what you're doing.

Our educational diagnostician assessed Ginny that day and confirmed her strong reading and spelling skills, although even in these domains there was noticeable fluctuation, as her output was marred by frequent careless errors. Math was indeed a formidable stumbling block. Ginny showed that she understood the concepts and procedures, but her solutions to problems were erratic. She would sometimes forget what she was doing while in the middle of a computation. As part of her educational evaluation, Ginny was asked to write a page-long essay about what she liked and disliked in her school. Her very brief written response is seen in Figure 4-1.

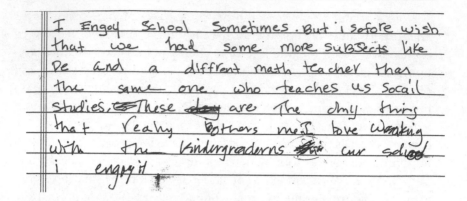

I Engoy School Sometimes. But i sofore wish that we had some more subsects like pe and a diffrent math teacher than the same one who teaches us socail studies, These ~~day~~ are the only thing that really ~~bothers~~ me. I love working with the kindergraderns ~~in~~ our school i engoy it.

Figure 4-1.   Ginny's brief paragraph was written hastily. As she proceeded down the page, even in this very short passage, she started running out of mental energy and so she made careless errors that she had to cross out. When asked later to correct her writing, Ginny found all of her spelling and capitalization errors and fixed them accurately.

Finally, our child psychologist interviewed Ginny. He felt that she was basically a normal early adolescent (if there is such a thing). However, there were indications that Ginny's self-esteem was in decline. She rated herself as not nearly as smart as other kids and seriously wondered if she would even finish high school. It was thought that she might be at risk of depression in the future.

Our social worker interviewed Mrs. Caldwell, who explained that Ginny's father hadn't come with them and did not approve of his daughter getting evaluated. He insisted he'd been just like her when he was a kid. A lineman for the electric company, he had been laid off a few months earlier. But Mrs. Caldwell was especially bothered by a comment her spouse had made as she and Ginny left that morning: "Ginny's just gonna be a waitress and have kids like her mom. She don't need no high school education. Nowadays they got these computers—you don't need no math to figure out the price of a barbecue plate, hush puppies, and slaw!"

The family lived on a nine-acre farm, where they kept Appaloosa horses, chickens, and Nubian goats. Ginny had one brother, B.J., age nine, who was described by their mother as "no great shakes as a student." His mom commented that B.J. had lots of "people sense" but no "book sense." He loved most of all to go hunting with his dad.

Apparently Ginny and B.J. were engaged in nearly constant verbal warfare, with occasional hand-to-hand combat, which their parents intentionally ignored. Since he wasn't working—except for some odd jobs—Mr. Caldwell had plenty of quality time with B.J. When the social worker asked about her husband's unemployment, Mrs. Caldwell stated that after numerous warnings he had been fired for being "so unreliable." He had been regularly late for work because he overslept or somehow just didn't feel like doing much of anything. But she was quick to point out that her husband was a good man and had never had a drinking problem. She added with some pride that his fellow workers claimed that Eddie Caldwell couldn't be beat when it came to tough repair work—"when he was on." Not surprisingly, Mrs. Caldwell told the social worker that sometimes Ginny reminded her of her husband. She admitted that she often wondered if Ginny would ever be able to hold a job.

Mrs. Caldwell suspected that her spouse's comment about Ginny's future was right on target. She pointed out, "Even though she's gettin' nothin' out of school and doin' nothin' in school, it might be that it's just God's will, and we should stop yellin' at her and let her be whoever the Lord meant her to be." But then tears welled up in Mrs. Caldwell's eyes, and she sighed. "Of course, bein' so pretty and sociable and all that, before we know it she could go and get herself a baby. That's what happened to me before I could get me an education."

Ginny's current circumstances certainly raised an abundance of psychological, educational, and ethical issues. How hard should you push a child? How often can a kid endure criticism without giving up and losing all motivation? Aren't there many trades that require little or no mathematical active working memory? Why not aim for those? Should we try to change Ginny or should we alter our expectations? I've come to believe that the answers rest somewhere in the middle. We can still teach Ginny math but perhaps at a slower pace. We cannot expect her to sustain her concentration as well as her classmates in view of her chronic mental fatigue, but we can give her frequent breaks and find better ways for her to stay alert. We can also take advantage of her people skills and her creativity to enable her to have some leadership responsibilities in school. Whatever we do, we must help Ginny feel good about who she is, what she is, and what she is likely to become. I really liked Ginny. I remember thinking how she would make a terrific child actress; she always seemed to be putting on a show, and it was a very entertaining and well-intentioned display.

EXPLORING GINNY'S MENTAL-ENERGY-CONTROL PROBLEMS

To work out, climb a mountain, mop a floor, or conduct an orchestra, you need physical energy, power generated through the burning of calories. We now know that heavy-duty mental labor also saps one's energy. However, little if any mental energy is required for talking to a friend on the phone, watching a soap opera, or playing your newest video game. Those activities call for minimal effort, but a lot is needed to study for a history test, fill out tax forms, write a report, or memorize historical dates.

The flow of mental energy ordinarily comes under the tight regulation of attention. Attention is the administrator of many crucial brain activities and agendas, including what I like to call mental-energy control. Attention also regulates the quality of output (see chapter 5) and the processing of incoming information. Of course, Ginny's problem was mental-energy flow. She lacked the spark to ignite mind work and the stamina to complete it.

Clearly, in people like Ginny (and, in all likelihood, her dad as well), there's a strong connection between low output and low mental energy. Individuals with inadequate mental energy flow and distribution are like automobiles with defective fuel lines; somewhere between the gasoline pump at the station and the engine under the hood, not enough fuel is getting where it needs to be. The result is a vehicle that's hard to start, that keeps stalling, or that may never make it to its destination. In the case of a child like Ginny, the mental energy sometimes may be getting sent to the wrong parts of her mind, preventing her from getting work accomplished.

Ginny got into trouble in school because she kept walking around or repeatedly asked to go to the bathroom. When I asked her about this, she confessed, "I have to keep moving or my mind will fall asleep on me." Many kids with low levels of mental energy actually do try to wake themselves up by substituting physical energy for mental energy; they fidget, contort their bodies, and wander like nomads in a desperate attempt to reach a more satisfactory level of alertness. That was certainly true in Ginny's case. Isn't it odd that kids get criticized for being fidgety when they should be commended for implementing a strategy that significantly elevates their attention?

Sophisticated scans have revealed a low or misdirected flow of mental energy to critical brain areas in some individuals with attention deficits and some other learning differences. So sleeping on the job or in school may often have a physiological explanation.

Our primary mental-energy controls are located at the base of the brain, in the brain stem. Four basic controls are employed at that site: alertness, mental effort, sleep arousal, and consistency. In Ginny's case they were pretty much all out of control.

- Alertness control seems to be the spigot that delivers the mental energy needed to concentrate, enabling a student to sit and listen to directions or explanations in chemistry class. It ensures that the driver of a car will remain alert on the highway at 11:30 P.M. It helps an infantryman stay focused while on guard duty. When alertness control is not functioning, concentration is likely to be superficial, erratic, or too readily diverted. A person may then feel bored and restless when required to sit still and concentrate. Like Ginny, she or he may too readily run out of intellectual steam.

- Mental-effort control relates more directly to output. Mental-effort capacity is your ability to conduct mind work that may not be fun. Almost by definition, true work may not be easy. When I mentioned to the author Tom Wolfe that I was writing a book on output, his face lit up with delight and he recalled that a 1921 edition of the *Encyclopaedia Britannica* had characterized work as "irksome toil." I became instantly enamored of that phrase—as he was. And it appears that different minds, much like engines, feature different levels of working capacity; they pull different loads and tolerate different intensities of "irksome toil." For some children and adults, sustained brain work is too much work; it drains far too much effort. These people are not lazy; they just tire easily. Ginny kept trying to explain this to me and also to her parents and teachers.

- Sleep-arousal control is another key component of mental-energy control. This process enables you to sleep adequately at night and to be mentally energized during the day. A web of nerve cells in the brain stem works like the mute button on the remote control for your TV set. These cells switch off the volume in your brain so you can fall asleep without hearing all the sounds outside your window and fretting over your troubles in life. In the morning your brain gets a wake-up call and that mute button is disengaged, so you can feel awake and tuned in. Regrettably, some kids and grown-ups, like Ginny, have what we call a sleep-arousal imbalance. That is, they are not sufficiently asleep at night and their daylight hours are clouded in mental fatigue.

• Consistency control is the fourth and last of the mental-energy-control knobs. Its job is to provide an even flow of mental energy throughout the day, year in and year out. It allows us to perform in a way that is reasonably consistent, dependable, and reliable. Many individuals with mental-energy-control problems show high levels of performance inconsistency. You may recall that Ginny's father was said to be unreliable. When he was on, he was a terrific mechanic, but frequently he didn't even show up for work. That's performance inconsistency. You can't count on someone like that; his performance is all over the place. Like streak hitters in baseball, these people vacillate unpredictably from superstar status to extended slumps.

Ginny frequently committed errors on her math tests that made no sense whatsoever: she would succeed on the first three items, then mess up the next three, only to triumph on the next four (our streak hitter at work). Or else she would dazzle her teacher with her clever solution to a very difficult problem, but then proceed to blow two very easy ones. She would come to school one fine morning admirably prepared for her social studies test. Then on a subsequent day she'd be at loose ends and not ready for much of anything. Inconsistency of this type causes widespread adult bewilderment and anguish. The pattern most often leads to heavy moral accusation and condemnation—typically, "We know he can do the work when he really makes up his mind to apply himself; we've seen him do it." Affected students and grown-ups become accustomed to hearing that they are lazy, but in reality, they are working hard, perhaps harder than most other people. They are working to overcome the effects of a fuel-deprived mind.

EXPLORING GINNY'S ACTIVE-WORKING-MEMORY PROBLEMS

Ginny's other significant academic liability lay in the area of active working memory. Some children and adults, like Ginny, have limited space for active working memory. While they're engaged in one part of a task they are apt to forget some or all of the rest of it. In school, active-working-memory dysfunctions cause the greatest damage in writing and in mathematics. That was certainly true for Ginny. But gaps like hers can also bludgeon everyday life. On the way to the refrigerator, you stop to wipe off the kitchen counter, but does that interruption make you forget what you wanted from the refrigerator? While repairing a broken fan, you put down the screwdriver and pick up the pliers. Then you need to use that screwdriver again. Can you remember where you just put it? Ginny described how, recently, she'd had to remember the combination to open her locker. While turning the dial, she'd forgotten that she had gone to her locker to fetch her math book. She'd grabbed her lunch instead, arriving textless in math class. Many an absentminded professor may struggle with a dysfunction of active working memory. Strengths in other domains help them nonetheless mount the academic ladder.

Active-working-memory dysfunctions make extended writing difficult for students like Ginny. They can't seem to keep together in their minds all the different strands of thought and all the rules that have to be maintained until written work gets done. While puzzling over a tough spelling word, Ginny would lose her train of thought or forget about punctuation, even though she really understood how to punctuate. This can lead to output failure and make a kid shut down when it comes to demands for written output.

COMBINED EFFECTS

So Ginny certainly fits the description of a child with mental-energy and active-working-memory dysfunctions. By the way, it is very common for people to have more than one reason for their struggles. Many different combinations of neurodevelopmental dysfunctions can be found eating away at an individual's output. Ginny's problems in writing and in mathematics are very likely to have stemmed from the combined effects of both weaknesses. She found it hard to mobilize and keep up mental effort when she tackled a taxing academic demand, such as composing an essay or studying for a test, and she displayed conspicuously low working capacity. She endured a significant sleep-arousal imbalance and was likely sleep deprived through the school day. Further, she confused everyone (including herself) with her extreme performance inconsistency. To make matters worse, her attentional woes were complicated by her weaknesses of active working memory; so even when she concentrated, her work was apt to have missing parts.

One further issue is worthy of emphasis in Ginny's profile: her high level of "social distractibility." This child could not seem to filter out, even temporarily, all the interpersonal activities in her classroom. She was overwhelmingly preoccupied with people, with relationships, with her own status within the group. During class and throughout much of her school day she was part social anthropologist (studying her peers), part gossip columnist (devouring and publicizing impending scandals), part child actress (displaying, especially for the boys), and part aspiring young political leader (campaigning for widespread approval). Her social agendas pretty much eclipsed everything else. Ginny was ever the social butterfly—and had been so even as an infant. Such social performing has its advantages, but, as we've seen, it can undermine output, particularly academic productivity.

A certain level of keen social awareness can be a tremendous asset during the school years and in a career, as it can make you especially sensitive to the needs and feelings of others you work with or for. But some adults are so overly focused on the social dynamics and petty political intrigues of the workplace that their work suffers. They talk too much about other people (sometimes unkindly), and they think too much about other people rather than thinking about salient issues and missions. Ginny might be like that someday.

HELPING GINNY

After her evaluation, we set about working to bolster Ginny's output in school. We had an unwilling client who kept denying that she was in any academic peril. I demystified Ginny's plight for her and her mom, describing in some detail the mental-energy controls and active working memory. I wanted so much to reach Ginny but sensed the barrier between us, as impenetrable as a bank vault. I often encounter this barrier among early adolescents. They are in such heavy denial that they want us to leave them alone (with their friends, of course), and they shun adult advice as if allergic to it.

I discussed Ginny's numerous strengths, including her excellent reading and language abilities. We also talked about her creativity and her special love of theater and design. I praised her for her terrific social cognition and her success with peers and suggested that she had potential as a leader, since other kids respected and often followed her (for better or for worse). However, we did deal with the possibility that sometimes her social interests got a little out of control and stood in the way of her accomplishing work. Of all the matters we covered, the suggestion of social concerns was met with the most vociferous denial, bordering on hostility. That's about what you expect from early-adolescent kids. The social arena is a forbidden kingdom; adults are unwelcome—especially an invasive clinician like me.

Despite some theatrical stoicism and her gloomy mask of sheer boredom, I think some of what we talked about made an impression on Ginny. It certainly interested her mother, who concurred with our team's assessment.

In a report to the school and her parents, we recommended that Ginny be allowed to get up and walk around when she needed to in school. We also suggested that she squeeze a soft rubber ball or manipulate some other object to legitimize her fidgetiness. We mentioned ways her mom could help her with her writing, emphasizing, in particular, Ginny's need to write in stages instead of trying to do it all at once. We provided additional advice of the type described in chapters 10 and 11. In math she was encouraged to whisper under her breath while solving problems. She was also urged to form real-life pictures in her mind (i.e., scenery) while tackling word problems. That would tend to keep the spotlights of her theatrical mind focused on what she was doing, preventing her from drifting off. She was also prompted to write down as much as possible during problem solving to reduce the load on her active working memory.

We suggested that Ginny try to get into bed at the same time each evening—even if she didn't go right to sleep. She could read or listen to country music, but she shouldn't get out of bed. I pointed out that eight good hours of sleep would make schoolwork a lot easier for her. I reassured her that her lack of sleep would not hurt her health. Too often kids worry so much about not being able to sleep that then they can't possibly sleep. I also told her that if things didn't improve, at some point we could consider some sleep medication. Such treatment used over a few months sometimes corrects a problematic sleep pattern.

I explained to Ginny and her mother that some kids with mental-energy problems benefit from taking medication that helps wake them up during the day. I was thinking specifically about using a long-acting stimulant medication, a form of dextroamphetamine. Such a drug is never the whole answer to a student's low output, but in some instances it definitely makes a difference. Her mother seemed interested in this therapeutic option, but Ginny got furious and rejected medication. "You think I'm some kind of mental case. No one's gonna drug me up and make me a dope addict." A phone call from Mr. Caldwell three days later reinforced Ginny's stance: "Sorry, Doc, no daughter of mine gonna be on no drugs. She's just lazy, that's all, lazy like a possum. And I know where she gets it."

Ginny's school was extremely cooperative and sympathetic. Her teachers came up with plans to help her in math and to give her more after-school supervision on writing assignments. Since she loved theater, her teacher decided to have Ginny write some short plays that the class could perform. Ginny did so reluctantly, but her classmates were in awe of Ginny's skits. She wrote and directed two such productions, then refused to create any others. Like many confused and ambivalent early adolescents, she seemed to fear success.

It was obvious that the school personnel felt for this girl and wanted to do all they could, even though Ginny could be pretty obstinate. I knew just how they felt. I too wanted very much to help Ginny, and I was sure that down deep she was crying out for help, but she just couldn't or wouldn't allow herself to admit her distress and her need. Maybe she was too afraid. Some people decide not to try to change because they are fearful that their attempt to do so will result in yet another failure in life.

I lost contact with Ginny for several years. She and her mother didn't come back for follow-up visits, in large part because Ginny refused to see me again. Then out of the blue, at age sixteen, Ginny, who was failing three subjects in ninth grade, asked if she could talk to that doctor in Chapel Hill. We set up a return appointment. This time her father came along. At that point he was still employed only part-time.

The not so subtle smell of alcohol was on Mr. Caldwell's breath as he entered my office. He then revealed that Ginny had been drinking a lot, had recently undergone an abortion, and had a court date after having been caught shoplifting for the third time. All that turbulence seemed to have triggered serious reflections for Ginny and her dad. She'd decided she didn't much like herself. I was told that while searching for money in her mother's dresser drawer, she had come across my tattered four-year-old report, the document she had originally refused to examine. That led to her request for a return appointment. This time Ginny could not have been more receptive and friendly. She was a different kid; she wanted help, and wanted it badly. She was beginning to acquire a value called ambition. Feeling ambitious can either help a person become more productive or add to the frustration of output failure.

Our follow-up testing revealed that profound weaknesses in math and writing continued to plague Ginny. We suggested specific forms of tutorial help, which she accepted and her school provided.

Ginny asked me to put her on Ritalin to help her concentrate, largely because one of her friends was taking it (a universal adolescent decision-making criterion). I spent time reviewing Ginny's mental-energy and active-working-memory problems with her and her parents. Her father kept nodding his head, and at one point he blurted out, "Doc, tell you the truth, you're talkin' about me much as her." Mr. Caldwell felt so desperate that, against his better judgment, he okayed Ginny's treatment with medication. As it turned out, she improved dramatically. There were still some problems, especially with written output, but she became much more conscientious and motivated, and her writing did show some improvement. She talked about becoming a cosmetician. That sounded good to me. Incidentally, Mr. Caldwell subsequently called to say that he thought he was getting back his full-time job as a lineman with the power company and wondered if he should take Ritalin too. I referred him to a knowledgeable physician who treats adults.

5

SCOTT MURRAY

Controls Out of Control

I have detected in my son an outstanding fault, that he is far too easy-going, too indolent, that he has the sum total of all those traits that render a man inactive; on the other hand he is too impatient, too hasty, and will not abide his time. Two opposing elements rule his nature, I mean there is always too much or too little, never the golden mean. If he is not immediately in want, then he is immediately satisfied and becomes indolent and lazy. If he has to bestir himself, then he realizes his worth and wants to make his fortune at once. Nothing must stand in his way; yet it is unfortunately those who possess outstanding genius who have the greatest obstacles to face.

—Letter from Leopold Mozart describing his son,
Wolfgang Amadeus, 1782

Human beings differ profoundly in regard to the tendency to view their lives as a whole. To some it is natural to do so, and essential to happiness. . . . To others life is a series of detached incidents without directed movement and without unity. The habit of viewing life as a whole is an essential part of wisdom . . . and is one of the things which ought to be encouraged in education. Consistent purpose is not enough to make life happy, but it is almost an indispensable condition of a happy life. And consistent purpose embodies itself mainly in work.

—Bertrand Russell, *The Conquest of Happiness* (1930)

Duxxxxring a ski trip to Vail, Colorado, Scott Murray totaled his sporty white Lexus when he rounded a curve and collided with a tree. He suffered only minor contusions and strained neck ligaments from whiplash. But his girlfriend, Courtney, seated next to him, fractured her pelvis, ruptured her spleen, and sustained three broken ribs. She spent several weeks in traction. The teenage couple in the back seat were fine.

At age seventeen Scott loved to drive and seemed to use his car to test his limits.

At the time of the collision, Scott Murray was launching his second junior year at a new school, his third joust with prep school since ninth grade. He was turning over a new leaf. This time he was determined to hit the books, to settle down and finally realize all that "awesome potential" everyone had always assured him he possessed. He would no longer be a "slacker," as he put it.

Shortly before the accident, Mrs. Murray reported that Ron Murray had really let his son have it. He'd called him a lazy worthless playboy, nothing but a parasite and a disgrace to the whole family. Scott had been forced to absorb similar verbal knockout punches in the past, but never had they been so ferocious. "I should have quit after Sean. You have just as much ability as your brother, maybe more. Look what he's been able to do with his life. Why the hell can't you do anything right? You're nothing but a goddamn lazy loser." Scott had struggled to rein in his emotions and not strike back. Besides, he'd thought, his dad was basically right.

Scott was perpetually a disappointment to his parents, in vivid contrast to Sean, six years older. Sean had been a decorated student athlete. He was a product of Andover, from which he'd graduated with distinction, and a magna cum laude graduate of Yale. A captain of the Eli swim team, Sean had also earned a letter in varsity lacrosse. He'd been a finalist for a Rhodes scholarship but hadn't made the cut, and Scott, with barely perceptible guilt, had felt relief when Sean was deprived of this honor. Sean was currently at Harvard pursuing an MBA.

Ron Murray was one of the most successful entrepreneurs in America, a self-made man who'd climbed the career ladder like a veteran fireman. He was unstoppable, ambitious, innovative, and sharply decisive at every turning point in his life. Starting out with paltry resources, he had built a regional airline, competing successfully with the high-flying giants. At the same time he had made numerous shrewd investments in technology and real estate. He was, as they say, wisely diversified. One business magazine listed him among the five hundred wealthiest individuals in the country.

Catherine Murray, Scott's mom, was equally successful in her own right. She was well known in philanthropic circles. The local children's museum had basically been her idea; she and a group of her friends had raised the money for it in record time. She also was active in supporting research in AIDS and breast cancer. Mrs. Murray seemed incapable of slowing down, but whatever she did led to laudable results. She was an output marvel.

Although they often had too little time for one another, the Murrays were a reasonably close family. They were owners of several homes scattered around the globe and regularly embarked in their private Learjet for vacations together. Mr. and Mrs. Murray and Sean loved golf and had low handicaps. Scott was not a golfer but shared the family's enjoyment of skiing and always went along to stay at their home in Vail during winter weekends and over Christmas. He was the best skier in the family. It seemed that any activity that featured rapid motion resonated with the rhythm of Scott's kind of mind.

I first was asked to see Scott for an evaluation when he was about to turn eighteen and in the eleventh grade. The headmaster of the New England boarding school where Scott was on probation referred him to our center. Most of the faculty members who knew Scott had recommended outright expulsion. But the headmaster was fond of him, and, besides, he was interested in having Mr. Murray join the school board. He had heard me speak at a meeting of the National Association of Independent Schools and seriously wondered if this bright and likable young man could have some kind of hidden neurodevelopmental dysfunction that was leading to his abysmally low academic output and causing him to earn failing grades in three of his five courses that year. The dean of students disagreed with the referral, fervently maintaining that Scott was nothing more than a spoiled brat. The headmaster was snared in an unenviable trap, since Ron Murray had just contributed $300,000 toward the school's new center for the arts, and there might well be more to come.

SCOTT'S HISTORY

I was able to splice together historical information about Scott from our questionnaires and an extended interview with Mrs. Murray, who turned out to be a lovely, devoted, but confused mom. Once I succeeded in diverting my eyes from the megacarat diamond anchored on her right hand, I found myself listening to a biography reminiscent of many I had heard in the past.

As a baby Scott had been impossible to satisfy; he always seemed hungry or cranky, constantly yearning for something he didn't have. His sleep patterns were not a big problem, but he was seriously colicky. Throughout his toddler and preschool years, he was active, but always manageable and lovable. At the same time, he was more demanding than a drill sergeant. When he wanted something or wanted to do something, he would not let you alone until his desire was satisfied. In this way, he often wore out his mom and his nanny.

In preschool, Scott emerged as the master sergeant of a three- and four-year-old, mostly male battalion. His followers especially appreciated Scott's innovative silliness. In every way Scott's intellectual abilities appeared to be developing normally; in fact, his preschool teacher described his language functioning as "quite precocious." Scott then went on to academic distinction during his first three grades. He attended a well-respected private academy in Connecticut, where he earned the plaudits of demanding teachers. However, scattered comments alluded to Scott's provocative behavior; he was becoming a troublemaker. He knew how to goad an entire classroom from perfect tranquillity to agitation. Nevertheless, his second-grade teacher pointed out on a report card, "Scott is simply a delight to have in class. He gets his work done, helps others, and he's always polite. And I must say I have never seen anyone have as much fun as Scott does when he's having fun!"

In fourth grade, the work starts to get more challenging and the workload more ponderous. This is typically a turning point in elementary education when output demands soar. Scott's academic decline, his output failure, set in. His basic skills at that point were quite respectable. He was reading at a fifth-grade level and performing comparably in the steadily cumulative subskills of mathematics. The only exception was writing. Scott never ran short of creative ideas, many of which glittered like gold nuggets during class discussions—mostly blurted out, as Scott was never the sort of participant who waited to be called on. However, this young verbalist was either unwilling or unable (or most likely both) to represent his fertile thinking on paper. Most of the time he steadfastly refused to write. His seeming writer's block was a mystery to all concerned, since Scott had neat handwriting and strong oral language. So why his writing paralysis? We'll come to that later.

Scott's academic performance went from bad to worse during the pivotal years of middle school. He seldom handed in assignments, and when he did, they were mostly substandard. He became a first-rate class clown and was typecast by his peers as supercool and lots of laughs. Other kids sought out Scott when they wanted to cut up. Such an as-signed role often becomes an integral part of a kid's personal identity and self-image, a skin that's very tough to shed.

Throughout middle school the boy's perplexed and somewhat em-barrassed mother and father sought all forms of help. In sixth grade he was tested and found to have a superior IQ with intact academic abili-ties (they didn't check out his writing). It was decided he must have "ADHD" (attention deficit/hyperactivity disorder). Sooner or later any kid who's not in line with expectations gets tattooed with those sooth-ing letters. So Scott was put on a drug called Adderall. The results were equivocal. He was given some tutoring, with equally undramatic change. Scott managed to go through two psychologists and two psy-chiatrists over the subsequent five years. His medication kept getting altered, and the diagnoses were custom-fitted to justify these periodic chemical shifts. He went from mere ADHD, to oppositional defiant disorder, to dysthymia (relatively mild angst), to clinical depression, to the inevitable label of bipolar. For some reason, perhaps an oversight, he was spared obsessive-compulsive disorder (OCD). Ron Murray con-cluded that the parade of professional kid labelers was a waste of money; despite the impressive use of terminology mixed with phar-macology, he could discern no appreciable improvement in his boy's academic productivity or, as he put it, in his totally "lazy, hedonistic, and self-centered way of life." The final knockout blow for the scholas-tically unproductive Scott came in seventh grade, when he was caught with marijuana and beer in his locker; one of his peers had blown the whistle. Scott was not asked back to his prviate school for eighth grade, despite the fact that Mrs. Murray had been a loyal board mem-bers for years—obviously a tough decision for the school and a humil-iating setback for the high-flying Murray family. They scurried to find a place for him. He ended up spending eighth grade in the local public school, where he generated virtually no academic output, undertook some predictable minor disciplinary incursions, experimented regu-larly with drugs and alcohol, acquired a tattoo on his groin (which only his most privileged friends of both genders were welcome to view), and became infatuated with skateboards and his Suzuki dirt bike.

In public school Scott succeeded in finding a flock of peers who were like him and who liked him. He seemed euphoric, learning to disregard the relentless assault of adult criticism and pessimistic prophecies regarding his future.

Scott next found his way to a boarding school, lasted one year there (possession of marijuana plus failing grades in two classes). He repeated ninth grade at a somewhat less academically competitive venue and was barely clinging to academic survival there (on probation) when I first encountered him a couple of years later.

At the conclusion of my interview with Mrs. Murray, I asked her what her worst fear was when she thought about Scott. She seemed relieved that I'd inquired and went on to describe her own younger brother, Tom, now in his late thirties. She said Tom had been exactly like Scott when he was growing up. He couldn't or wouldn't accept responsibilities. Her brother had been a social whiz kid; everyone had adored him. But he had always been a bit of a con artist. He'd never completed any schoolwork and had dropped out of college during his freshman year. Since then, he had been married and divorced twice. He had held numerous jobs. Whenever he appeared to settle into a career, he'd get restless and think of things he'd rather be doing. He often got sucked into get-rich-quick ventures, and Mr. Murray had had to bail him out a few times. Tom was presently unemployed and manifesting a serious drinking problem. He was under investigation for extorting money. His life was a mess. Mrs. Murray expressed the fear that Scott possibly had "picked up Tom's bad genes," that her son's life might well replicate that of her lost soul of a brother. I have to say it's not unusual to find such a skeleton in the closet.

GETTING TO KNOW SCOTT

I liked Scott from the moment he marched like a star cadet into my office. In retrospect, I'm pretty sure he did a number on me. He could have written the manual on clever ways to charm and manipulate grown-ups, and his accomplished subspecialty was handling clinicians like Mel Levine. His radiant smile showcased perfect teeth. A firm handshake, penetrating eye contact, and a gentle pat on my back were designed to let me know who would be in the pilot's seat. This kid had seen so many professionals over the years that he was a veteran consumer of do-gooders. My own self-esteem was at stake, as I realized I was joining a long succession of clinicians who'd earned failing grades from Mr. Murray; no doubt, I would not be the last.

At our center we use a standardized interview and questionnaire we developed to help us evaluate teenagers with academic difficulties. The tool is called the STRANDS (Survey of Teenage Readiness and Neurodevelopmental Status). We use this in conjunction with the results of any assessments the student has undergone in the past, along with our own testing of academic skills plus reports from the school and parents. We are always in search of what I call "recurring themes," patterns of performance that emerge from these multiple sources that shed light on a kid's wiring—specifically, his breakdown points as well as his strengths. I also performed a neurodevelopmental examination of Scott. I was most interested in accounting for Scott's chronic output failure. It had been obvious from his history that he had always been better at taking in and processing information than at manufacturing his own academic products.

The interview and a self-administered questionnaire were dramatically revealing. Scott was upbeat and responsive as I posed questions about his ability to get thoughts into and out of language. He claimed to have world-class receptive and expressive language abilities. I think he was right. As we systematically reviewed the eight different neurodevelopmental systems, Scott also pointed to strengths in his spatial perception, all aspects of his memory, and his creativity. And, of course, he immodestly portrayed himself as "a social genius."

Scott admitted to some problems that were troubling him, but it was obvious to me that he had never before thought in depth about his specific areas of weakness. When we talked about the production controls of attention, a set of regulating functions housed mainly in the prefrontal lobes of the brain that guide academic, behavioral, and social output, the charismatic Scott became uncharacteristically glum, as if dark clouds had suddenly shrouded a sun-drenched beach. I reviewed with him the five different production controls, which I will discuss in more detail later in this chapter.

Scott acknowledged that he had "big-time" trouble planning and looking ahead before he did things. "Look ahead? I don't think I ever look ahead; it's as though it's raining hard all the time and my mind has no windshield wiper. I can't see what's ahead, and I'm not so sure I want to. I live life in the present." He added spontaneously, "I guess I'm the kind of dude who always likes to do the first thing that comes to mind. I don't worry much about what will happen if I do something. I just follow my gut." He laughed, "Sometimes that gut's right on and some-times it gets me into deep doo-doo, if you know what I mean." He added, "Hey, one other thing, Doc: I'm a guy who likes closure. I like to do things fast and I like to do things you can do fast. I hate the slow stuff; it makes me bored and impatient. I guess that's the part of school that really gets to me, having to slow down and work on something that takes too long to do. That's just not my rhythm. I'm into action, real ac-tion, big time."

I asked Scott whether he senses when he is getting into trouble or whether he can tell he's in hot water only after he's done something wrong. He responded, "By the time I realize I blew it, it's always too late to do anything about it." When I asked if he was the kind of person who learned from experience, Scott answered abruptly, "Hell, no." He went on to say, "Wherever I go, whatever I do, I treat it like a whole new thing. I erase the past like a teacher erases a chalkboard."

Scott and I talked some about his nearly violent aversion to writing. With a raised voice he exclaimed that trying to write a report blew his mind. "It's like the worst torture known to man," he added. His ideas went too fast a lot of times, and he couldn't stop making "dumb careless mistakes." And, mysteriously, he asserted that he could never see where writing was taking him, where all the words were going to end up. He could write and write without it getting anywhere. And all that made him detest writing. He also indicated that it wrecked his thinking. By the way, it's supposed to do just the opposite. Many students and grown-ups find it helpful to think on paper.

Scott seemed to experience problems with his attention whenever it came to satisfying output demands. He could concentrate while read-ing but not when he wrote. Put a pen in his clutch, and Scott's mind would blow a fuse. Besides, writing was no thrilling adventure. Scott told me, "The older I get, the more excitement I'm after. I can't stand doing boring stuff; it drives me up a wall, right up a f——in' wall."

Our educational diagnostician evaluated Scott and discovered some-thing unexpected: this boy who had always been described as a strong reader was delayed more than one grade in his reading comprehension. He also was falling behind in mathematics, and his writing remained as inadequate as ever. Scott's written output was stingy, the content con-crete and unsophisticated. The first paragraph of his writing sample is shown below.

JEEPS
by Scott Murray

I have to tell you I'm an incurable total Jeep freak. And Jeeps are
something I know a lot about. I'm even working on fixing up one now
a red 1968 Jeep Pioneer. No one knows for sure how Jeeps got themselves named Jeep. A comic strip named Popeye had a creature in it
called Jeep who could go anywhere and do just about anything—like
a Jeep. The Army, which was big on Jeeps, called them GP (general
purpose) cars. That's sounds like close to Jeep. Usually they have 4
wheel drive and can anywhere. Like they went to Asia and Africa some
wars. So they were big, real big, in history, and Jeeps go like in deep
mud or snow. They zip up mountain trails and water if it's not too
deep I mean like up to the doors. It would be cool to take a Jeep on a
beach I could go surfing the same day. Surfbords are kind of like Jeeps
going fast through rough stuff I mean wicked high surf and all . . .

The passage was written at a frantic pace, without forethought, and
was lacking in any attempt at proofreading. There is no real topic sentence, and the flow of the ideas seems to lead nowhere, as the sentences reflect free association rather than a coherent argument. The
thoughts expressed seem more like those of an early elementary school
student than a seventeen-year-old. Interestingly, Scott's oral language
had always been much more sophisticated than his writing. The need to
plan and coordinate the diverse elements of written output crowded
out his higher thinking and verbal expression.

At the request of his mother, our social worker and psychologist did
not meet with Scott. Mrs. Murray said that he had been "overdosed"
with counseling and with assessments of his emotions. She and her husband wanted us to focus exclusively on Scott's academic needs, which
we did. There were family problems, but we complied with the parents' desires. I eventually recommended that the family continue getting counseling. Often neurodevelopmental dysfunctions interact with
other psychological issues to inflame the situation. I was well aware
that there had been damaging clashes between Scott and his father and
that the boy felt his mother had always favored Sean and neglected him,
issues that sorely needed sensitive discussion and management.

Because of the lack of input from a social worker or psychologist,
I spent more time than usual talking with Scott, who was never at a loss

for words. He was so frank that it sometimes made me uncomfortable. That hypercandid state is characteristic of seasoned advice recipients. It also is a common finding in adolescents with drug problems. Sometimes you feel as if they're telling just what they think you want to hear as they try to make you feel that you are their sole confidant. Scott would come to see me wearing his dressed-down preppy garb, which consisted of a fastidiously untucked, wrinkled ecru button-down shirt with the collar buttons undone, unironed khakis, and running shoes with no socks. His hair always looked as if it had been uncombed professionally at a local dog-grooming salon. And he would alternate within a kaleidoscope of cool poses; watching his legs assume their succession of studied casual postures was like attending an underwater ballet. He was a compulsive displayer, a habitual marketer of his personal coolness.

We talked about his family life. I asked what it was like to have such an incredibly successful dad. Scott first claimed that he never gave it a thought. Then he allowed, "Not that easy . . . damned hard." He admitted that his father "was always in my face and on my case." At one point his dad had told him to stop seeing all those worthless shrinks (I felt relieved about being a pediatrician) and instead get off his butt and start dealing with his own "f——ing laziness." Despite all the chastisement, Scott displayed no obvious resentment toward his father. Instead he saved all his antipathy for Sean, his "sickening golden boy complete phony of a brother." He said he couldn't stand "the dork," but was resigned to the fact that someday Sean was destined to take over the family businesses; he was like a digital image of their father. I asked Scott where he thought he would fit someday. He responded, "It's something I don't even think about. I just put it behind me." I wondered how anyone could put the future behind him. But I see plenty of adolescents who are trying to do just that. They live only in the present, seeking immediate gratification. Maybe it's because they are so frightened of the future.

I once cautiously inquired, "Scott, tell me something. Your family has plenty of money. Your father is one of the wealthiest persons in the United States. He loves you very much, and I suspect he's set up a trust fund for you, an account that can make you secure throughout your whole life." Scott inserted, "That's right. He told me about it." I went on, "You're not doing very well in school; in fact, you're failing and may be about to get booted out of another school." "I know that," Scott admitted. I then posed a loaded question (infused with a modicum of devil's advocacy): "Scott, does it matter? You're fixed for life. Why are your grades in school of any importance at all?" For about ten or fifteen seconds, he acted as if he hadn't heard my question. But then this chunky hulk of an adolescent with the face of a model, this young man who looked more like twenty-three than seventeen, started to choke up and tear up. He actually cried. "Because as long as I live I have to stare at this pretty face in the mirror every morning and wonder if I'm worthless, if I'd be a nothing and a nobody without my dad and all his money. Somehow, I don't know how, I have to do something on my own besides partying. But maybe that will never happen. I might never be able to make it happen because I'm such a f——in' loser. I'm not good for anything." This was a very scared kid, in a way afraid of himself.

UNDERSTANDING SCOTT MURRAY

From all of our evaluation results, it was obvious that over and above all his superimposed emotional turmoil, Scott's productivity had been obstructed over the years. I had to figure out where the breakdowns were occurring and then share this understanding with Scott so he could get to work on his mind's "assembly line."

PRODUCTION-CONTROL DIFFICULTIES

Specific possibilities had to be ruled out in Scott's case. He had endured no difficulties with language at any point in his history. He had advanced through the early school years as a fluent speaker and a good reader as well as an accurate speller. He did develop reading-comprehension delays during secondary school, but I was pretty sure those were due to the fact that Scott had turned off to school and had ceased reading much of anything, thus failing to reach the higher plateaus of language development. Scott had never shown evidence that problems with his memory were clogging his productivity. To the contrary, when we conducted tests of Scott's memory function he turned out to be advanced in all the different remembering tasks administered. Scott's history also did not include the kinds of trouble with organization that result in output failure in some individuals. Nor did he have obvious problems with his mental energy. There was no history of sleep difficulty or persistent mental fatigue during the day.

As we learned about Scott from his teachers, his mom, and Scott himself, one very clear pattern emerged: Scott was highly impulsive. By his own admission, he did most things too fast, without thinking or planning or looking ahead and without watching what he was doing. When I tested Scott, I could observe that pattern clearly. For example, I gave him a graph-paper copying task (Figure 5-1), which is part of our neurodevelopmental examination. Scott was given two minutes to copy the design at the top of a page of graph paper, making use of the graph-paper grid to locate his design in the same position as the one he was copying and to reproduce its size and proportions accurately. You can see that his rendition was poor. He failed to show any planning behaviors, and instead his impulsive approach prevailed. He completed the exercise in under twenty seconds. And he never looked back; there was no quality control. When I prodded him to go back and draw the identical design but at a slower rate, he executed it reluctantly with much greater accuracy.

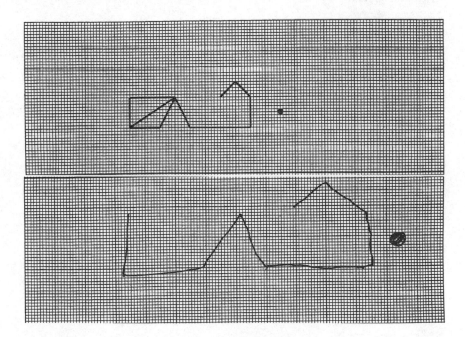

Figure 5-1.   This task, designed to show whether a student can plan, pace, monitor, and organize a form of output, brought out Scott's impulsivity. Despite careful instructions to make his design the same size and shape as the one he was copying and also to put it in the same location below the line as the one above the line, Scott ignored the squares on the paper, engaged in no thoughtful planning, and failed to check his work.

That was the rhythm of Scott's life. He often got into trouble because he did things without thinking them through, a trait that had gotten him booted from one school for bringing drugs onto campus. Scott seldom gave thought to consequences; he rarely asked the all-important question "What if I . . . ? "

Scott's impulsive tendencies led me to think he might have been having problems with his attention controls. But Scott was quite different from Ginny in the last chapter. She had weak mental-energy controls, but Scott did not. His deficiencies resided mainly in the production controls of attention, those brain-based knobs that regulate the quality and efficiency of output. The production controls are housed largely in the prefrontal lobes of our brains, a region that undergoes its greatest rate of development during the adolescent years. There are five fairly distinct production controls, each of which was ineffective for Scott. The controls are described in the following table, along with the ways they failed in Scott's life.

THE PRODUCTION CONTROLS AND SCOTT'S FAILINGS

Production Control	Role	Scott's Symptoms
Previewing control	Looking ahead, having a destination, anticipating, having a goal in mind	Doing things without thinking about their consequences, trouble envisioning academic results
Options control	Thinking about choices rather than doing the first thing that comes to mind	Tendency to act or do things impulsively, not pondering best moves or methods, failing to inhibit the execution of "bad ideas"
Pacing control	Regulating output speed, so actions are not too rapid or too slow	A tendency to do everything too fast and frantically
Quality control	Monitoring quality of output, so improvements can be made	Frequent careless errors, lack of awareness of how he was doing
Reinforcement control	Learning from experience and using the past to shape judgment	A pattern of making the same mistakes or wrong judgments repeatedly

Previewing control is a production control that enables us to look ahead and foresee an outcome, a likely result of something we're about to do or attempt. In building a bookcase in carpentry class, a kid starts by picturing what a project will look like when it is completed. A competent mathematician estimates the rough answer to a problem before she tackles it. A socially aware teenager anticipates his friends' reactions when he wears his newly acquired sweatshirt; in fact, that previewing influenced the tension-filled selection of its color and style. A tactful employee predicts how her boss will react when she tells him the company was outbid on a contract; by anticipating his response, she can be ready with her response. An artist has a "feel" for what he expects a statue to represent when it's finished. So it is that previewing affects social interactions, academic work, and behavior. Some people are well-attuned previewers, while others, like Scott, do most things without considering likely outcomes.

Probable consequences seemed to be of no consequence to Scott, despite the fact that he paid a price for almost never looking ahead when he fooled around in class, experimented with recreational drugs, failed to hand in assignments, or drove a car recklessly. In addition, Scott's lack of previewing made his writing a muddle. To write well you need to sense where your writing is headed, what it's leading to. As we saw in Scott's case, writing was stream of consciousness, not much more than a chain of random associations. Its shapelessness from the outset made writing feel suffocating to Scott. So he'd shut off his writing spigot at an early age. The subsequent lack of practice made his written output ever less manageable (a discouraging snowball effect).

Effective output calls for some deliberation. Deliberation most often consists of a review of options, such as, What's the best way to do this? What are my choices here? If this doesn't work out, what else can I try? Such problem-solving queries are subsumed under the second production control, *options control.* Scott, unfortunately, had poor options control. He made no behavioral or academic choices!

Successful options control enables a person to slow down or postpone a first response to anything, at least long enough to check out available alternatives. Scott mostly went for the first action that came into his mind. He seemed incapable of decelerating his decision making, reflecting, drawing upon his values, and thinking through options, a process that fosters something we all should seek, namely, good judgment. Unlike someone blessed with refined judgment, Scott could not pause to review alternatives, pick the best one, and maintain a couple of alternatives as "backup plans" in case that top choice didn't pan out. Thinking up choices, opting for the best of the lot, and having back-ups together comprise solid options control. Throughout his young life, Scott generally did the first thing that came into his mind, and if that didn't work he was sunk. That made it hard for him to regulate his behavior. It also thwarted Scott's writing as well as other projects in school that require one to stop and think about the best next steps or strategies.

An author keeps asking himself about the clearest way to express an idea or the best order in which to unfurl a plot or the details of an analy-sis. If you keep putting down the first thing that comes to mind, you're likely to get into a jam midway through your writing. What you're get-ting down isn't making much sense. This was another writing trap that snared Scott early on.

Effective output also calls for an appropriate tempo, so quite natu-rally *pacing control* must operate. Our product-assembly lines work best at an optimal turnover rate—not too rapid and not too sluggish. Scott conducted almost everything at a frenetic pace. Endeavors such as writing that demand time and the delay of gratification were unnatural acts to his kind of mind. Pacing control also allows for the tight synchro-nizing of different functions that have to work in harmony to accom-plish something; the members of an orchestra need to play together, and in many respects individual brain functions are just like players in orchestras.

Writing demands exquisite synchronization; the flow of language and finger movements needs to keep pace with the outpouring of ideas. If one gets too far ahead of the others, a writer is likely to lose track of what she is trying to write. It is as if her mind is an orchestra without a conductor; she can't seem to get the strings, the tympani, the woodwinds, and the brass instruments to play together in har-mony.

Quality output entails ongoing monitoring so that adjustments can be made as needed. That's *quality control.* Proofreading a report or checking a work sheet in math, watching the expression on your teacher's face when you tell her you forgot to do the assignment, and noticing that you've strayed off the topic during your contribution to a class discussion are all instances of self-monitoring. Once again, there is a great deal of variation in any classroom or workplace. Some individu-als have well-worn feedback loops; they watch what they're doing and make corrections as needed. Others, including Scott Murray, are oblivious. They lack quality control in what they do and sometimes also in how they act. So they don't get a chance to self-correct. Scott fit this description to a tee. Probably the most intricate quality control needs to kick in while you're driving a car. You have to monitor your speed, the traffic around you, and your steering as you proceed with caution. You might even be trying to listen to a CD while doing all this. That explains why so many kids (for some obscure reason, especially males) with production-control problems run a high risk of demolishing a car before the age of twenty-five. Scott fit that trend.

Reinforcement control informs output through keen hindsight. It influences us to apply our previous experience to help guide our current actions. If it were operating favorably, reinforcement control might have prompted Scott to warn himself, "I'd better not keep acting like that; that's what got me booted out of school in the past." But Scott treated each scenario in his life as if he'd never been there before. There was little cumulative wisdom. He was only weakly reinforceable. His parents had always noticed that both punishments and rewards were ineffective instruments in rearing their son. His teachers reported that they could teach Scott strategies and study skills that worked beautifully for him, but that he would subsequently fail to apply them. In retrospect, because of his weak reinforceability, Scott forgot how much satisfaction he had gotten from using the newly acquired strategies.

Together the production controls of attention are what make output efficient at the same time they enhance its overall quality. They promote sound judgment, effective problem solving, and commendable decision making. Scott committed countless errors of judgment. He was too impulsive to be a thoughtful problem solver. He made more than his share of unwise decisions. His production controls were not doing their share.

THE BEHAVIORAL IMPACTS OF INSATIABILITY PLUS SOCIAL DISTRACTIBILITY

Scott manifested one other troubling trait apart from his poor production control and recently acquired linguistic difficulties. The boy had always been insatiable. He'd been hard to satisfy from the earliest days of life. As a baby he was cranky, colicky, and perpetually hungry, then he became a whiny, overly demanding toddler.

Throughout his school years Scott was chronically restless, unable to delay gratification, seemingly starved for excitement. Often his provocative, disruptive behaviors represented frantic attempts to get satisfied. He became a thrill seeker, a risk taker, a troublemaker—all in his quest for some elusive satisfaction. I encounter insatiability in about half of the children I see with attentional dysfunction. Their insatiability may erupt into behavioral outbursts in school and at home. I've also seen it lead to substance abuse, alcoholism, marital instability, and career problems (much like Scott's uncle Tom's).

The trait of insatiability can infect and obliterate output. An insatiable child may be so preoccupied with stimulation and having fun that he fails to develop his working capacity. Entertainment becomes so attractive that work becomes a letdown, a drag, perhaps a dull afterthought in an overstimulated life. In Scott's case, his insatiability combined with a high degree of social distractibility, traits we also saw in Ginny. The result was a kid who prized and worshiped friends with the reverence of religious objects. Certainly nothing academic could compete with Scott's interpersonal adventures.

SCOTT'S COMPLICATIONS

Scott kept contending with several common complications of output failure. First, he had lost all motivation, and as we noted earlier, he was unwilling to ponder his future. He had decided that academic effort was futile, that he could never succeed no matter what he did—he felt he was born to fail.

Second, because he had disengaged from schoolwork late in elementary school, by age seventeen Scott had fallen behind in some essential language functions. He had not accrued the successful learning experiences necessary to propel his verbal abilities up into the higher plane of sophisticated conceptualization, abstract ideas, technical vocabulary (in math and science), and inference (especially in literature). This intellectual ascent ordinarily occurs in sixth or seventh grade, but it bypasses kids who are totally turned off by school. They are doomed to add a language deficit to their academic suffering. Such was the case with Scott. That's why his reading comprehension and math scores had declined so conspicuously.

There was also one final side effect of chronic failure: since fifth grade this boy had pretty much stopped accumulating knowledge. Whatever he was learning in school, he was learning passively, nothing in depth. So new knowledge mostly evaporated soon after his exposure to it. Having a growing fund of knowledge is like constructing a house. With sparse knowledge, there's not much intellectual content to build on or base anything on. It's not that Scott was unable to consolidate knowledge; it's just that his output problems drained him of all interest in learning and led him instead to a life of adventure and leisure, almost exclusively on the high seas of adolescent social life.

SCOTT'S HOME ENVIRONMENT

Scott grew up thinking of his home as a playground. His mother admitted that his bedroom looked like a miniature theme park! I vividly recall once when Scott came to see me during his sophomore year in college. He had recently moved off campus, and he told me that he and his roommate had just returned from buying furniture for their oversize shared quarters. He described with relish the new purple leather couch, the queen-size beds, the red oak dressers, and the phenomenal stereo cabinet. There was never any mention of any desks or bookcases. Scott pointed out, "You ought to see that room now. What an awesome place to shack out—if you know what I mean." I thought I did.

When a child reveals early signs of insatiability and is reared in a culture that nurtures this trait, the symptoms are especially accentuated. She or he becomes an obsessive pleasure seeker. I suspected strongly that this was the case for Scott, but the same is true for many contemporary children from all socioeconomic levels. Scott had an inborn tendency toward insatiability and grew up in an environment that brought it out, one that was fast paced, highly stimulating, and based on immediate rewards. Scott's life was saturated with music that had brief, catchy, obvious themes and rhythms, TV programs replete with calamitous car chases and stimulating special effects, videos whose plots resolved swiftly, often violently, and always predictably, recreational extravaganzas that stressed fast, thrill-packed motion (i.e., skateboarding, racing about in his all-terrain vehicle, skiing, flying in his dad's plane, and playing video games). Scott's material insatiability was also overfed. He was forever amassing cherished possessions, each of which fueled his hunger for more, bigger, and better stuff. In fact, it was difficult to see what adult life was going to add to Scott's worldly experience and precious possessions. Childhood was going to be a hard act to follow.

HELPING SCOTT

I felt deep sympathy for Scott; somehow, this overprivileged kid was in a way underprivileged, a tragic figure, a pathetic setup for calamity disguised under a rock-hard layer of social poise and bravado. I don't know where it came from, but I was haunted by a sense that his story would not have a happy ending. I felt frustrated and inadequate. From my first visit with him, I knew that this boy had undergone all manner of testing and mental-health assessments in the past and that, for the most part, the resulting recommendations had been ignored or only partially carried out.

After our evaluation, I offered to follow Scott because I thought he and his family needed some continuity. They had seen so many interveners over the years. They agreed to come back periodically but went on to make things hard for me. These were such busy and important people, a family with a lot of irons in the fire. They often failed to keep their follow-up appointments. Sometimes they called and canceled, but mostly they simply didn't show up. I had the sense that I was one of a crowded troupe of performers in their lives, a cast that included, among many others, their private pilot, their personal trainers, their golf and tennis pros. Once my assistant called to find out why they hadn't shown up for an appointment. Mrs. Murray confessed that their lives had been so hectic she'd forgotten. I received calls only when there was a crisis or when I was requested to write a letter or fill out a form getting Scott out of some requirement or obtaining extra time on tests (imagine Scott wanting more time for something).

Only several times a year do I see an individual kid for follow-up visits. During his late adolescence and college years, Scott acquired a new psychiatrist who specialized in medication. Various drugs were attempted (a recurring theme in the biography of Scott), with only marginally positive results. At one point all the pills were discontinued because this altruistic undergraduate, ever the accommodating nice guy, was dispensing the tablets gratis to his fraternity brothers to help them study for exams.

In the four or five years I knew Scott, I never met his busy dad, despite my strong hints that I should. I wondered if Mr. Murray had pretty much given up on his son by the time I came on stage. I think I got to see Scott about five or six times during that period. At each meeting he was polite and affable, but I still had the impression that I was just another service purveyor in his life. Scott was in control. He had mastered the art of looking adults in the eye without really processing what they were saying to him, a technique that made me uneasy as well as a little annoyed and intimidated.

I spent considerable time demystifying Scott during several visits. I explained to him about the production controls, and we explored the implications of his insatiability. I think he was unable or perhaps unwilling to see the connections between these dysfunctions and his daily performance, particularly his output failure. Typically he would resolve to work on these issues, but I doubt there was much follow-through.

I also periodically reviewed Scott's strengths with him; he seemed to have more trouble accepting his strengths than acknowledging his deficits. We explored all kinds of career possibilities based on his interests (mainly cars, movies, travel, skiing, and females), his remarkable social abilities and orientation, and his outstanding spatial and language capacities. We talked about the entertainment field; Scott mentioned that he would like to produce music videos. Although Scott had stated that he didn't want his triumphs in life to come from his father's success, we nevertheless explored possible important contributions Scott might make working in one of his father's businesses. He admitted, as if resigned to it, that employment in a family business was the most likely outcome, but I was surprised to find out that he'd never had a summer job in one of these companies. The opportunity had been offered, but Scott had repeatedly declined. On subsequent visits I never detected any sense of direction, any spark of commitment to any of these very promising vocational trails. I felt frustrated and wondered whether I was of any value to Scott and his family.

After his initial evaluation, I had located a psychologist in Connecticut who had been trained to help adolescents and adults with attentional dysfunction through what is called coaching. He agreed to meet with Scott (yet another adult telling Scott what to do and how to do it). I found out that Scott barely tolerated the coaching and showed up only erratically for sessions. Nevertheless, the coach appeared to help Scott slow down, preview, and check out his options or possible methods before writing a report or undertaking a science project. There was a stress on self-monitoring. Also, Scott kept a log of examples of his insatiability. He and his coach explored constructive ways of dampening his appetite for intense stimulation. Building his body turned out to be a healthy way to satisfy himself, as were investing in the stock market and restoring a 1957 Camaro. The coaching support seemed to help Scott paddle his way through the rapids of upper school (barely). In college he discontinued it in favor of a psychopharmacologist. Scott then had to fend for himself, and he couldn't.

While in college Scott declined all help, claiming he knew what he needed to do and was set to do it. As it turned out, he didn't. College life consisted of heavy drinking, a succession of volatile ill-fated romances, several semesters on leave of absence, one mostly completed drug-rehab program, an assortment of abortive part-time jobs, serious academic drought, and countless unfulfilled resolutions to "start buckling down." Scott hit rock bottom during his sophomore year. After his girlfriend of six months suddenly spurned him, Scott attempted suicide with a drug overdose—yet another impulsive action. He received emergency psychiatric help and confessed that he had been too confused to think things through. But sometimes a kid like Scott needs to reach the depths in order to bounce back.

I last saw Scott a year or so after his suicidal gesture. He was his usual ingratiating, cordial self, but this time there was a tone of remorse, of authentic concern about himself. He no longer acted like someone playing a party game called Con the Doctor. He said he wanted to apologize to me for being "such a bad patient" and admitted that he knew he was lucky to be alive. He said he had given more thought to our career discussions. He was now majoring in communications and was determined to succeed this time. When had I heard that before? He wasn't certain whether he would start his own video-production company or join the marketing department of his father's airline. He had been through drug and alcohol rehab once more and was completely dry. He was taking antidepressant medication but was doubtful it was doing anything for him.

I had the impression that Scott finally was serious, not just reading the tattered script he had saved for clinicians like me. I told him to stay in touch, that I would keep my fingers crossed and be available to him anytime he needed me for anything. He departed, saying, "By the way, Doc, I think my production controls have tightened up a lot in the last few months."

I could only hope that he meant that.

6
DARNELL MASON
Words That Can't Describe

My hesitancy in speech, which was once an annoyance, is now a pleasure. Its greatest benefit is that it has taught me the economy of words. I have naturally found the habit of restraining my thoughts. And I can now give myself the certificate that a thoughtless word hardly ever escapes my tongue or pen. I do not recollect ever having to regret anything in my speech or writing.
—MAHATMA GANDHI, *AN AUTOBIOGRAPHY* (1927)

Whenever the police telephoned Darnell's mother, Ruth Mason, to come and pick him up at the precinct, she felt as if she were viewing a rerun of a stale TV show—only she was part of the cast. The calls had become routine at the Mason apartment on West 119th Street in Manhattan. Their building straddled the border between a middle-class neighborhood and some hard-core inner-city housing. Sixteen-year-old Darnell had a penchant for entangling himself in webs of adolescent temptation, often in the form of petty crime. Mrs. Mason's fear was that these infractions were leading him toward bigger and worse transgressions.

One night Darnell barely evaded charges of disorderly conduct. He and his friends had been disruptive and destructive at a party they had crashed. Hurling beer cans and a few bricks as they departed, they'd smashed several windows and hit one boy in the head, causing a serious concussion. Darnell and his partners in crime received a stern warning from the police, to whom they responded with well-practiced feigned remorse. A detective took Darnell aside and informed him that he might be hearing from them further about some "serious charges." Darnell seemed to dismiss this threat entirely. When Mrs. Mason arrived on the scene, he made no eye contact with her. He was his usual unfeeling, icily stoic self, and she could tell that he was stoned. She launched into one of her eloquent lectures, knowing full well it wasn't registering. Darnell had mastered the fine art of tuning out maternal reprimands.

At about this time, Mrs. Mason, who taught at a public middle school, attended our Schools Attuned training program in New York City. Through this project we educate teachers about neurodevelopmental function and variation among students, including how to observe students and gain a sense of their strengths and weaknesses in the brain functions essential for academic success at various grade levels. While attending the seminars, Mrs. Mason wondered whether Darnell could have some kind of "hidden handicap" that was turning him off to school and maybe even condemning him to the wretched life of a felon.

During one of my frequent visits to New York, Mrs. Mason asked if I would have time to talk to her about her high school son. I explained that I do not have a medical license to practice in New York State, but that I could listen to her informally and maybe come up with a few general ideas about him. I was taken with her deep compassion for her son and her clearly desperate state. She was unwilling to condemn or give up on him. This lovely and loving mother was convinced that her Darnell had an excellent mind but somehow was unable (not just unwilling) to be productive. Over coffee later that afternoon she related his chaotic academic and behavioral history, then informed me that her son was awaiting trial for running drugs and for the rape of an eleven-year-old girl. Mrs. Mason was in an understandable panic.

Ruth Mason was a single black parent with three children, fourteen- and eighteen-year-old daughters on either side of Darnell. Their father, an automobile mechanic who had always had a drinking problem, had left more than ten years earlier, but he still saw the kids periodically and fairly reliably sent money. Both daughters were scholarship students at prestigious Manhattan private schools.

A ninth grader at a city high school, Darnell's output was a trash heap of academic waste; he looked as if he were being sucked into a vortex of repeated failure—seemingly a downfall of his own doing. His mom described him as his own worst enemy. He handed in no homework and sat in classes wearing his coat and backward cap, several heavy gold chains encircling his neck, while sporting a facial expression that blended boredom with defiance and arrogance, an almost snobbish detachment and passive resistance. He slung his baggy trousers lower and lower every day, proudly exposing his multicolored boxers. His hair was an extra-long partially and randomly braided dust mop. He wore unlaced hiking boots with no socks, making it clear symbolically that school was only a minor stopping-off point, not a destination. He was an intimidating presence in the classroom, suspiciously quiet, hostile in a passive-aggressive way, and inscrutable. He brought on his teachers' paranoia because he gave the impression that he was a student terrorist plotting their violent overthrow. The other students accepted Darnell; although he certainly wasn't popular, he was very much a follower, and in his characteristically unassertive manner, he tended to hang around with a clump of kids who were for the most part considered losers by the local educational jury.

Mrs. Mason had intended to try to place Darnell at a private middle school, but her plan had been scuttled by Darnell's deteriorating schoolwork. His academic meltdown had taken place gradually. Although quiet and never a participant in classroom dialogue, he'd had no trouble learning to read and, in fact, had loved and devoured books, which had delighted his mother and older sister. During Darnell's first four grades, mathematics came easily. Additionally, the boy took pride in his neat handwriting and lit up with a thousand-watt smile when his copied sentences and works of art were exhibited in the classroom.

It was in late fourth grade that Darnell transmitted some early-warning signals of an impending academic drought. Most conspicuously, he refused to write. Writing was not an issue for him when he was copying or filling in blanks on a work sheet, but Mrs. Carver, his fourth-grade teacher, required her students to write stories or describe experiences on paper each week. Darnell steadfastly resisted this demand. In his characteristically passive manner, he never objected to writing assignments; he just didn't do them. The few attempts he made resulted in simplistic prose devoid of content and lacking any grammatical sophistication. What he put down on paper was a brief rendering of simple sentences. He was retained in fourth grade. Repeating the grade did no good whatsoever—which is usually the case. It merely demolished his self-esteem.

Over the next several years, Darnell became increasingly bored and continued to ply his passive resistance to writing assignments. In sixth grade he even gave up on mathematics work, his earlier badge of academic prowess. Sometimes he turned in tests and quizzes with only his name atop the page. In third grade he had been in the seventy-fifth percentile in reading comprehension and the ninetieth in mathematics; at the end of sixth grade he had slipped to the thirtieth percentile in reading and the thirty-fifth percentile in mathematics. It was as if Darnell's mind had disconnected itself from the power supply for learning.

Darnell reached puberty rather early and was six foot two by the end of sixth grade. That he played basketball with some success seemed to be the boy's saving grace. He loved sports. He also enjoyed rap music and was thinking about taking up the trumpet.

Middle school was calamitous. Although never a discipline problem, Darnell was oppositional. He refused to do the necessary work and offered no excuses. As a result of his stubborn reluctance to produce anything on paper, everything in school seemed to cave in on top of him. Clearly, Darnell felt inadequate; but worse, he was overwhelmed, suffocating under the demands for productivity, especially writing. His mother said he had "writer's block." If so, he had a bad case of it! She showed me the following fragment of Darnell's eighth-grade writing, which she had typed out:

HUMAN RIGHTS

When somebody has rights they should know about it. Your rights are what lets you be free. It should be that like every dude got the right to be free, some people they act like they got no rights. Some people they act like they have more rights than they should so they get in trouble. Don't know a Right from a Wrong. Your rights are what you can do, Rights don't get you in no trouble. They are all yours You don't like steal them from your govermint they are in you. The law it says you got rights. Some places take away your rights. You gotta Fight for rights. Or you could lose Them.

This was the entirety of what was supposed to have been a two-page report. The boy's sparse written output could be described in three words: simplistic, brief, concrete. Was that because he had nothing to say or couldn't remember or couldn't focus his attention? Or did Darnell have ideas that he found too hard to get into words? The latter became a strong possibility when Mrs. Mason admitted that when I'd talked about language-production problems during my lectures, I had described her son as vividly as "a portrait on the wall."

I could tell at a glance that Darnell's writing was typical of students with oral-language dysfunctions. His mother mentioned that Darnell had "absolutely letter-perfect" handwriting but what he wrote was always extremely short and simple, and the wording extremely "immature." Like others with language-production problems, Darnell consistently violated rules of punctuation and capitalization; that's because a person's use of writing mechanics is partly dependent on having a feel for the structure of language. Darnell was missing that language-construction intuition. Mrs. Mason said she had plenty of reason to believe that her son was a very deep thinker but that you'd never know it from what he managed to get down on paper.

Darnell was a promising basketball forward but had been kicked off the middle school squad because of failing grades. Ironically, the activity that seemed to be his sole source of gratification, adult praise, and self-respect had thus been stolen out from under him. He acted as if it didn't matter, but I suspect it dealt a mortal psychological wound. At a pivotal age, he had lost the opportunity to perfect his developing basketball talent. It was the abrupt lights-out for a dream of becoming a professional someday.

Darnell was held back again in the seventh grade, yet another blow to his fragile self-esteem. Nothing is quite as ego crippling as being in the same grade as your little sister or brother because you were held back. Eighth grade was more of the same, except that Darnell then became part of a quasi street gang and felt immensely proud that they'd accepted him into their fraternity. These guys seemed to be the only people in his world who allowed him to feel good about himself. They all shared an aversion toward school, which helped Darnell legitimize his stance. He would do almost anything to seem cool when he was with them. Besides, roaming with his friends made Darnell feel somehow invulnerable, as if nothing could hurt or deter him. This was in dramatic contrast to his feelings of constant vulnerability in the classroom, or when he was by himself, or even at home, where he was forced to compare himself to his ambitious siblings. It was as if Darnell needed his friends as shields to protect him from the effects of personal despair.

As his mother and I spoke, it became increasingly likely that Darnell was a teenager who might harbor a long-standing gulf between his comprehension of language and his ability to get his own thoughts coded in language. To put it simply, he understood better than he talked. His advanced reading during the early grades suggested that he possessed a solid command of the sounds of language and so could match them up to symbols. He never had trouble following instructions or comprehending stories in class, and he readily incorporated new vocabulary words. He could answer questions about things he had read with reliable accuracy, although he never elaborated on those responses. His mother reported that he almost never spoke in full sentences; he seemed almost to "dumb down" his thoughts to make it easier to find the right words for them and he spoke slowly and often hesitantly. She admitted that she was forever "putting words in that boy's mouth." Whenever he faltered and labored to say something complicated, she felt compelled to jump in and express his ideas for him. For years she'd attributed this need to the fact that he was the only male in a verbally saturated household where "anyone had trouble getting a word in edgewise." Also, she was perplexed that Darnell, although always the quietest member of the group, was reasonably fluent when talking with his friends. She wondered if he was simply intellectually inhibited.

Interestingly, Darnell had not had trouble learning to talk. In fact, all of his developmental milestones were normal in infancy and throughout his toddler and preschool years. It was only when he had to find more difficult words, formulate sentences, and elaborate on ideas that his underlying problems with language production emerged and started to erode his school performance. As kids go through fourth grade, their language-output demands intensify, and that may well have precipitated Darnell's academic mayhem. Hearing of his onset of trouble in fourth grade reminded me that not all learning difficulties show up early. We have to be vigilant at every grade level and even throughout adult life for the possible emergence of those buried handicaps as the demands on minds change.

I suggested to Mrs. Mason that Darnell undergo educational testing and a thorough language evaluation. I referred her to an excellent speech and language specialist, Dr. Rose Bennett, who later offered to go over the results of her testing with me the next time I was in New York. Her findings confirmed the suspected discrepancy between Darnell's language interpretation (relatively strong) and his verbal output (very weak). The boy was delayed by more than two years in mathematics and reading comprehension. I was convinced that these delays were not direct manifestations of any dysfunction but the result of Darnell's total withdrawal from active learning over the last several years. This was similar to the decline we'd encountered in Scott Murray. Even Darnell's understanding of language, previously a strong suit, was not nearly as solid compared to others of his age as it had been, because he was not allowing himself to gain exposure to sophisticated linguistic material. To put it succinctly, he had ceased reading and listening. His receptive language had undergone what we in medicine call "disuse atrophy," a progressive wasting away from lack of use. Normally, as children go through school and the ideas become increasingly complex, they enhance their understanding by putting thoughts and concepts into their own words—but not if they have trouble with language production.

HOW DARNELL'S LANGUAGE PRODUCTION BROKE DOWN

Because there are multiple pieces in the puzzle of language output, Dr. Bennett and I had to consider how Darnell was functioning in specific aspects of verbal ability. First, there was the basic sound system, the phonology of language. Clearly, the accuracy and the efficiency with which you can pronounce word sounds will have an impact on language production. Some children who have speech-articulation problems early on seem to have a hard time catching up with language-output demands throughout their lives. But this was never an issue for Darnell. He never stammered, mispronounced words, or struggled very long to articulate new vocabulary.

Dr. Bennett and I then talked about another aspect, the word level of language—vocabulary and the ability to readily access from long-term memory the right words required for talking or writing. Some individuals suffer from chronic difficulty thinking of the right word fast enough during a conversation or while shaping an argument or an explanation. To test his word retrieval, Darnell was shown a series of pictures and asked to name them as rapidly as he could. Darnell had serious problems with this activity. In completing the exercise, he was noticeably hesitant and often used stall tactics like "Umm" and "Let me see" and "It's a . . . like a . . ." He sometimes substituted a definition for a word (a symptom with the impressive name of *circumlocution*). For example, when he was shown a picture of a lamp shade, Darnell called it a "bulb cover." It often took him too long to come up with a word, and sometimes he was stymied altogether.

On a vocabulary test we found that he was delayed in acquiring new words. It was as if new entries in his mental dictionary had been turned away at his brain's turnstile for the last several years. Interestingly, the sentence or syntax level of language, which has to do with how effectively you can make use of word order to extract meaning, was more than adequate for his age on a test of his understanding of complex sentences. He could decipher complex sentences that had clauses buried in them, and he seemed sensitive to the effect of word order on the meaning of sentences. But Darnell was sunk when he was asked to formulate his own sentences using two or three words Dr. Bennett provided. For example, he had to use the words *who* and *although* in the same sentence. After struggling for nearly ninety seconds, he offered, "Although he wanted the dude who it was." His mom admitted that he usually stuck to simple or incomplete sentences. It appeared that Darnell could understand but not implement the grammatical rules and conventional constructions of language.

Dr. Bennett next examined Darnell's effectiveness with discourse, his ability to produce language in chunks larger than sentences. These include, of course, well-designed and -executed paragraphs, passages, stories, extended descriptions, and arguments. Discourse requires a speaker or writer to organize the flow of ideas so they follow logically or cohere nicely as a description, explanation, argument, or narration. Dr. Bennett engaged Darnell in a conversation and, with his permission, recorded it. When she played it for Mrs. Mason and me, I found it agonizing to have to listen to this kid in obvious stress as he labored to get his ideas into verbal messages. In struggling to talk about his views on the death penalty (a topic he'd chosen), Darnell seemed to free-associate rather than develop a coherent discussion of pros and cons. His sentences were all monotonously simple, and some conspicuously incomplete.

Over the years I have encountered many students like Darnell who are academically asphyxiated because they cannot meet schools' language-production requirements. Inevitably their verbal impairments culminate in serious output failure. Often these handicaps are subtle, but their effects are not. The language gaps may go undetected by parents and teachers and last a lifetime.

One reason the diagnosis is missed is that affected individuals may sound fairly normal during everyday conversation. That was certainly Darnell's case. His language output with his friends was pretty much intact, but serious problems ensued when he needed to express more complex concepts rather than deploy social lingo. He could speak credibly about last weekend's party, but he buckled under and failed in a classroom when it came to explaining how compound interest works or why an income tax might be fairer than a sales tax. Social language is far more concrete, referring mainly to one's direct experience. Everyday conversation requires less vocabulary, less demanding word retrieval, less complex sentence construction, and less organization and variation of text. Although we sometimes detect some glimmers of language difficulty, we can't reliably judge someone's language output by tuning in to his or her everyday chitchat. Additionally, I have found that parents like Mrs. Mason may be so accustomed to the way their child speaks that they don't notice what an unrewarding effort it is. Not only that, but when adults notice that their child is hesitant and imprecise in his speech, they may not perceive the connection between that observation and his struggles in the classroom. It took years for Mrs. Mason, a very caring and perceptive mother, to connect her boy's hesitant speech to his output failure.

Darnell's school failed to diagnose his language-output problems. In part, this is because traditional tests of intelligence, aptitude, and achievement are not good measures of expressive language. Therefore, a child with oral-language gaps, like those crippling Darnell, often falls through the cracks. And I have found over the years that even relatively mild weaknesses of this type create turbulent ripple effects across a child's behavior and learning.

How, then, are we to detect dysfunctions of language production? The answer is surprisingly straightforward. We need to learn how to listen to a person who is verbally grappling with relatively sophisticated subject matter, and we need to know what to listen for. There are several things his school and his mother might have noticed in Darnell.

Problems at language's sound level are some of the most obvious indicators of malfunction. Affected individuals may mispronounce words (well beyond the toddler years, when such mistakes are normal), stumble over specific sounds, or arrange sounds in the wrong sequence (*pasghetti* for *spaghetti*). Or they may stutter or stammer when they speak. Children with trouble at this level of language may show steady improvement over time, but they may be left with a tendency toward language inhibitions. They speak as little as possible and therefore don't keep pace with the need to bolster their language-production capabilities. Ultimately, they may reveal gaps at the word, sentence, and discourse levels.

There are several ways we can tell if a child or adult is at a loss for words. While speaking, she or he, much like Darnell, may keep hesitating and making liberal overuse of what are called "stall words": "Those, um, people, the, uh, whatchamacallit terrorists, they like, they think, uh, like everybody has to, um, believe what they like think, you know what I mean? It's like, uh, they think their way is, umm, the only way; everyone else is like wicked or something." Listening to a kid speaking like that, an adult feels tempted to jump in and put words in his mouth. As one teacher commented to me, "I can tell Susie has good ideas and knows what she's trying to say, but the effort required to go from ideas to words frustrates her and me too. I have all I can do to resist finishing her answers for her."

Often kids like Darnell use a limited vocabulary consisting of only common words when they speak or write. Their speech is devoid of any learned, technical, or abstract vocabulary. They are also apt to generate amusing malapropisms. Darnell's mother recalled him once noticing how his little sister loved to kiss everyone and commenting, "She's full of infection."

Darnell's sentences were most revealing. Mostly he didn't use any. Instead he talked in sound bites or word clusters. Some students overuse direct simple sentences or never vary sentence structure during speech or in their writing. They might also commit various grammatical sins, such as poor subject and verb agreement or incorrect use of the pronouns *me* and *I*—"Him and me are good buddies."

Sentences need to be linked smoothly for discourse to sound right. Some writers and speakers make little or no use of what are called "cohesive ties," the tiny bits of verbal mucilage that bind sentences together. When they talk, it sounds as if they are reading a list of unconnected sentences:

> They had a meeting. They wanted a cease-fire. They disagreed about everything. They argued. They met for hours and hours. Nothing got decided. There was no cease-fire.

A literate user of cohesive ties would say or write:

> They went to a meeting at which they tried to negotiate a cease-fire. Although they met for hours and hours, they disagreed on everything. So nothing got settled, and as a result, there was no cease-fire.

Phrases and words like *at which, although, so,* and *as a result* are examples of cohesive ties, elements of language that are rare in the spoken and written output of most people with expressive-language shortfalls. In listening to Darnell's recording and in examining his writing samples, I found no evidence of any use of cohesive ties.

Writers and speakers need to be acutely aware of their intended audience and its needs. But many individuals can't size up the intended recipients of their thoughts. This problem with "taking perspective" is a common affliction among people with language-output trouble. Darnell might say to his teacher, "I went to that party with Michael last weekend." What party, and who is Michael anyway? The speaker didn't ask himself whether his teacher knew about the party or had any idea who Michael is. Any with-it conversationalist would have taken the listener's knowledge into account and tailored his verbal output accordingly: "My niece had a birthday party Saturday, and I went to it with my cousin Michael." That tells it all. (You will encounter this phenomenon among adults as well.)

I recently watched a television interview of a noted thoracic surgeon. Oblivious to the needs of his audience, he described an operation using technical vocabulary that would have challenged a surgical senior resident. He had obvious expressive language gaps (which may have influenced his choice of a surgical career). Often people with language difficulty either give you too much information (that you already know or don't need or want to know) or fail to provide you with necessary background data you obviously couldn't know.

Perceptive speakers also modify their language to suit the characteristics of their audience. This is called code switching. The way you talk with your close friends is different from the way you speak with your teacher, your grandparents, your kitten, or your baby sister. You can adjust your tone of voice, the rhythm of your language, your choice of words, and the length and complexity of your discourse depending upon who's listening to you. Some individuals talk or write the same way to every audience.

Language is intended to convey ideas. But in some cases too much language is used to express too few ideas. We call this "low ideational density." On the tape recorded by Dr. Bennett, Darnell talked for two minutes and said a lot less than a fluent speaker could have communicated in three sentences. By the way, I am sometimes condemned to attend meetings where the adult speakers exhibit alarmingly high levels of low ideational density; they go on and on saying virtually nothing. Some religious channels on television feature alleged clergymen whose interminable sermons are classic examples of low ideational density! Many politicians have the identical proclivity.

Perhaps the most transparent finding in many individuals with language-output obstructions is their inability to elaborate. Darnell was a classic example. He was a short-answer guy. "What do you think of your math teacher?" "He's okay." "Do you agree with him about giving surprise tests?" "Nope." "Why not?" "Not fair." "What's unfair about it?" "Lots of stuff." "What aspects of it do you find unfair?" "Taking tests and like that." Darnell was failing to use language as a tool for extending, linking, or developing ideas.

It has been shown that many nonelaborative individuals with language problems have serious difficulty forming an opinion about anything. An opinion is a point of view that you can argue for, that you can verbally justify, unlike points of view that are mere biases or prejudices. I'm always impressed with how many hate crimes are committed by irrational individuals who are described as very quiet. I wonder how many of them have sustained long-standing deficiencies of language production.

One final point concerning elaboration: there seems to be a tight linkage between verbal elaboration, the ability to stretch or extend ideas through language, and the effectiveness of long-term memory. One of the principal strategies for remembering something is to elaborate on it rather than to try to retain it by rote. Sure enough, students like Darnell with expressive-language dysfunctions often encounter problems remembering factual material for examinations. As tests in school required more recall of facts, Darnell's scores sank.

So simply listening to Darnell and knowing what to listen for could have resulted in an early diagnosis of his language-output impairment.

A person listening carefully to him could have detected his pronounced hesitancy, trouble finding words, very slow and simplified construction of full sentences, absent ties between the sentences he did make, a conspicuous lack of elaboration, and very flat expression.

DARNELL'S COMPLICATIONS

Darnell illustrated vividly how children and adults whose language output is problematic become susceptible to a number of emotional and behavioral complications that are more destructive than the language dysfunction itself. In particular, they often seem to underutilize a vital process called "verbal mediation." We guide and regulate many of our feelings and behaviors through a kind of internal coaching mechanism. That is, we talk things through to ourselves, which helps to slow us down, so we don't act rashly. Imagine a teenager like Darnell cruising with a group of peers, one of whom offers him an illicit and dangerous drug. He is tempted to be cool and accommodating, since accepting the offer would ingratiate him with the group. But if the voice of reason within him talks about the perils of taking the pills, he is more likely to refuse the offer. His internal language might even provide him with an evasive excuse. Darnell apparently had little or no verbal mediation influencing his actions and reactions.

There is strong evidence to show that many incarcerated violent offenders have expressive-language dysfunctions. I was involved myself in one such study of adolescents who had been committed to the Division of Youth Services in Massachusetts for having committed violent crimes. We performed complete assessments on these teenagers and discovered that, by far, these teenagers' most common area of dysfunction was language output. It may well be that they lacked verbal mediation. If you can't talk out your temptations, you capitulate. Incidentally, very similar findings have arisen from investigations of adult prisoners. So Mrs. Mason was not at all overreacting when she worried about her son's future.

Even more commonly, reduced language facility can demolish self-esteem and lead to a total obliteration of academic motivation. This self-defeating pattern was certainly operating in Darnell. Moreover, when a person like him is unable to use internal language to deal with personal feelings, to reassure himself, to cope with stress, he may experience deep feelings of despair. We might wonder how often mental-health problems stem from misunderstood underlying dysfunctions such as expressive-language impairments.

HOW DARNELL WAS DONE IN

Darnell was plagued with a significant expressive-language dysfunction that went undiagnosed for too many years. Eventually his written output, reading comprehension, and mathematical understanding deteriorated, as he was never able to talk through complicated material to clarify it for himself. In math and science some kids with language problems are able to compensate by visualizing and relying on nonverbal thought processes, but Darnell wasn't resilient enough to shift to his strengths and instead wrote himself off. Perhaps he didn't have the appropriate role models or a strong, supportive father to help him find his way over the barriers he faced in school. If he had understood at an earlier age that he was a smart kid with some expressive-language dysfunctions, he might have discovered ways of working around his impediments. Instead, he stopped producing and plummeted into output failure. Unfortunately, Darnell followed the path of least resistance, joining low-achieving peers to test society's behavioral limits by committing petty crimes. Now he stood accused of a much more serious charge.

From fourth grade on, Darnell was made to feel lazy. At first he worked very hard in school—without rewarding results. It was not that he was lazy; he was swimming against the tide of his dysfunctions. In many ways, Darnell was a victim. First, he should have been diagnosed and helped while in elementary school. Second, he never should have been retained in fourth and seventh grades. It obviously did no good; it seldom does at those ages. It's often a near-fatal blow to a kid's life aspirations. It doesn't work, and it leaves scars. Third, despite his failing grades, telling Darnell he couldn't play basketball was a serious error. I don't think you should take away the only form of output that's going well in a kid's life, the sole product that earns him praise from the outside world. Fourth, there seems to have been no effort to strengthen Darnell's strengths. In addition to sports, he showed promise both in art and in music, but these areas of passion and potential talent were ignored. His mother was preoccupied, holding down two jobs to support the family. His school had all it could do to control the moment-to-moment discipline of its students. Besides, there were plenty of early adolescents in Darnell's middle school who were much more severely delayed or impaired than he was. So he got misplaced and misunderstood. Like many others in very large urban schools, Darnell was lost in the crowd.

After Mrs. Mason had digested the results of Darnell's testing, she made an appointment to share these findings with the head of special education and the principal at Darnell's school. They felt that he would be unlikely to qualify for services, since his math and reading scores were still pretty close to grade level even though his I.Q. had fallen. So they maintained that he was performing as expected for someone of his modest intelligence (a not-too-subtle put-down) and insisted that there were no indications of any real "learning disability."

Apparently the principal went on to say that he thought that Darnell's evaluation was culturally biased. He reported that two-thirds of the kids in his inner-city school didn't speak well. They weren't exposed to complete sentences at home. They used lots of profanity and single-word exclamations. Their sentences frequently lacked verbs, not to mention subject-verb agreement. He implied that the tester was using middle-class white norms to evaluate Darnell's language.

Mrs. Mason told me that she had argued with the principal that her daughters were thriving at private school and were perfectly able to switch from any neighborhood dialect or ebonics to the language at school. This was impossible for Darnell and maybe for many others too. The principal remained skeptical.

Mrs. Mason thought that schools in the area should place a heavy emphasis on the development of oral-language functions in kids from an early age. That means loads of oral presentations, speeches, storytelling, and the like. I concur but would add that *all* schools ought to stress oral-language development. I encounter increasing numbers of students and adults who are terrible at expressing themselves. In the United States during the eighteenth and nineteenth centuries "rhetoric," public speaking, was a core part of the curriculum at every grade in school. Let's revive it.

HELPING DARNELL

Mrs. Mason's first action, of course, was to hire a lawyer for her son. I later discovered that she told him she would like to show the court that Darnell's alleged criminal behaviors were the direct result of his lan-

guage difficulties and wanted me to testify as an expert witness. But before the trial began, one of Darnell's friends admitted to having raped
the girl and having made it look as if Darnell had done it. Darnell was
also cleared of the drug charges before a trial date could be set. It was a
sad commentary that Darnell had not felt confident enough in his language abilities to deny the accusations and explain his innocence. He'd
just remained quiet and sullen. Mrs. Mason was deeply relieved that he
had not been tried but sensed that there could still be trouble ahead, as
Darnell seemed to have learned nothing from this brush with the law.
He was still hanging around with the same peers and participating in
their disruptive adventures.

Mrs. Mason called me one day to say that she was thinking of suing
the New York City public schools for not diagnosing Darnell's language
dysfunction. She was incensed that her son had been kicked off the
basketball team and left back in fourth and seventh grades, in a sense
punished for the school's inability to understand and help him. To my
knowledge, she never went through with this threat, but she met with
some other parents in similar situations and launched an active advocacy group in Harlem. I heard that they met with school officials on
frequent occasions and ran some evening meetings of parents of struggling students in the area. I'm afraid they never accomplished much
change in an overstressed and underfunded school system.

As I mentioned, I have never actually met Darnell. I suggested to his
mother that the educational specialist and language professional who
had tested the boy might spend some time explaining his strengths and
weaknesses to him. Darnell was in dire need of demystification to halt
his self-destructive momentum. He would need encouragement to
practice elaborating ideas, beginning with areas that interested him. He
could read the sports page (which he did on his own) and then be encouraged to deliver a sports commentary in class. It would help if he
could brainstorm his ideas in a bulleted list on a computer before trying
to figure out the best way to put them into words. He could be encouraged to write without regard to grammatical correctness and careful word choice. Then his mother (luckily an English teacher herself)
could help him beef up the language. It is so easy to make changes
when using word-processing software, a blessing for kids who have to
sand and polish their prose to make it acceptable. Also, Darnell needed
more time on tests, more time to encode his ideas into words. This was
eventually granted him.

During my last direct meeting with Mrs. Mason, I found out that as a tenth grader Darnell got back onto a basketball team and was playing the tenor saxophone, which he seemed to be picking up nearly intuitively. Most important, he was staying out of trouble. Mrs. Mason had noted considerable progress, although her son still had a long way to go to catch up in school. She attributed his recent transformation to the demystification, to Darnell's realization that he was not stupid or lazy. He was beginning to see some promise in himself.

By the way, I received an unexpected phone call from the principal at Darnell's high school. He had read the report of the language specialist and said that he was very interested in students with language impairments. He felt certain that he had many kids with that kind of wiring deficit. He said he was meeting with the whole faculty to see how their curriculum might place a much heavier emphasis on the development of oral language. He wanted all of his students to have more opportunities to make oral presentations in every class. He also was thinking about requiring all ninth graders to take a public speaking course. I heartily endorsed his initiatives but said I would begin the process in the elementary grades.

What do we learn from Darnell? First and foremost, language production is a major player in school achievement—and in later life. Articulate and fluent speech enables a person to engage actively in classroom interchanges or collaborative planning on the job; it enables an individual to respond to questions in a way that goes beyond single words or terse utterances. It is a key to meaningful dialogue, and oral language is also a prerequisite for written language. Chances are, if you don't speak well, you're not going to write well. That was certainly true for Darnell.

Throughout life, fluent and accurate oral-language ability equips you to sell your ideas and to sell yourself (such as during a job interview). It also enables you to get thoughts down on paper and to use writing as a means of thinking.

As our oral-language functions are honed, we talk through ideas as a way of understanding them more clearly. By putting ideas into our own words we can comprehend and retain them more firmly. In fact, it's been said that the best way to learn something is to have to teach it! Throughout childhood and our adult years, oral language has an inner life as well. We all talk to ourselves. Such internal monologues help us explore options, cope with our anxieties, control our behaviors, and decompress potent pent-up feelings without offending anyone.

So there's little doubt that a person's ease and precision with language output will have a weighty influence on the outcome of many a quest for mastery in life. For a lot of individuals, the translation of ideas into verbal form occurs with little effort and with effective results. For others—the Darnells of our realm—verbal expression is a hidden cause of confused frustration and output failure. It's never too late to work on oral language, to undertake language workouts. In fact, many adults who are now good speakers could not talk or write on a literate level when they were kids.

7
ROBERTA CHAN
Deflation Ideation

Remember that writing is translating, and the opus to be trans-
lated is yourself.
—E. B. White, *Letters of E. B. White* (1976)

It was the second time I had given a seminar at this high-powered West Coast Catholic high school. This time a group of teachers asked to have lunch with me so they could present a case for discussion. A week before my visit, I called and asked what kind of issue they had in mind. They hadn't decided, so I went into the big event cold turkey (consistent with the wraps they served). They ultimately chose to tell the simple tale of well-behaved, hardworking Roberta Chan, a Chinese-American ninth grader who consistently got A's and B's in school. Roberta's parents gave permission for the presentation, and, in fact, her mother sat quietly absorbed in the corner during the session.

Now, you might be wondering, "What's a kid like that doing wasting precious pages in a book about output failure?" Wait and see. Her teachers described Roberta's notably advanced skills in all academic areas as confirmed recently on the ERBs (Educational Records Bureau), a widely used test of achievement. She was said to be near the top of her class in math and a superstar in advanced-placement biology. This achievement was especially gratifying, since Roberta's mother worked as a technician in a marine-ecology laboratory. Her father, incidentally, was the proprietor of a successful and reportedly "highly innovative" art gallery and antique store.

The teachers circulated an excerpt from a recent report Roberta had written for history. A section of it follows:

Hitler thought that Germany could attack Poland with no risk of British or Soviet intervention and so he gave orders for the invasions to start on August 26. News of the signing, on August 25, of a formal treaty of mutual assistance between Great Britain and Poland caused him to postpone the start of hostilities for a few days. He was still determined to ignore the diplomatic efforts of the western powers to restrain him. Then at 12:40 P.M. on August 31, 1939, Hitler ordered hostilities against Poland to start at 4:45 the next morning. The invasion began as ordered. In response, Great Britain and France declared war on Germany on September 3 at 11:00 A.M. and at 5:00 P.M. respectively. World War II had started.

I read over the meticulously word-processed work and thought it looked just fine to me. It reliably (to the best of my knowledge) covered a short chain of events culminating in the outbreak of the Second World War. But then the teachers pointed out that Roberta's essay was pure description, pretty much lifted from the Internet and modestly reworded. They added that the entire report was nothing more than a listing of events in the right order, much of it not even in her own words.

No one was accusing Roberta of plagiarism; her teachers were getting at something else. One of them actually charged her with having "a lazy mind," implying that she always took the easy way out and was unwilling to think things through. He described her as displaying a "cut-and-paste mentality," meaning that she would find facts and ideas and simply stick them on a page or in her mind. Here again were clear allegations of laziness.

Apparently, Roberta was hard to stump on a spot quiz in any subject. She applied well-crafted study skills and was always in a state of high preparedness. She was at her best with multiple-choice, fill-in-the-blanks, matching, and other short-answer assaults on long-term memory. She also could write well-organized, information-saturated essays when required to do so. You would be hard-pressed to find any errors in her spelling, punctuation, or sentence structure. She had fully conquered the mechanics of writing. I also discovered that she was the envy of her classmates during class discussions. She always knew the answers to factual questions and stated them quickly and cogently, as if she were extracting the data from a fast hard drive embedded in her cerebral cortex. What's the problem here? I wondered.

The problem was that Roberta, truly a first-rate, world-class absorber,

retainer, and retriever of information and skills, was woefully inadequate when it came to generating ideas of her own. She was the very
model of what we call a "bottom-up" processor of information. She
could conquer and tame any corpus of knowledge with relative ease.
Her mind could penetrate and digest thick layers of detail and somehow sort it all out and remember it the next day. And, for better or for
worse, Roberta always stuck to the facts as they were delivered to her
highly receptive brain. She was a phenomenal information recorder, a
human paper copier. But this industrious student never seemed inclined or able to put anything of herself into that which she was processing and remembering. Her own imprint was nowhere to be found
in her output. There were no personal interpretations or extrapolations
of what she was learning about in any of her classes.

I reexamined Roberta's excerpted essay and, sure enough, it contained all the personal reflections of a lawn-mower repair manual. How,
then, was Roberta getting such super grades in school? Was this the
high school version of college grade inflation? Could it be that her
mixed A's and B's were placing Roberta in the lowest 20 percent of her
ninth-grade class? No, not at all, I was assured. Roberta was performing so splendidly because she consistently tested so well. That made
me suspect the tests were designed to tap only rote recall, factual regurgitation.

So it was that Roberta was having problems with the ideational
component of output. Her teachers reported that they were forever
prodding Roberta to form her own interpretations, her personal views
and reactions. When forced to do so, she produced responses that
were painfully uninspired, constricted, bland, and somehow childish.
And she was as concrete as a sidewalk. For example, when her English
teacher asked her to share her feelings about the characters in *Oliver
Twist,* Roberta said she hated Fagin. When asked what Huckleberry
Finn's life on the raft might be symbolizing, she said it was like someone running away from home.

Apparently, whenever a teacher instructed the students to write an
essay on a topic of their choice, Roberta became noticeably agitated.
Often she would ask the teacher to provide the topic and let her know
the exact length required. She craved structure and highly specified expectations. Brainstorming was repugnant to her. Her English teacher
lamented, "It's hard to believe how such a brilliant girl can be so entirely
uncreative." Roberta had problems constructing ideas.

I asked Mrs. Chan if she wanted to make any comments about her daughter. The first thing she said was that Roberta liked her friends but couldn't stand school. Mrs. Chan commented, "For years now she has learned well yet gotten absolutely no joy at all from learning. She derives plenty of satisfaction from getting good grades, but that's about it. And she works very hard; we all do in our family. We work together at the dinner table every single night after supper. She and her two sisters are close in age. None of them is allowed to date. We have no TV set." She went on, "Roberta is completely different from Susan and Anita. They both love to write and make up stories. Susan wants to be an English teacher, and little Anita says she will write songs. Roberta doesn't know what she wants to do. But they are all three happy. Even Roberta, although she does not like school too much, she is a happy person inside. She has many strong interests—her flute playing, her gymnastics, her deeply held religious faith, her several close friends. I think she'll be all right."

A very animated and provocative discussion ensued after Roberta's mother left to get back to work. First of all, the issue of whether or not Roberta was really a "problem student" fueled considerable disagreement among the faculty. I stayed safely neutral. Several teachers felt that Roberta was manifesting a particular kind of mind, a distinct "learning style," as one of them put it. He insisted that there are plenty of great opportunities for extremely bottom-up people like Roberta. The world doesn't need everyone to be a creative genius. There are loads of competent teachers who stick to the curriculum, talented musicians who follow the score, and skilled nurses who carry out the doctor's orders. We'd be in trouble if everyone in the world spent their workdays producing original ideas. Besides, what right do we have to rewire the mind of one of our best students?

This view had some vociferous opponents. They argued that Roberta wasn't really learning; she was memorizing and imitating. Her English teacher adamantly stated that the essence of learning was somehow integrating new knowledge and skill with your own values, perceptions, and feelings. Using that mixture, you create rich and relevant products rather than recycling information in history or biology and mimicking processes in mathematics. These teachers felt the school had as much of an obligation to teach Roberta how to generate ideas and infuse them into products as they did to teach her the laws of geometry. Even if it turned out that such an undertaking was not entirely natural for her, it was essential that she experience the germination and cultivation of ideas—by deploying her knowledge base to help shape those ideas.

Inevitably, the teachers turned to their lunch guest and asked what I thought. After some verbal fumbling, I found myself headed for the temperate middle ground—a compromise position, perhaps even a cop-out. First I said that I did think Roberta had a problem in that she was getting no joy from her education. That could lead to getting no joy from a career. Education should cultivate a taste for learning and productive output in all students. She was learning and producing in a way that was arduous and not at all satisfying or joyful. I suggested that we ought to honor, admire, and cultivate Roberta's bottom-up kind of mind but that someone needed to demystify her, so as to help her understand ideation and how it's supposed to work, and then assist her in generating some original thinking and personal perceptions of things. Since Roberta obviously craved structure and specific instructions, she should be given directions that explicitly required that she include original thoughts. We'll talk about how this might be done in the next section.

As I left that appetizing lunchtime discussion, my mind was percolating like a coffeepot. I started to think about a classmate of mine at Oxford University, a Rhodes scholar from Oregon. Richard had graduated from Dartmouth College, a political science and math major at the top of his class. He had scored 800s on his math and verbal SATs and achieved results nearly as impressive on the Graduate Record Examinations. Richard's brain was both hungry and penetrating, an omnivorous digester of all manner of data. He read whatever he could find. He seemed to have leased space in the Bodleian Library, and he got himself deeply in debt at Blackwell's Bookshop.

After our years at Oxford, my friend returned to Harvard, where he received his Ph.D. in economics at the same time that I was a student and then an intern across the river at Harvard Medical School. Later Richard became a junior faculty member at a leading university. Some years after that I received a troubling letter from an obviously distressed friend. Utterly despondent, Richard reported that he had dropped out of academia. He reminded me that he'd always been an outstanding student, at or near the top of his class since nursery school, but he now revealed that his academic career had offered little but frustration. He just couldn't seem to catch on. He had been turned down for promotion to associate professor because of his lack of publications and grants. It was a colossal blow to his self-esteem; his pride felt irreparably wrecked from this, the biggest defeat, perhaps the only substantial setback in his entire life.

Richard and I met a few months later in New York. Over lunch he recapitulated his plight and pointed out that throughout his education he had never had truly original ideas or creative insights. He had been a popular teacher, but he'd had a sense that in his field everything had been done already. He could go on acquiring more knowledge, but he couldn't add to it. He was unable to get papers published in peer-reviewed journals, and the few grant proposals he'd managed to write were not reviewed favorably by funders because they seemed like a rehashing of old stuff. He was hoping to venture into a new career in the computer industry as a management consultant, a business troubleshooter. He eventually did this and succeeded. He found a niche and felt gratified but thought he had wasted a decade. He told me subsequently that he believed he was very good at his new profession but added, "I must say that it doesn't take much imagination to do what I'm doing." Nevertheless, Richard had come to terms with his kind of mind. He had high output, and he felt secure that he was making a contribution. His earlier output failure had been turned around when he'd found a niche that worked for him. That happens for some people and not others.

Flying back from San Francisco the next morning, I kept thinking about Roberta and my friend Richard. I also examined my own kind of mind. I had always been the exact opposite of these two individuals, inexorably top-down. Whenever a teacher doled out an assignment, I would convert her commands to a task I preferred. When given a topic, I would exercise my questionable license to modify it liberally. I thrived in a creative writing class and consistently underachieved on multiple-choice tests, including the SATs. When I wrote and contributed to class discussions, I was far more interested in exploring my own views (often thinking out loud) than describing the perspective of anyone else. If any authors had perused my book reports and read my interpretations of their stories, they would have been horrified. Like Roberta and Richard, I got mostly A's in school. The majority of my teachers tolerated my compulsion to invade all subject matter with my own personalized weaponry. A few teachers couldn't handle it (those were my B's). Some subjects didn't allow for it; one couldn't be too top-down in trigonometry. But I was able to modify my style in such courses. During medical school (a phase of one's education not celebrated for the cultivation of creative thought) my errant mind was pretty miserable. I felt as if my insufferably top-down brain had been deposited in cold storage for four years. Throughout my career I have continued to tread my own original pathways and often have found myself repeatedly rejecting the intellectual structures (such as the labels for kids with learning and behavior problems) and the ways of thinking that I have been expected to assimilate and disseminate. Believe it or not, I even pulled this off during my two years as a captain in the United States Air Force. I do things my way. I march to my own drummer.

In contrast to my idiosyncratic ways, some adults reveal an abundance, perhaps an overabundance, of what is called "vertical loyalty." They don't dare deviate much from the traditional approaches and structures of their chosen disciplines. Their thinking firmly adheres to the ideas and approaches they inherited from their college or graduate school professors or perhaps their first bosses. Top-down types like me can't wait to break away, to reconstruct the manner of thinking imposed on them, to come up with novel paradigms. As you might surmise, many top-down people lack much admiration of and respect for their bottom-up colleagues, and vice versa. I am convinced that our world needs both kinds of minds. We'd get nowhere with just one or the other. In reality, most adults operate snugly in the midrange between extreme "bottom-upism" and heavy "top-downism."

HELPING ROBERTA GENERATE IDEAS

Roberta's output problem was far from unique. As I travel around the country and abroad, more and more teachers lament to me that their students are reluctant to think things through and come up with their own ideas.

The generation of ideas occurs through a number of slightly overlapping processes. Here we will consider five of them, all closely related and all at least partially obstructed in Roberta's case: 1) brainstorming, 2) creativity, 3) critical thinking, 4) personal interpretation and analysis, and 5) problem solving.

Brainstorming is the process through which a student like Roberta searches her own mind to come up with some worthy thoughts or solutions. Topic selection is a prime example of a challenge to brainstorming. Recall that Roberta didn't like to choose her own topics; she preferred to have them prescribed by a teacher. Brainstorming barriers may make it hard to come up with a thesis topic, determine what subject you want to portray in a painting, or figure out what to tackle for your civics project.

Brainstorming can be thought of as a state of mind, a flexible openness to the wide-open exploration of options. Your mind keeps flowing freely, into and out of possibilities, ultimately choosing the optimal one or ones. In the course of brainstorming a person conducts various miniexperiments: If I pick this topic, what will the report have in it, and will that be any good? If I criticize the president's foreign policy, what good points can I make and how will they impress this teacher? Brainstorming is not totally unfettered; it usually acknowledges certain limits (imposed by laws, rules, moods, available time, and space constraints).

In my opinion, all students need plenty of practice brainstorming across subject areas. Roberta was never a patient of mine, but I suggested to her teachers that she form a partnership with a dynamically brainstorming classmate. Together they could pursue some projects or writing activities. Roberta could do a lot of the research, digging up relevant background information, while serving initially as the junior partner in the brainstorming effort. Over time she might assume heavier brainstorming responsibilities. As an exercise Roberta could sit down with a blank sheet of paper and just list topics or ideas for a report or project and then submit her brainstorming work sheet to her teacher. She might even be given a grade for coming up with an impressive number of alternative topics and ideas. We always like to take a vital and perhaps troubling step in a process like brainstorming and set up activities that end at that step—that's why we'd want Roberta to hand in her proof of brainstorming activity. I advocate requiring kids to come up with bulleted lists of ideas for topics, projects, new inventions, or better commercial products. They should be evaluated on the richness and spontaneity of their ideas.

Creativity is a close kin of brainstorming, but you can be creative without doing much brainstorming, and you can brainstorm without being creative. For example, you might brainstorm to pick a topic you think your teacher would like. But true creativity invariably features originality, unorthodoxy, imagination, and novel approaches. It brings out divergent thinking, your willingness to take off on intentional tangents and ponder and mentally toy with just about everything that you can think of.

Creativity often calls for you to be naive and make believe you don't know much, so you can reconstruct your universe. A teenager like Roberta has trouble with this in part because she is so narrowly beholden to the conservative accumulation of knowledge. Creativity involves taking intellectual risks, possibly bucking currently accepted trends and values. A highly creative person therefore may be forced to function at the fringes of society, to be considered eccentric. Finally, creativity seeks a vehicle. No one can be creative at every endeavor. Will it be sculpture, poetry, music, inventions, landscape design? And once the medium is identified, creativity can be melded with acquired technical skill. Roberta had not yet found her medium, but she needed to actively immerse herself in that quest.

A third component of ideation entails *critical thinking.* This process should become a part of schoolwork and career work in a range of contexts and circumstances. Roberta needed help to become systematic in evaluating ideas, products, other people, and even herself. She also needed to be able to evaluate evaluations—for example, the critical thinking of her peers and their parents.

Critical thinking involves, first of all, a clearly thought out description of what is being assessed. There needs to be as well a bit of a self-evaluation (e.g., "I tend to believe only what Democrats have to say."). Then, with the facts straight and your personal biases accounted for, you can go about finding and using criteria to evaluate your subject, which may be someone's opinion, a commercial product, or the performance of a person. The steps in critical thinking result in your own ideas, which can enrich your writing, your comments in class, and your decision making in general. Critical thinking is protection against gullibility unless it gets carried to the point of unbridled cynicism. Roberta was not a critical thinker; she echoed what she learned. She needed overt guidance from her teacher to identify contradictions, to take a personal stand, and to defend her position. Such requirements should have been part of the specific instructions Roberta and her classmates always received. I think students should be graded both on their reporting of information and on their ability to assess that information.

Personal interpretation and analysis yield some additional raw materials for idea production. A student can reflect on what she is learning, in part by relating it to her own experiences and prior knowledge, a process that can yield answers to such questions as What does this mean to *me*? How does all this agree with, add to, or contradict other things I know or have experienced in my life? How can I apply this in the future? Doing so provides an open invitation to introduce your own top-down thinking, your highly personal imprint while you write or talk or think.

Some people engage in this mode of analysis spontaneously, while others, like Roberta, have to make use of a map, such as one I developed called Point-Counterpoint. A student lists within a column of boxes the major points made in a text and then to the right of each completed box provides his or her response to the information. An example of this format is illustrated in Figure 7-1 that can be used to enhance both critical thinking and personal interpretation. I fervently recommended this exercise for Roberta. Alternatively, such a student should be instructed to add to any factual essay she writes one or more paragraphs of personal interpretation, perhaps addressing some of the questions raised in the text.

When we encounter an area of weakness in a student, we try to set up a system in which that weak link becomes a totally separate stage in the output chain. So we might say to Roberta, "You've done a great job presenting this information on the outbreak of World War II. Now please go back and add a section describing what you would have done differently if you were a leader of one of those countries."

Output can be used in *problem solving.* For example, a writer may be struggling with a highly enigmatic issue or dilemma. In the process of writing about it, she may unravel or even resolve the inherent conflicts. An architect might tell you that the drawings he has just rendered are solving a space problem. He could not have worked it out without drawing it out. Robert Frost once wrote, "I go into a poem to see if I can get out of it." That's a form of problem solving. He also pointed out, "A poem should begin in delight and end in wisdom." That, too, is problem solving—namely, how can I express my most personal feelings and learn something from them?

Students like Roberta need to realize that many forms of output require problem solving. This is most obviously true in mathematics, but only when students comprehend what they are doing and are not just

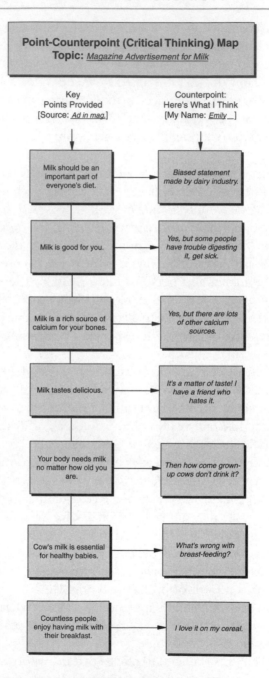

Point-Counterpoint (Critical Thinking) Map
Topic: *Magazine Advertisement for Milk*

Key
Points Provided
[Source: *Ad in mag.*]

Counterpoint:
Here's What I Think
[My Name: *Emily*]

| Milk should be an important part of everyone's diet. | *Biased statement made by dairy industry.* |

| Milk is good for you. | *Yes, but some people have trouble digesting it, get sick.* |

| Milk is a rich source of calcium for your bones. | *Yes, but there are lots of other calcium sources.* |

| Milk tastes delicious. | *It's a matter of taste! I have a friend who hates it.* |

| Your body needs milk no matter how old you are. | *Then how come grown-up cows don't drink it?* |

| Cow's milk is essential for healthy babies. | *What's wrong with breast-feeding?* |

| Countless people enjoy having milk with their breakfast. | *I love it on my cereal.* |

Figure 7-1. This template can be used to help a student come up with personal reactions to information conveyed in a book or article. Such a technique can be used to encourage active processing of reading material and sharp critical thinking.

imitating the procedures handed down from their teachers. As with creativity, people are likely to vary dramatically in the media they can use or the kind of subject matter they feel comfortable with for problem solving. Some are terrific problem solvers when it comes to repairing cars, while others can use problem solving to unravel the meaning of a poem, and still others are great at problem solving when it comes to the personal troubles of their friends.

A couple of years ago I visited a seventh-grade science class at a middle school in Harlem. We were there in collaboration with WGBH in Boston to film a video library on learning issues. One particular student, Arnaldo, looked conspicuously confused while his dynamic teacher was lecturing on various forms of energy. But when the teacher asked the kids to design a heating system for a house with no source of electrical energy, the challenge jump-started Arnaldo's brain. He eagerly reached for some paper and crayons and quickly sketched a typical rectangular New York apartment house, on the outside of which he created a complex network of ducts and pipes. When I asked him what that apparatus was, he explained that the conduits would carry water that would be heated by the sun, then stored inside water tanks, and so on. As he drew up his plan, he saw some troubling impasses in his ideas.

During an interview we taped after class, I pointed out to Arnaldo that I thought he was probably a hands-on kind of guy. He liked to do his thinking while he was producing something. He laughed and in his almost musical Hispanic accent he agreed completely. This early adolescent was an active problem solver. He learned by creating. His teacher mentioned that Arnaldo failed most quizzes but was fantastic at doing projects; he was just the opposite of Roberta. This was a high-output guy, not about to star on multiple-choice tests, yet quite possibly destined to be an impressively productive and inventive worker (if he gets the opportunities he deserves). He was a great kid, but I feared for him when I thought of end-of-grade testing.

The production of ideas is a critical ingredient of much high-quality output. Sometimes students like Roberta fail to receive sensitive help with ideation, so they may miss out on a crucial aspect of education. They may be rewarded over and over for their mastery of knowledge and skills without sensing the need to build up their ideational richness and fluency in the ways I have cited in this chapter. Using writing as the prototype, Roberta and the many others like her should discover that the goal is not merely to report knowledge but to transform it in some constructive way. It is through such transformations that individuals experience fun and satisfaction while making insightful contributions.

A couple of years later I received a call from the head of Roberta's school asking me to come back and make another presentation. I asked how Roberta was faring as a senior in high school. I was informed that she had survived some rough times. When she was in eleventh grade, Roberta's father had died unexpectedly of heart failure. His art gallery, which had been on the verge of bankruptcy, had accumulated substantial debt and closed down. Mrs. Chan had had what was described as a psychotic breakdown after the loss of her husband and could not work anymore. Roberta's paternal grandmother had moved in with them, and she provided some much-needed moral strength. Meanwhile, Roberta had hardly missed a day of school and continued to meet expectations meticulously. This was all the more impressive since she needed to work part-time in a local Starbucks to help pay her tuition. She never complained. Heroically, Roberta insisted on enrolling in three advanced-placement courses during her junior year. She told one of the nuns that that's what her father would have wanted her to do.

I was informed that Roberta's teachers were stressing the kinds of idea-production tactics I had recommended, and that they saw some modest improvement in her capacity or willingness to become more top-down, more of a brainstormer, a more vigorous critical and creative thinker. They had decided not to be too heavy-handed with her since she had so much on her mind and was continuing to do solid work in school. Interestingly, the principal let me know that our lunchtime discussion had catalyzed a sequence of chain reactions so that teachers in this notably and notoriously traditional parochial high school were now working hard to teach kids to engage in what they were calling "distinctive thinking."

The principal informed me that Roberta had come through her tumultuous junior year reasonably unscathed. Having managed phenomenally high scores on her (bottom-up) SATs, Roberta had applied to Stanford, UCLA, and Berkeley, with the intention of studying biochemistry. During a conversation with her school's college-placement adviser, Roberta confessed, "I love biochemistry. And, like, for sure, I'm not going to win any Nobel Prizes or find a cure for brain cancer. But I think, like, I'll be really good at knowing everything you can know about my subject and doing all kinds of research experiments in the lab using the right techniques just the right way." Roberta appeared to be suppressing a giggle when she added, "Maybe someone else I work with will have to think up the ideas for our experiments, and then I'll do them. Who knows, someday maybe I'll be thinking up my own theories." Minds grow and diversify over time. I would never write off this tenacious girl. She and her partner just may win a Nobel Prize someday.

8

SHARON AND MARK TAYLOR

Falling Prey to Disarray

He who would do good to another must do it in Minute Particulars;
General Good is the plea of the scoundrel, hypocrite and flatterer:
For Art and Science cannot exist but in minutely organized Particulars.
—WILLIAM BLAKE, "JERUSALEM"

Like many people, Dr. Sharon Taylor was a tangle of contradictions, a mixed assortment of stunning strengths and exasperating flaws. There are some individuals whose talents and shortcomings are openly displayed day after day, as if on a massive highway billboard. That was Sharon. She was genuine. Those who knew her really knew her. What they saw was what she was.

A brilliant child psychologist, Sharon worked under my supervision in Massachusetts before I moved to North Carolina. She served as clinician in various programs for children with learning and behavior problems and was a mainstay in our multidisciplinary team evaluations of kids. She also saw patients on her own. You had to be impressed with her profound expertise and perceptive judgment when it came to evaluating students with learning difficulties, as she was laserlike at pinpointing their specific deficits and strengths. She was as effective at unraveling twisted family problems as she was at understanding the emotional nuances of a child's struggles. Furthermore, she could analyze learning and behavior problems without feeling compelled to label or categorize those who ventured through the doors of her office. She gave parents and kids heaps of great advice, and from what I could see, they all admired and loved this woman. And she got results. I saw countless children regain their self-esteem, improve in school, and modify their behavior for the better under her care.

Sharon was also fun to have around. Her wry sense of humor, her consistently upbeat mood, and her unending altruism attracted our admiration and affection. She was the first to roast a turkey or bake one of her apricot meringue pies for someone who was ill. She was, as well, a first-rate communicator and collaborator on a diagnostic team.

Over the years our trainees learned a great deal from Sharon. They valued her clinical judgment, and she provided them with inspiring guidance. Most important, she nurtured them; they could tell she really cared about their lives.

It sounds as if Dr. Sharon Taylor was the very model of a model psychologist, but, in truth, she was a problem, a significant problem for me and for our department. Major components of her output were abysmal.

Writing reports on our patients is one of the principal responsibilities (or chores) of everyone who labors in our evaluation programs. These written descriptions of our findings, along with treatment recommendations, make up the tangible products of our evaluations. The reports are read by parents, by school personnel, by outside clinicians, and often even by the children or adolescents themselves. Without a timely, clearly written description, an evaluation comes close to being a waste of time. Sharon's report writing (or lack thereof) was a seemingly insurmountable problem for us. She was always months and sometimes years delayed in getting them out. We all spent time on the phone fabricating excuses for her tardiness, but the reports were not forthcoming. On occasion some staff members felt compelled to write a report for her. Her output failure was a puzzling mystery, one that could not have been solved by invoking any of the explanations covered in earlier chapters of this book. Sharon had no motor problems, nor did she emit the telltale signals of attentional dysfunction (she could concentrate for hours on end and usually worked a ten- or eleven-hour day). Her language abilities were intact, and there were no signs that she had any glitches in her memory system.

Sharon's negligent report writing was by no means her sole output shortfall. The time warp she lived in was another. Sharon was predictably late for almost everything. She'd get to meetings or conferences absurdly tardy and for some reason always seemed to be out of breath upon arrival. She often appeared as if she'd just escaped an automobile wreck.

I would be understating the truth if I described Sharon's office merely as a mess. I have no idea how she ever located anything in that

panorama of heaps, some of which had been demolished by recent
paper landslides. There were Himalayan mountain ranges of journals,
reprints, folders, and test manuals as far as the naked eye could see
(which wasn't all that far, due to a tall mound near the doorway). Even
her computer monitor was partially obstructed with her memorabilia. I
don't think her training had ever included advice on the use of waste re-
ceptacles. Sharon, like a squirrel in mid-October, hoarded everything.
She claimed she knew where each item was buried, but I had reason to
doubt that, since she also regularly admitted to losing things.

When Sharon first came to work for me, at the age of twenty-nine, I
thought she had enormous potential as a scholar. I felt sure she would
ascend the academic ladder within a tenure track in the psychology department at our university. She had great ideas and possessed an excellent command of the research literature on a wide range of topics. Also,
she was obviously ambitious and hardworking. At the time she and her
husband, a successful certified public accountant, had two young children and had made effective day-care arrangements for them.

Sharon was an eager candidate for her Ph.D. She had completed all
her course work and had started doing the research for her thesis (on
social problems among children with learning difficulties). Eight years
later she was still working on it. Ultimately it took more than a decade
for her to complete and defend her thesis successfully.

I encouraged Sharon (as well as others who worked for me) to develop an area of expertise all her own. I wanted her to be the world's
leading authority on something so she could develop an international
reputation, produce papers in her domain, and derive the satisfaction
that comes with intellectual depth. But it seemed that almost every
week Sharon showed up in my office with a new scheme, a new area of
focused interest that she wanted to pursue. Her topics ranged from depression, to gifted children, to autism, to bed-wetting, to child abuse.
She never followed up on any of her inspirations. In fact, Sharon was a
veritable geyser of terrific ideas but a dry creek when it came to implementation or follow-through. She had no trouble with ideation; you
couldn't beat her at brainstorming. But this woman couldn't complete
anything. My own boss at Harvard, Dr. Mary Ellen Avery, used to call this
the "promises, promises syndrome," and she claimed she encountered
it often—people who were always telling her what they were going
to do but never actually did. In Sharon's case I found myself cringing
whenever she came to see me with another set of great ideas she was al-

legedly about to pursue. I was overwhelmed with a deep sense of irony, along with a bit of annoyance that she was wasting my precious time.

I detected yet another consistent troublesome trait in Sharon. She could never prioritize. She would spend hours writing a one-page assessment of one of her trainees (that in all likelihood no one would ever read) and then entirely neglect her reports on patients. She would go to lectures in the medical school on topics she had heard hundreds of times, only to be late to or miss an important meeting. Sharon had an uncanny knack or dys-knack for allocating too much time to things that had no payoff and too little time to high-stakes activities. It was as if she were totally blind to relative importance.

I was forever trying to help Sharon make the grade in academia, where the rule is publish or perish. She certainly had the intelligence, the motivation, and the knowledge to do so, despite lacking that vital ingredient called focus. One time I arranged for her to write a chapter on autism for a very prestigious pediatric textbook. It was a great opportunity for Sharon to get national exposure along with a nice item on her curriculum vitae. She diligently visited the library and compiled a mammoth bibliography on the subject, but she just couldn't manage to produce the chapter. After repeated requests from and pleading by the editor, she was still three months beyond the deadline with nothing to turn in. The angry textbook editor finally went ahead and wrote the chapter by himself. This scenario was repeated at least twice when Sharon missed deadlines on grant proposals. Each time the proposal started out well written, well thought out, and original; she simply couldn't finish it.

I was always striving to help Sharon make use of her strengths. That's why when a terrific opportunity arose to obtain a contract for training day-care personnel in the psychological needs and problems of children, I seized the chance, believing this would be a perfect fit for Sharon—lots of teaching, no reports to write. She accepted this part-time segment of her job with her usual unbridled enthusiasm. I soon received very positive feedback regarding the quality and practicality of her teaching. Alas, after a few months the project director requested that Sharon be replaced because she was showing up late for just about all of her training sessions and, on several occasions, had failed to show up at all (claiming she'd forgotten about them or had had car trouble). The project director told me he could not tolerate her "obvious laziness."

So that was Sharon: intellectually tantalizing, well meaning, kind, creative, skillful, knowledgeable, ever industrious, but, alas, malignantly disorganized. I passed through cycles of admiring Sharon, feeling very sorry for her, and resenting her. There were times when I came close to firing her, but I couldn't quite bring myself to do it. And yes, of course, I had countless long talks with her about her performance.

I can't claim that my discussions with Sharon did much to cure her problems. In fact, one of my colleagues once told me that adults don't change much. That is, what you see is what you're going to keep on getting! (By the way, I keep trying to explain this to my spouse, but she won't give up trying.) If true, this would imply that you have to work with someone's strengths and at some point give up on trying to reform or rewire his or her mind. I don't really know if I believe that—I don't feel comfortable giving up on anyone's deficiencies if they are thwarting output.

Despite my therapeutic ineffectiveness, I learned a great deal during my discussions with Sharon. What I found out added to my understanding of people like her—both children and adults. At the outset, I should report that Sharon was candid and seldom defensive, although from time to time she accused me of not knowing what it's like to be a single mother (eventually her husband left her, possibly for someone more organized).

In several of our conversations, we focused on Sharon's report-writing famine. She kept using the word *overwhelmed* to describe how she felt when she sat down to tackle a report. She described writing a report as like trying to do a gigantic jigsaw puzzle without having a picture of the completed work to refer to. There were always so many pieces, and while she felt she had a handle on the individual pieces, she found it nearly impossible to put the puzzle together. Sharon had problems integrating information, knowing what to include and what to exclude, knowing how much to report and how much to elaborate on what she was reporting, knowing where to put what in the flow of a narrative. She couldn't select the scattered strands of her knowledge and weave them together cohesively. So Sharon's problems with written output were actually a manifestation of organizational failure; she had serious trouble orchestrating knowledge.

Obviously, Sharon's organizational deficiencies extended well beyond the writing of reports. In fact, she stands out in my mind as a model of all the common forms of disorganization, in her case tragically rolled into one human being. First and most obviously, Sharon was struggling with time management. She had no idea how to estimate time, allocate time, meet deadlines, and know what to do when and for how long in order to get something done on schedule. So work of all kinds would accumulate and overtake her. Sharon also seemed to lack an internal clock. As a result she had no sense of when she was running behind—or ahead. Instead she seemed suspended in time, which made her chronically tardy. I remember becoming intensely annoyed when working on a team with Sharon. She would exceed by more than thirty minutes the time she was allocated for her part of the evaluation—not because she was more thorough than the rest of us but because she had no awareness of the passage of minutes or hours. As she reflected on it, Sharon told me that her time warp had been an issue for her since the earliest days of childhood. As it turned out, she'd been delayed in learning to tell time, and it had taken her forever to memorize the months of the year in the right order.

She had experienced two other problems stemming from her weak sense of time. She predictably became unglued when faced with anything resembling multitasking. Sharon had to do one thing at a time and became confused if there were multiple to-do items on her agenda. For example, she had trouble on a day when in addition to her hours at the office, she was also working at the clinic, shopping for the right items on the way home from work, returning telephone calls, and paying her bills. Those servings were too large to fit on her small plate. Second, Sharon had problems knowing what to do when she undertook a substantial task. She lacked what I like to call "step wisdom," which is the innate knowledge of how to break a challenge down into achievable, "bite-sized" steps. Sharon tried to do too many steps at once, a quick route to feeling overwhelmed.

Sharon's time-management weaknesses were complicated by problems with material management. She had long-standing difficulty keeping track of possessions and the various props or tools needed to accomplish the day's activities. Endless hours were devoted to prolonged treasure hunts for car keys, glasses, pens, and, yes, incomplete clinic reports. As a child she'd often lost things and had had major problems organizing a notebook, a desk, or a locker. Her childhood bedroom had been the coming attraction for the state of her adult office.

Sharon never denied that she had these problems, and, in fact, at my urging she got extended periods of counseling. She even underwent a neurological evaluation at one point, but it failed to explain anything. One psychiatrist decided (of course) that she must be "an adult ADD." I didn't agree at all, especially since I knew that in our era sooner or later anyone at loose ends inherits the ever convenient catchall label of attention deficit disorder. Naturally, Sharon was given the stimulant medication Ritalin. This therapy helped, but just a little. Eventually she was switched to Prozac, which didn't do anything for her. She also had a course of lithium for presumed bipolar illness, but there was no real benefit and (fortunately) she developed side effects, so the medicine was discontinued. In summary, despite her cooperativeness, Sharon could never be described as "a therapeutic triumph" for the mental-health professions!

I never really got into Sharon's personal life; such matters are not within my domain of clinical expertise or comfort. I do know that during the last couple of years she worked for me, her two children, a boy and a girl, were mid-adolescents. Her daughter was very competent and doing well in school. But her son, Mark, was said to be just like his mom, complete with a bedroom rivaling the local landfill and an extensive track record of overdue homework assignments and brusque summonses for tardiness. He was having serious problems in ninth grade. Daughter Julie, on the other hand, inhabited a bedroom right out of Bloomingdale's furniture floor and tended to be early for all appointments. She had recently submitted a history term paper on American experiments with socialism a week before it was actually due, a gesture that had totally detonated her older brother and led him to characterize her as a complete "dorkette."

One day Sharon came to see me about "something very personal." It turned out she desperately wanted my help, or at least some advice, regarding Mark. She said he was getting counseling and taking medication prescribed by a psychiatrist friend of hers (who never actually saw Mark—believe it or not). She readily confessed that Mark was just like her, completely at loose ends all the time. She wanted me to see him as a patient, but apparently the boy was refusing—too embarrassed to reveal himself to his mom's boss. Eventually she coerced the fifteen-year-old to come in. There is almost nothing more unsettling than dealing with an adolescent patient who doesn't want to see me (or anyone else, for that matter) for an evaluation. Anyway, I spent about two awkward hours talking with Mark on two separate occasions. His most common, predictably noncommittal responses to any queries I made were "Not that much," "It doesn't matter," and "I don't really care."

One of our educational diagnosticians tested him and informed me that Mark possessed grade-level reading and spelling abilities and was about a year ahead in mathematics. His writing was described as "labored and difficult to follow but containing a good many good ideas expressed in rather sophisticated language."

Over time, I had a series of follow-up visits with Mark. Eventually he relaxed and no longer responded blandly to my questions. From our discussions, it appeared that his worst headache in school was his trouble handling the workload. He confessed that he seldom met deadlines, hated written assignments, and felt hopelessly behind in getting work done. He said he couldn't stand school and blamed his teachers (an all too common reaction in adolescents with output failure). From everything he told me, it was clear that Sharon's boy was struggling with the organization of output—big time!

His poor school performance contrasted with the good grades his mother had earned as a child. It may be that Mark was even more disorganized than she had ever been. Mark insisted he didn't have any kind of learning problem. As he announced almost defiantly, "There's nothing wrong with me; I'm just lazy, that's all." Incidentally, kids with output failure commonly accuse themselves of being lazy. I believe that's because they have no other explanation for their low productivity.

I always try to think systematically about an organizational problem to isolate any specific breakdown in an individual kid. To help Mark, I reviewed with him the four most common forms of organizational problems I encounter in kids:

- *Managing complex tasks:* planning written reports, studying for final examinations, launching projects
- *Managing time:* multitasking, accomplishing tasks in steps (knowing what to do when), meeting deadlines, not procrastinating
- *Managing materials:* arranging a notebook, finding what you need when you need it, imparting physical order (e.g., in desks, closets, bedroom)
- *Prioritizing:* knowing and attending to what's most important, not wasting too much time, not spending too much time on trivial pursuits

Guess what? After talking with Mark, examining samples of his schoolwork, and reading years of comments from his teachers, I arrived at the inescapable conclusion that poor Mark suffered from all of the above! I know of many students who harbor one or another of these four organizational problems but relatively few who suffer them all. He had been genetically invaded by the identical quartet of organizational saboteurs that had undermined his mother throughout her career. Such familial patterns of disarray are common. A complex task requires the assembling of multiple pieces or components. Mark had difficulty pulling together the various parts of any such assignment. When undertaking such a project or a substantial writing challenge, Mark couldn't get all the information he needed, figure out how he would use that knowledge, present the material in the best order, and incorporate other elements (such as good grammar, logical thinking, and punctuation). Tasks like that, with a lot of moving parts, made Mark feel as if he were being buried alive.

Time management was another barrier. Mark was often late for classes, and was a record-breaking procrastinator, dependably failing to meet nearly all deadlines. He had trouble allocating time, sensing in advance how long any undertaking might take, and knowing when he was running out of time. To make matters worse, there were also problems with material management. Mark invariably misplaced his belongings. Consequently, he would spend hours on end in desperate searches for missing books, writing utensils, and notes.

Lastly, Mark appeared totally incapable of prioritizing. His mother lamented that he "wastes his time on little activities that amount to nothing more than dawdling and then has no time or energy left to complete work or get closure on things that really matter."

As a pediatrician, I readily admit to my dearth of expertise regarding the organizational tactics suitable for career success, although I know when they're lacking, as in Sharon's case. Looking back, I believe there are some thoughts I should have shared with her regarding each of her organizational gaps. I didn't feel qualified to help Sharon (nor was I asked to do so), but I was eager to try to rescue poor Mark, who had convinced himself he was suffering from a terminal case of laziness and was rapidly plunging down through a failure vortex in high school.

HELPING MARK MAKE HIS MARK

I tried to tackle Mark's organizational glitches one by one. I offered him advice and also sent a report to his teachers. Three or four times Sharon and I got together with him to go over some management techniques. You never know whether an adolescent will accept advice from an adult, and you can be even less sure that he will apply it if he does take it. Nevertheless, I feel it's worth the try, and I've had enough successes to justify trying.

Complex Task Management

Imagine a contractor responsible for putting up a new building. It's her job to coordinate the work of the bricklayers, drywall people, electricians, plumbers, and carpenters with various subspecialties. That requires complex task management.

Writing a report or doing a project for school is a complex task that involves assembling multiple components. A student may have to decide on a topic, figure out how to research it, splice information together, add his own ideas or interpretations, figure out how best to express the ideas, and create a written first draft. That's a lot of work for most kids, and for some, like Mark, it's too much. Sharon confronted the same obstacle when she had to create reports. I can think of many other career challenges that require people to engage in complex task management: preparing a proposal or business plan, rebuilding an automobile engine, planning a wedding, creating a new history curriculum for a high school, assembling a brief for a courtroom trial.

I have encountered many children with output problems similar to Mark's. Like him, they succeed when an assignment contains only one significant component or step. Such a student may occupy a vaunted niche in his class's highest reading group but may have problems doing the research and assembling the ideas for a project or written report. He just can't seem to cope with multifaceted tasks.

One very common situation involves the child who is a whiz with computer games but rejects word processing. Mark fit this pattern perfectly; he could defeat almost anyone at games and was widely respected by his peers for his brilliant gaming know-how. His computer wizardry shone through during these satisfying cyber-forays, in part because they are not such complex tasks; they tend to involve vigilance and a relatively small package of neurodevelopmental functions. Word processing, on the other hand, demands the integration of multiple operations (e.g., saving, selecting, deleting, cutting and pasting, formatting). I sometimes worry about computer-game addicts because they may not gain the experience of weaving a lot of different strands together to achieve a goal (a vital requirement in almost all careers). While we're on the subject, I'll mention that watching TV, transmitting instant messages over the Internet, riding a skateboard, and filibustering on the phone also fail to qualify as complex tasks. Mark was addicted to all of these forms of passive time wasting. On the other hand, athletic pursuits, arts and crafts and construction projects, and musical performance are healthy opportunities to handle output complexity.

In my report, I urged his mother and his teachers to help Mark stress the planning stage of any complex task. Adults and children who shun output complexity should be discouraged from simply diving into an endeavor. They need help strategizing and articulating efficient approaches before they launch any effort. Much of their advanced planning should be aimed at breaking down the activity into steps to make it more manageable. In general, Mark needed first to identify the bits and pieces of a task, then to work on them one at a time. Once the parts are completed, a separate step pastes everything together. After sanding and polishing, a final finished revision can be produced. Writing a story is a good example of a complex academic task faced by many children and teenagers. The Story Developer, somewhat abridged from my book *Educational Care,* can be seen in Appendix B. It serves as a development plan for breaking a complex task into manageable chunks. As different components fall into place, the child fills in the appropriate blanks on the planning form.

Should adults too make use of developers? One could do worse, I think. At our newly established Student Success Center in North Carolina, we recently developed report-writing technology, which would have been a godsend for Sharon. On a computer monitor, a clinician can bring up the skeleton of a clinic report, a template that guides his diagnostic reasoning as well as his writing. For the most part, the person creating the report then fills in blanks and responds to questions on the screen. I believe analogous software is becoming available across a range of vocations and project types. There are computer programs for planning projects, writing business plans, filing income taxes, and writing your will. I find that those individuals who could benefit the most are probably the most reluctant to rely on these complexity-taming systems. They need to be cajoled and coerced—perhaps even threatened—to do so.

Complex tasks can also be tackled through collaboration and division of labor. Every child should have experience as a project manager or editor in chief. The challenge involves setting goals for a task (previewing the desired outcome), breaking it down into its components, doling out assignments, and then putting it all together. Incidentally, it's often that last step that eludes and discourages kids like Mark.

Having a clear vision of the intended final product helps a lot. A contractor's job is simplified if he has blueprints to refer to. The author of a thesis may need to work from an outline. A speechwriter could start by constructing a tentative concluding paragraph. In other words, knowing where you're headed helps you pull together all the necessary pieces. I noted the importance of such previewing in the story of Scott Murray (chapter 5). At each point in the complex task, you ask yourself how each part that falls into place is moving you closer to your anticipated conclusion or end product. It's not too different from peering at the picture of a model rocket ship as you assemble the model.

The bottom line is that when a task looks and feels like an enemy attacking you, the job is to disarm the adversary, to make the task easier. Some people achieve this nearly intuitively, especially within their chosen field. Others, like Mark and his mother, consciously have to break the job down into its specific ingredients and tackle them one at a time.

Time Management, Multitasking, and "Step Wisdom"

A person's sense of time can be a blessing. There are countless students like Mark, as well as many employees like his mother, whose problems with output can be traced to a diminished sense of time and timing. Like Mark, many of them have difficulty following schedules, accomplishing all the things they should do during the day (i.e., multitasking), and knowing what to do when (having step wisdom) and for how long. Some become world-class procrastinators, doing everything at the last second (often in a state of panic). Time sneaks up and ruthlessly ambushes them. They have trouble allocating the right amount of time to what they need to do, estimating how long something will take to achieve, and knowing whether they are on time or running late (the latter being the more common state of affairs).

Trouble with time management, including problems with punctuality, chronic difficulties meeting deadlines, and never sensing how long it will take to do something, can resist the most well-intentioned efforts to improve, yet I have seen cases where students have gotten in step with life's temporal demands.

When people lack a feel for time, we try to offer them ways to find some temporal structure. In Mark's case this involved a whopping dose of schedule planning. Parents have to try to be their kid's time tutor. At regular intervals, a parent and a child need to confer as they work out tentative schedules for each day of the coming week (for more details, see pages 203 to 204). Interestingly, Sharon felt totally unqualified to play this role, so she hired Barbara Bates, a retired high school teacher and a friend of the family, to be "Mark's organization coach." Sharon told me that Mrs. Bates had always been considered an outstanding teacher and a "fanatic for fine detail, a totally together person." So Mrs. Bates served as a pipeline during her weekly sessions with Mark; I offered advice, and she made sure that it was applied. I know quite a few people who would benefit from such organizational tutoring.

Increasing numbers of adults depend on pocket computers to help them with time management, multitasking, and step wisdom. Most of them are likely to be people who were organized to begin with, at least sufficiently organized to find ways to get even more organized. Yet this technology holds promise and may be the salvation of some low-output workers engulfed in a time warp. It could also be helpful to temporally disorganized children. It's worth a try—unless, of course, the individual is also plagued with material organization, in which case the pocket organizer may well vanish from the pocket of the organizer. Mark tried one but lost it within a month. That's why I haven't gotten one.

Material Management

As a person who is severely challenged in terms of material management, a chronic loser of vital objects, I feel hypocritical writing this section of *The Myth of Laziness*. I spend much of my day searching for misplaced objects. All those who work with me know not to give me the original copy of anything. If they need me to sign something, they stand there while I do so, as they know that otherwise they might never see the document again. If I need a Phillips screwdriver for a chore at home, it consumes much less time and anxiety if I buy a new one than if I try to locate the one I bought six weeks ago. But if you'll forgive me for not always practicing what I preach, I will try to describe some interventions that I suggested to Mrs. Bates and that I've used with many kids who suffer from a kind of disappearing-objects syndrome.

Mark was apt to walk the high school corridors with his notebooks hemorrhaging crumpled papers. The rings on his loose-leaf notebook paper always seemed to rupture, and the doors of his overstuffed locker in school would never close completely; some fragment of paper or twisted remnant of clothing invariably jutted out through the cracks. The boy's jam-packed book bag was so heavy it probably resulted in unchecked overgrowth of his latissimus dorsi (i.e., upper-back) muscles.

As kids like Mark mature, the stifling challenge of many activities re quires getting more and more things together—bringing home the right books, locating a usable sheet of paper, clearing the T-shirts and underwear off a desktop to expose a workable surface. As adults they misplace the tools of their trade and are bewildered by the need to organize desks, computer files, closets, and all the props and facilities needed to accomplish tasks. Even everyday routines fall prey to material oblivion. The parents of one eleven-year-old mentioned to me that she would take a shower with her socks on if she were not reminded to remove them. Mark might have done the same.

How, then, do we teach material organization to a kid at loose ends like Mark, one whose output is in jeopardy? It's pretty straightforward. The answer is consistency. We have to establish for that child or for an adult like Sharon a rigorous set of consistent (possibly also boring) routines that in the long run will save time and alleviate suffering. I believe parents have to play a leading role in establishing and enforcing habits of material order. Adults have to do it on their own. For example, I now have rather neat offices at home and at work. That's because I have discovered that I can't think in an organized manner in a chaotic environment. My technique is quite primitive: I throw away most things!

Some of the worst material disasters seem to occur at critical transition points during the day. I have found that I misplace most objects and suffer other material organizational catastrophes as I am progressing from one activity or scene to the next.

Many of us afflicted with material disarray have a way of rushing through the day's transitions without taking inventory. So one very useful intervention Mrs. Bates tried with Mark was to get him to identify the day's principal transitions and learn to slow down at these critical points (e.g., leaving to catch the bus, getting ready to exit the school, changing classes, or finishing homework). At these junctures, he was encouraged to talk to himself, asking, "Is there anything I've left behind or misplaced? What things do I need for what's coming next?" or even, more specifically, "Do I have the stuff I need to finish that report for history?" In severe cases, a child can be given little checklists to use at several key points during the day. These can be pasted on his or her assignment pad. Mark refused this option, protesting that it would make him "look weird," always an issue in secondary school life.

In my own case, I have been helped immeasurably (but not cured) by applying what I now call my "lump checks." I carry three stable objects with me: a wallet, mostly for credit cards and my driver's license; a billfold for paper money; and a cell phone. The phone is like an escape artist; I have left it in taxicabs, hotels, airport lounges, and restaurants during my existence as an academic nomad. But now, thanks to modern ingenuity, every time I cross a physical threshold (a minitransition of sorts), I pat my pockets for the three telltale lumps. At the same time, I subvocalize and say to myself, "Lump check leaving airport parking lot." Then when the cell phone later gets away from me, at the very least I know where and when to commence the search—that is, at a locale I have traversed since the last lump check!

Several of Mark's teachers cooperated with our strategy. For example, at the end of English class, Mark would stop at the teacher's desk for a moment to mention what materials he'd need for the night's homework. He did this for a few weeks, until one of his friends made a nasty comment about it (the kiss of death for any adolescent tactic). Nevertheless, he was showing lasting signs of slowing down at the transitions.

Prioritization

As we have seen, Mark's organizational woes were confounded by his inability to gauge task importance. Consequently, he would expend far too much time and effort in low-yield trivial pursuits and then lack sufficient time and energy for the things that really counted. For example, he would spend hours searching for one questionably useful bit of information for a report he was writing and then be too tired to write the paper. Therefore, as his mom had informed me, Mark was a professional time waster. And he was always at loose ends, because when you don't prioritize you get disorganized.

There are quite a few Marks out there who are drowning because they can't prioritize. Before the age of eleven or twelve few kids are proficient prioritizers; fortunately, their lives are arranged for them, so they don't need to make distinctions of importance. But once they start reporting to multiple teachers, engaging in varied recreational activities, seeking several forms of entertainment, actively dealing with peer relationships, and fulfilling obligations or responsibilities, they need to rank the relative importance of the competing priorities in their lives. Mark's failures to prioritize created some of his most formidable academic hurdles.

Prioritization is pretty intuitive for some kids, but for those like Mark everything seems to be equally relevant to their needs in life, or else (an even more hazardous situation) they have inappropriate or distorted priorities. The latter phenomenon can be observed when a student decides that his main priority is to get all of his work done in school, so he won't have to take home any books and waste his evening writing a report. Thus he rushes through his work during a study hall, and the resulting output is skimpy and shoddy. The students like Mark who fail to prioritize much of anything are our main focus, and they need our help. In chapter 11, I will explain the use of a prioritization chart that seems to be helpful to many children and grown-ups.

I think poor prioritization infects careers even more than schoolwork. Sharon needed to ask herself repeatedly, "What are the truly important things I'm trying to accomplish on this job? And what percentage of my time am I engaging in activities that don't further these core missions?" Having posed such questions, one can go about the artful craft of whittling away the questionable routines and rituals that play havoc with an individual's high-payoff output.

In my own career, I have to say I have been brutal, possibly excessive or even obsessive, when it comes to prioritizing. More than anything else, I know I want to dedicate my energies to helping misunderstood children who are failing in life. To meet this aim, which I consider vital, I try to serve on no committees in the university. I attend as few meetings as possible, for which I have been occasionally criticized. I engage in no ceremonies of any type, unless I'm trapped into one where I'm receiving some kind of reward I didn't seek. Meanwhile, I devote my time to doing as much reading and writing on my subject area, traveling around the world to work with teachers and clinicians (I write a lot of turbulent prose on planes and in hotel rooms), and seeing as many patients as I can so that I don't lose touch with the real problems facing kids in school. That leaves little time for what I consider trivial ventures. Luckily, many university faculty members have very different priorities from my own. Some want to be leaders in the university, so committee membership becomes a high priority and they are avid participants in meetings. (I fall asleep at them.) Of course, we are all obligated to do certain things to be polite, to make others feel good, to help out, to have some fun, and to be sociable. Such actions and activities do add to the pleasure and gratification in our lives, even if they don't foster high output.

Thank goodness there are all kinds of minds with all kinds of priorities. Problems occur mainly when people fail to sort out and follow through on priorities they have established. Low output ensues. The charges of laziness may be heard echoing in the distance.

Mind functions that are nearly instinctive to some people have to be trained in others. Some folks are natural mathematicians; others need to learn math formally. Some seem to have been born with musical talent; others require oppressive lessons and extra practice to succeed with an instrument. Organizational problems are no exception. Sharon's ex-husband and her daughter, Julie, were tightly wired to be organized, while Sharon and Mark needed to have such wiring installed. I believe that adults can change for the better when they understand clearly what's at stake. I have mentioned some ways we could have helped Sharon. More suggestions are contained in subsequent chapters.

But I believed we could assist Sharon and Mark only if they became active collaborators in their own destiny, that is, if they knew what they needed to do and why they needed to do it. Sharon at one point acknowledged to me that she had many of the same needs as her son, yet she seemed reluctant to change. You might argue that she was too set in her ways. But I know some adults who have shown improvement in their weaknesses. I suspect it is more likely that Sharon was afraid she might try to organize herself and fail at it.

I am hopeful that *The Myth of Laziness* will help people like Sharon and Mark come to grips with their dire organizational needs before it's too late to mend a needlessly crippled career or life.

SOME FOLLOW-UP

I met Sharon's former husband, Mark's dad, a few times. He was a quiet guy, always well dressed and immaculate. He exuded efficiency. In his job as an accountant, he obviously needed to be organized and productive. Output failure wouldn't sit well on April 15. I couldn't help wondering if theirs was a match that was not quite made in heaven, a poor fit neurodevelopmentally. Who knows if that contributed to the failure of their marriage? It may well have been a factor.

Eventually I left Boston to move to North Carolina. About two months before my migration with the geese, Sharon came to see me and told me she was resigning. She said she needed to earn more money than academia was providing, and besides, she had come to believe that she wasn't cut out to succeed in research. She had gotten an offer to go into private psychology practice with a former classmate from graduate school. There was not much I could say. I wished her luck and told her we should keep in touch. She informed me that she had to start her new job the next week, giving us no time to recruit a replacement for her. A big mistake: you should never burn your bridges behind you. I've always believed strongly that how you leave a job is more important than how you start one. But then Sharon had never been able to carry things to a smooth completion.

Several of my colleagues in Boston had accused me of being much too tolerant of Sharon's "lazy, lackadaisical ways." I was under steady pressure to "do something about her" while she worked for me. But I harbored a strong belief in her and a sense that she wasn't at all lazy. In fact, she was one of the hardest working clinicians I have known. It's been more than fifteen years since I worked with Sharon, and since that time I have developed a clearer understanding of the kinds of organizational traps that snare otherwise competent and industrious people. I see these problems in kids all the time. I have become convinced that organizational problems such as those borne by Sharon and Mark are just as genuine and just as handicapping as disabilities in reading, writing, or math. But all too often disorganized individuals stand accused of first-degree laziness or indifferent carelessness. Well-entrenched patterns of disorganization can be tough to fix, but when the distress signals are detected, helpful measures can be taken.

About three years after moving to North Carolina, I received a Christmas card and annual newsletter from Sharon. She was enjoying private practice, although it was taking more time than she'd thought it would. Sharon's holiday card was postmarked January 16—yes, for some people, I guess, the more things change, the more they stay the same.

9
OUTPUT'S INPUTS

Canst thou bind the sweet influences of Pleiades,
or loose the bands of Orion?
—THE BOOK OF JOB

Johnson's first job was on the college clean up crew, picking up papers, rocks, and trash. Most of the students considered this unpleasant work, worthy of the minimum effort necessary to avoid being fired. But Johnson brought to it the same zeal he brought to everything else. He imagined himself in a race to determine who could clean up the most trash in the least amount of time . . . [and] his eagerness left its mark: when he applied for a better job, he received it at once, assistant to the janitor of the science building. At this post he again labored with extravagant enthusiasm, and again his efforts were rewarded: the next job he got was the one he had coveted all along—special assistant to the president's personal secretary.

—DORIS KEARNS GOODWIN,
LYNDON JOHNSON AND THE AMERICAN DREAM

Productive people abound—in every school, at every construction site, within every restaurant kitchen, and inside every scientific laboratory. How do they get that way? What energizes or motivates their high output? Somehow these achievers make wise use of their knowledge, skills, and ideas, and successfully blend them with their strategic wisdom, motivation, and energy to synthesize their mind's products. But we have seen what happens when a mind's assembly line breaks down and output failure sets in. That's when people may be unjustly accused of laziness.

OUTPUT FAILURE:
THE COMMON NEURODEVELOPMENTAL GAPS

In the preceding chapters, I have portrayed eight common forms of mind miswiring or misfiring that contribute to output failure. These patterns of dysfunction are depicted in Figure 9-1.

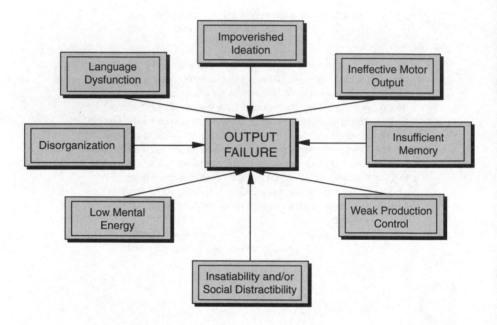

Figure 9-1.   Eight common neurodevelopmental breakdowns that may thwart productivity.

As we hold these concepts in our active working memories, let us seek answers to eight key questions about anyone with output failure:

  1. Could there be a motor breakdown?
  2. Could there be a memory shortfall?
  3. Could there be a verbal production problem?
  4. Could there be an impairment in the generation of ideas?
  5. Could there be poor regulation of mental energy and therefore low working capacity?
  6. Could there be a weakness in the regulation of output (production control)?

7. Could there be insatiability and/or social distractibility deterring output?

8. Could there be a deficit in one or more forms of organization?

And could there be a combination of several of the above phenomena?

I believe that one must answer these questions regarding any seemingly lazy child or adult. Although in my work I devote a great deal of time to the formal testing of children and adolescents with output failure, in many cases the reasons for their low productivity can be detected just by taking a good history and being aware of the eight neurodevelopmental trouble spots so readily observable in everyday life. Often, however, a teacher or supervisor or parent may be too close to the situation to see what's going on. They need to pause and ask themselves, "What am I seeing every day as I deal with this person?"

I recall one fourteen-year-old girl with output failure whose father was a psychiatrist and whose mother was a high school guidance counselor. They had always noticed that Donna was painfully slow and hesitant when she spoke about anything nonroutine or complex. They were in the habit (without thinking about it) of putting words in her mouth. But they never made the connection or related her obvious verbal hesitancy to the fact that she was unproductive in school. They didn't see that her verbal output was seriously obstructing her scholastic proficiency. We all need to be aware of these neurodevelopmental processes and become unbiased observers of their day-to-day operation.

It would be overly simplistic to assume that neurodevelopmental functions, such as language, motor function, and memory, make up our only output engines. These essential neurodevelopmental systems are perpetually interacting with a host of outside influences in daily life and in our immediate environment, as well as with our personal traits, feelings, and insights (or lack thereof) to determine the quality and amount of our output. A neurodevelopmental profile is constantly under the influence of both external and internal forces. Let's look at some key external forces.

EXTERNAL FACTORS INFLUENCING OUTPUT

Many outside factors affect the nature and quality of a mind's output. Most of these forces are beyond our control; they are environmental givens. What matters is how resistant we are to the negative influences and how susceptible we are to the positive ones.

The Influence of Affluence and Poverty

Poverty and productivity may not mix well. Children deprived of adequate living conditions and nutrition are at risk for learning difficulties of all sorts, especially output failure. Pressuring them to be productive in overcrowded, understaffed schools is like rubbing salt in their educational wounds. If they also bear the stresses of being from broken homes, living in violent neighborhoods, or receiving poor preventive medical care, the odds against constructive output mount steeply. Fortunately, some individuals resist these toxic elements and emerge from poverty to become productive performers. In many instances such resilient individuals have succeeded in coming up with a niche or a product line that works for them, often under the guided care of a caring adult.

While participating in the production of a set of videotapes on learning, I met a boy at a Harlem middle school whose family had immigrated from Barbados. This student had serious problems with written output: I think they were graphomotor breakdowns. However, he was a dazzling boy, a colorful and fluent speaker. His stunning rhetoric was helping him blaze a trail that would lead him out of the ghetto. At the age of thirteen Vincent was delivering many of the Sunday sermons at his local church. He was planning to be a preacher, a teacher, or both. Everyone who knew hardworking Vincent was sure he was going to make it. Being a great communicator during the teenage and young adult years is a common source of resilience for people reared in poverty. Many become preachers, politicians, entertainers, or leaders of worthy causes.

At the other extreme, affluence has its risks. This was all too transparent in the case of Scott Murray, who was supplied with whatever he wanted, never having to delay gratification to fulfill a whim. He was exposed to one exhilarating pleasure after another—from skiing in the Italian Alps to sailing in the Mediterranean to flying from continent to continent in his dad's Learjet. Childhood was an impossible act to follow! How do you come down from such juvenile ecstasies and settle your body at a desk to write a ten-page essay on humor in *The Tempest*? Despite his extensive scuba diving in the Caribbean, Scott failed to submit his sophomore marine-biology term paper on biodiversity in the coral reefs.

So it is that uncontrolled affluence may be as much a deterrent to output as abject poverty. Of course, we all know children from socio-economically advantaged homes who have successful role models and who learn how to work and produce. And you needn't be the child of a Fortune 500 multimillionaire to be overindulged. This phenomenon occurs and is just as destructive of output at all socioeconomic strata.

The Effects of Stress

A patient of mine, Matthew, put things succinctly when he lamented, "Almost every night while I'm trying to fall asleep, I can hear my parents arguing downstairs so much that I think they really hate each other. They fight over everything, and then I can't get to sleep. The next day in school I'm not much good for anything because I keep thinking they're gonna get a divorce, and it's hard to concentrate on getting work done when you're as worried as I am all the time." An eleven-year-old girl con-fessed to me that she had trouble working because she was so stressed out over other students teasing her. A third grader from an inner-city school confided in his teacher that he was always scared; all he could think about in school was that his mother was going to be arrested for drugs, and since he had no father, there would be no one to take care of him while she was in jail. Such weighty preoccupations often under-mine output.

Children differ in the degree to which they can withstand stress with-out its thwarting their productivity, and the same can be said of adults, who vary in their capacities to set aside their personal cares to get work done. Everyone endures stress, but those who do not cope well with it may have it spill over into their work. Of course, work-related stress in the right dosage can have a beneficial effect on productivity. It has been shown, for example, that students who feel a moderate degree of anxi-ety when they take a test are likely to do much better than those who are in a panic as well as those who are too complacent about the chal-lenge.

Examples That Are Set (Role Models)

In one way or another, we are all emulators. As they grow up, children and adolescents mimic role models, who will help them construct their own identities. Kids extract aspects of people they respect and try to incorporate those attributes into their own behavior. A child may be evolving into a composite of his best friend, his dad, his grandma, his favorite football player, and his fourth-grade teacher—to be merged somehow with his own inherent tendencies. Patterns of output are noticeably affected by the kinds of people kids identify with. Having high-output parents and siblings, for example, can energize productivity in a child. When revered or loved adults exhibit productivity shortcomings, their patterns of failure may be rubber-stamped onto a child or adolescent.

Schools That Produce Mind Workers

Some schools keep young minds in shape for high output. They challenge students not just with undertaking the intellectual exercise of building skills and knowledge but also with shouldering the workload. Having high expectations for student output enables a school to strengthen the mental working capacities of its students. So not only does a student learn to think and learn, he also learns how to transform thinking into products and to do so with efficiency and at a sufficiently high level of output. I know of some schools that give their students surprisingly little work to do, as if they've forgotten that building working capacity is an important aim of education. For the most part, this mission is accomplished through homework assignments. I confess to being a fan of homework, largely because it can bolster some of the most important components of high-quality output, such as the capacity to sustain mental effort, the ability to prepare for an important upcoming event (such as a test), the proficiency to organize materials and one's own thinking, the organizational insight to know how to manage time and meet deadlines, and the sense of producing independently outside the structure of a classroom. Those are important skills. We'll deal more with effective schools in chapter 11.

Family Life Shaping Working Life

It is my stubborn contention that schools are supposed to teach kids how to learn and parents are responsible for teaching them how to work. Mothers or fathers (or, preferably, both) need to take on the sometimes adversarial and perverse authoritarian role of taskmaster. This undertaking has been a very traditional ingredient of parenting but one that I think has been too often neglected in recent years. Nowadays many parents perceive themselves as entertainers and recreation coordinators, facilitating play rather than mind work!

The lack of an intellectual work life at home certainly can play a role in output failure. Some kids are naturally cognitively industrious, but most need to learn to work. And they require the right conditions in which to do so. The home environment ought to foster intellectual output, in part by providing fertile intellectual input. On a regular basis, parents should discuss with their kids news events, decisions in their own careers, moral issues, and other matters within the world of ideas.

One family I know quite well can serve as a real-life legend of home life providing the fertile setting for productive output. The Minh family—two parents, two sons, and one daughter—immigrated from Vietnam as boat people in the early 1980s and settled in Durham, North Carolina. No one in the family spoke English. Mrs. Minh had some skills as a seamstress. The Minhs had a very modest amount of money, so they borrowed a small sum from relatives in the area. With this money they rented a tiny space, where Mrs. Minh opened a tailoring shop, the only such establishment in the immediate area. The fledgling commercial enterprise soon prospered. Mr. Minh helped his wife with the business side of things and, despite his language limitations, manned the front of the store.

Meanwhile, the Minh children were enrolled in school. Every evening after dinner this close family congregated around the dinner table to work. Mr. Minh studied his English, Mrs. Minh did the same while hemming and finishing hand-sewn alterations, and the children did their school assignments and were encouraged to review what they had learned that day. The kids were also told to do more work than the teacher assigned because "that's how you get ahead in life." Everyone served as a consultant for everyone else; it was a highly collaborative educational atmosphere. Whenever the Minh kids had no assigned homework, they studied. This was not negotiable. And there was no seductive TV set competing for their attention. The Minhs all managed to learn English with rapidity. Mrs. Minh had the hardest time but compensated with her impressive fine motor dexterity and speed, which enabled her to support the family.

The three kids became superb and highly productive students. Both Minh boys were Moorhead scholars at the University of North Carolina, a highly prestigious honor. The older son recently entered medical school, while the daughter is a high school honor student taking ad-vanced-placement courses. A work ethic that values mental effort pays off. A set of consistent work routines has enabled this family to succeed. Mr. and Mrs. Minh also served as potent role models. You can't ask kids to do things you don't do yourself! Incidentally, the Minhs always have been a very close, jovial, and loving family. They enjoy eating out to-gether and share several recreational interests, but they are committed to productivity.

All parents want their children to feel happy. Unfortunately, some are so preoccupied by their self-imposed obligation to prevent juvenile re-sentment and foster contentment that they set up their homes as multi-media entertainment centers. The Minh children worked fastidiously. The satisfaction they derived from their own output sustained their happiness—not a bad way to feel good in the long run.

A work ethic can be a core family value. Many successful adults can testify to that realization when they fondly recall a mother or father who was a strong disciplinarian, a parent who forced them to do things they didn't feel like doing. In retrospect they feel deep gratitude.

I will never forget a fifth grader named Ian, a patient of mine from Newton, Massachusetts. I first met Ian when he was experiencing and causing frustration with his inadequate output, especially writing. His reports contained few developed ideas. Ian was a disastrous speller and a victim of serious graphomotor dysfunction as well. Poor kid: he wanted desperately to succeed but had tasted nothing but criticism and failure. Ian's dad, a graduate of Harvard College and Harvard Law School who had clerked for a United States Supreme Court justice, was a partner at one of New England's most prestigious law firms. Whenever he came to see me, Mr. Langston would always wear an immaculate three-piece Brooks Brothers suit with the same blue-and-gray club tie. He looked to be about six foot three and was as svelte as a cruise missile. While we would talk about his son's needs, Mr. Langston would scratch out copious notes on his yellow legal pad. I always wondered whether in the back of his mind he was preparing to sue me for malpractice! I was in awe of his obviously keen intellect and wholly intimidated by his stiff demeanor. Every single suggestion I made for Ian was written down and scrupulously implemented. Mr. Langston was a stickler for detail and an autocratic daddy; no one ever questioned his authority. I have to admit that he even shot barbed darts of fear into me whenever he en-tered my office.

Over time, Ian soared in school. He became productive and intellectually inquisitive. His problems with the use of his memory and his graphomotor function diminished significantly, and his attention improved noticeably without his ever having taken any medication. In seventh grade, a lanky six-foot-one Ian emerged as a star basketball player, which I think helped fortify his motivation and self-esteem during his stressful academic moments.

At the end of eighth grade, Ian was accepted into Roxbury Latin School, a highly respected, rigorous high school. He went on to Princeton, where he played varsity basketball. From there he entered medical school and is now a successful orthopedic surgeon specializing in sports medicine. When he was in college, Ian dropped by to see me one time. I couldn't help asking him what it was like to be brought up by his hard-nosed father, who put endless pressure on him to succeed. I'll never forget his answer. He said, "You know, Dr. Levine, my dad always did put heavy pressure on me, and he never let up, not for a moment. But I didn't resent it, no, not at all. Kenneth Langston was not the kind of father who could ever kiss or hug his son; he just wasn't the affectionate type. I think I always knew that, so every time he put pressure on me, I felt that that was his way of kissing me, his way of showing me how much he loved me."

When kids are not required or at least encouraged to fortify their mind's working capacity at home, they may come to regard school as the only place they have to use their minds (even if they don't especially want to) and home as an extension of the playground. This notion may make the school experience feel alien and boring. Education in such a vacuum becomes something you have to put up with rather than a positive and valued experience. Moreover, kids deprived of structured work experience at home may not acquire productive habits and the self-discipline needed for effective academic output. Good work habits make good work easy. Some students may feel overwhelmed when they sit down at a desk, in part because they have not steadily acquired efficient working habits.

A Work Culture and a Play Culture

We are always hearing that to be well rounded we must both work hard and play hard. But how is this balance maintained? What's the optimal proportion of fun and "irksome toil"? We know that many children are growing up within a culture that opts for immediate pleasure over long-term results and that many of childhood's current modes of stimulation may be at odds with constructive output. We have seen how productivity often demands mental energy, the delay of gratification, and the ability to organize one's effort. Electronic games, instant messaging, and pop music characterized by verbal and melodic redundancy (reiterating endlessly the same small bite-sized unsophisticated lyric and brief melodic theme) rather than gradual thematic development may be inconsistent, or even at loggerheads, with well-paced, guided, sustained output.

Prolonged television viewing may promote intellectual passivity, causing a mind to be out of shape when it comes to heavy-duty brainstorming and conjuring up its own products. Many contemporary forms of amusement demand little if any organizational proficiency, language fluency, memory access, or original idea generation. In other words, a cavernous gulf exists between the ingredients of effective output and the nature of the cultural diversions that tantalize and infatuate children and adolescents. Some can't seem to handle this disparity. I've encountered many children with output failure who are so addicted to their computer games, to TV, or to other inactive forms of pleasure and leisure that slow-paced schoolwork feels intrusive and out of step with the rhythms of their lifestyles. When a teenager's output failure is combined with an acquired passion for these immediately gratifying forms of stimulation, it can be especially hard to resurrect a capacity for mind work.

I am not suggesting that we ban all forms of passive recreational activities. However, parents and schools should take responsibility for maintaining a good balance, for not allowing children to become obsessed with all the highly stimulating electronic objects and fast-paced intellectual dead ends that engulf them. It's definitely possible to work hard and play hard. Many children and adults have succeeded in doing so.

Competition That Fuels or Douses Output

Competition can significantly foster or deter productivity. Many students and adults need to compete to generate good output. Competition becomes their prime motivator and energizer. There are, of course, countless examples of the role of competition in fueling productivity. Businesses compete with one another, and the employees within those companies, in turn, compete with one another for recognition, promotion, and bonuses. But some students and many adults shut down their assembly lines because they can't handle the competitive pressure. They may harbor an intense distaste for competition. Or else they feel they cannot compete with the accomplishments of a productive parent, sibling, classmate, or coworker. At worst, in abandoning the pursuit, they may gravitate toward self-destructive pathways, such as drugs, alcohol, or other addictions, to compensate for their lack of productivity.

I have cared for some older adolescents who have shaved the hair off their heads, joined a cult, or rationalized their way into some other quest for meaning in life. One girl, Fran, had run away from home at least three times by her fourteenth birthday. She had navel and nasal rings, dyed hair, and a chain-smoking habit, all to repudiate adult mores. She had also joined a rather bizarre group of dissident aging teens, virtually none of whom, I suspect, had earned a reputation for high academic output. This pathetic girl had battled significant output problems (trouble with production control and memory, as it turned out) well before I met her, at age fifteen. On her first visit, Fran openly confessed, "I just don't feel like trying to compete with my brother, my parents, and every f——ing kid in the neighborhood. They're all so 'wonderful.' I have no desire to do everything right, at least the kind of right they're thinking about. I'm after more meaning in my life. Besides, there's no way I could make it in their world." Fran was obviously afraid to compete, paralyzed by the prospect of losing.

Sporting a Track Record

A person's own record of accomplishment (or lack thereof) strongly influences his current and future output. Kids who have a sustained history of praised output are most likely to keep on producing. Those who come to feel they can't do anything right may stop doing anything at all. Productivity thrives on success. A mind keeps score of wins and losses. Individuals with chronic success deprivation feel like losers, and out of a sense of hopelessness they simply shut down their minds. Success and failure occur in spirals. Failure may lead to further failure, while success energizes the system for more success.

Opportunity, Timing, and Just Plain Luck

It's a bit unsettling to ponder, but praiseworthy output depends partly on a hefty dose of luck, timing, and opportunity. What would have happened if the first cellist in the Vienna Philharmonic Orchestra had never been exposed to the cello? What if an award-winning photographer for the Associated Press had never been given a camera by his aunt? What if a noted physician had never been given a tour of her local hospital at age fourteen by a surgeon who was a family friend? What if a leading electronics pioneer had not roomed in college with a budding entrepreneur eager to start a new company? Yes, being in the right place at the right time makes a difference. But success requires more than that.

Once opportunities occur, they are most likely to lead to productive output in primed individuals who have learned how to work and who possess insight into their own most effective modes of output. Parents should be on a constant lookout for sparks of all different kinds of talent in their kids and then should create opportunities for that which ignites those sparks.

The principal external factors are depicted in Figure 9-2.

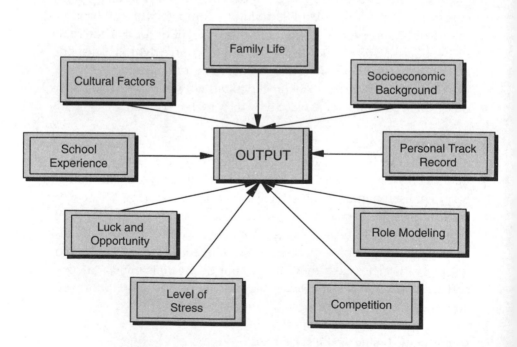

Figure 9-2.   Nine external influences on output, as discussed in this chapter.

INTERNAL FACTORS INFLUENCING OUTPUT

I have discussed some external factors that affect a person's neurodevelopmental profile to either encourage or discourage output. The culture, the school, the family, stress levels, one's own cumulative track record, socioeconomic forces, luck, competition, and positive or negative role models all seem to converge on a child's production lines. Clusters of influential productivity promoters are also lodged within a person's mind. Let's examine some of these persistent internal forces.

Motivation, Drive, and Ambition

A twenty-year-old college student who had been eking out low C's through the first two years of his undergraduate career was sent by his parents in Ohio to pay me a visit in Chapel Hill. Jonathan came on his own and declared that he didn't know what all the fuss was about. After all, he wasn't failing anything. As we talked for a while, the conversation went something like this:

> LEVINE: So, you're pretty satisfied with how you're performing academically?
>
> JONATHAN: Yeah. I guess.
>
> LEVINE: Your parents wrote to me and said they thought you were doing the bare minimum, just scraping by in school.
>
> JONATHAN (*smiling*): They're right on. I'm not what they call a hard worker.
>
> LEVINE: Why not?
>
> JONATHAN: I just don't care. I just want to get by.
>
> LEVINE: Jonathan, are you ambitious? [That's a question I like to ask a lot of high school and college kids.]
>
> JONATHAN: No, not at all. No. I just want to be happy. I have no desire to be rich or famous. And, to be honest with you, Dr. Levine, I don't feel like working very hard—now or in the future. What's wrong with that?
>
> LEVINE: Nothing, I guess. Some folks aim real high, and others don't. It looks as if you've decided to settle for not very good grades and maybe not an excellent job later on. That's okay. It's okay as long as you didn't arrive at this decision because you thought you wouldn't be able to excel even if you wanted to.

Jonathan took a look at his watch, making it clear that he wanted to leave. But we went on and tested Jonathan. While he did not particularly shine in any neurodevelopmental function or learning skill, we uncovered no severe dysfunctions. However, he did exhibit some impairment of his expressive language; it was quite hard for Jonathan to express complex thoughts orally and even more so on paper. He seemed to represent a case of low aspiration combining with a mild neurodevelopmental dysfunction to cause low output, but I felt that his language dysfunction was surmountable. I also had the sense that Jonathan was rapidly becoming what I call a conservative non–risk taker. He was so disappointed in himself that he'd unconsciously made the decision to pull out of the game of trying to achieve. He was not about to take any risks with performance. By setting low standards for himself, he felt he couldn't fail; he couldn't let himself down. He was playing safe with his ego.

When we discussed his policy of low ambition, I made it clear that this was his decision to make, but I did urge him to think about whether he might look back in ten years and be intensely angry at himself for following a pathway that led to a dead end. He might seriously regret the road not taken. Jonathan was unresponsive, but sometimes a message gets across, even if the recipient does not acknowledge it!

Although many outside factors can fuel ambition, I regularly encounter students like Jonathan who are inveterate "I'll get by" types. They are often conspicuously laid-back and seem almost to have a fear of success. You want to light a fire under them, but they don't appear to be combustible! They want to be left alone by people like me, and they have a right to be. All I ever do with them is discuss their strengths and help them see realistic ambitious possibilities for themselves just in case they ever decide to redirect their aims.

Then there are the individuals who symbolize the opposite pole, the hard-driving or driven juvenile workaholics, who display ultrahigh output and determination to excel. In a few cases, their ambition is far too transparent and emits socially obnoxious fumes. Most often it can be carried off with acceptable verve. I have watched a person's "ambition gene" emerge and grow over time. When I see such children in their preschool and elementary years, they also harbor a burning desire to please and impress others, to show off their wares—at the swimming pool, in art class, on the playing fields, wherever demonstrable output opportunities present themselves. That desire to please is satisfied when their products garner abundant praise, especially from the adult world. Somehow recognition for one's output becomes addictive; the more you get, the more you want. So these students go on to acquire a taste for work. And they are likely to keep seeing exciting possibilities for themselves in life as they mount that recognition ladder. For them, hard work promises a payoff, and they cling to an inner sense that output will keep on reaping satisfying rewards.

Not all output is driven by the quest for accolades and dividends. Many kids and grown-ups are fortunate enough to be what the sociologist David Riesman called "inner-directed." That is, more than anything else, they seek recognition for their actions and products from themselves. They are their own appreciative audience. I wish I knew how to inoculate students with that internal force, but I don't. Some have it and some don't. In any case, its presence or absence is a critical variable in determining output.

Optimism

One's level of optimism affects one's motivation to produce. To feel like putting in effort, it helps if you harbor an inner sense that you are likely to succeed at what you are undertaking. I recently saw a little boy with unacceptably low output in school and I was struck that, while I was testing this child, almost every time I gave him a task to perform, Isaac would say, "No way, I'll never do that" or "That's too hard." Then I would encourage him to go for it anyway, and he would almost always succeed.

His mother described seven-year-old Isaac as "an incurable pessimist." As she put it, "He gives up so easily; he's defeated before he even starts, and lots of times, I can't even get him to try something because he's so convinced he's going to mess up." If that self-defeating feeling is allowed to persist, kids like Isaac can lose all motivation. Fortunately, his mother and his teacher joined forces to teach Isaac the difference between optimism and pessimism and to give him positive feedback whenever he overcame his pessimism and put forth effort. Whenever Isaac succeeded in a challenge, which was most of the time, they would say, "See, you could have been optimistic." I'm always amazed by how much we can accomplish when we simply teach children and adults the words for what they need to be working on and then provide practice in applying those words.

Initiative

A highly respected professor (now emeritus) at the University of North Carolina was like a sorcerer when it came to garnering generous grants to conduct his research. I once asked him how he maintained his reputation with the foundations and agencies that kept on funding him so richly. He told me that every time he undertook a project he made sure that he did more than he'd promised to do in his original proposal (and I suspect he saw to it that his benefactors noticed). That's initiative, the willingness to deliver more than what's expected of you. I've seen students and adults who possess an innate capacity for initiative. Needless to say, they are most unlikely to have output failure!

Bill Charette is one of the most successful and talented TV cameramen in this country. I worked with Bill on a video library called *Developing Minds* that our institute All Kinds of Minds produced with WGBH, the public television station in Boston. During our travels, Bill recounted the early phases of his career. He grew up in Leominster, Massachusetts, then left school early to hold various retail jobs around town. But Bill had a raging desire to be a television cameraman and a specific interest in working in public television. He had taken courses in various aspects of theater. Camera work, his true interest, was a hard field to break into. There were no job opportunities for cameramen anywhere in the greater Boston area, so he remained in his job at a local shoe store. But one day a buddy of his came by and showed him a classified advertisement from *The Boston Globe*. WGBH was looking for someone to work in its mailroom. Bill took the job and spent the next six months being the best mailroom person ever. He worked countless extra hours without compensation, helped reorganize the mailroom, went out of his way for anybody who needed anything from him. Then the station had an opening for a cameraman. Everyone there already liked and respected Bill. He got the job, and his career momentum never abated. He became a true superstar at filming documentaries. He would typically show up at a site at 5:00 A.M. to prepare meticulously for a 10:00 A.M. shooting. His talent was liberally infused with initiative—an unbeatable output formula.

Here's the other side of the initiative picture. Recently, at about 6:40 A.M., I stopped at a supermarket that remains open twenty-four hours a day. I pulled up to the front of the store and went to the vending machine to buy a copy of the Raleigh *News & Observer.* As I was returning to my car, I noticed two boys roughly eighteen or nineteen years old passively perched on a four-foot brick wall in front of the store and staring mindlessly into outer space. With typical southern amiability, one of them said hi to me, and I reflexively asked, "What's up, you guys?" One of them answered, "Our shift doesn't start till seven." I was a bit startled. So I impulsively inquired, "Well, why don't you go in and start working now? That would really snow your boss." Both boys glared at me in disbelief. My kernel of advice had made no sense at all to them. Apparently they didn't grasp the concept of initiative. Somebody needs to tell them what that word means and how it can profoundly affect their destinies.

Flexibility and Adaptability

Have you known folks who get so set in their ways that they can't adapt to changing demands in the workplace? They have trouble adjusting to a new accounting system or a recently hired supervisor with a management style that differs markedly from her predecessor's. Similarly, some students may endure undue anguish in adjusting to the demands and teaching methods of different teachers. Their output dwindles when adaptability and flexibility are called for.

A similar phenomenon is seen in children who may be described by their parents or teachers as exceedingly rigid. I remember one stymied math teacher who spoke about a girl in her class: "Kendra is so completely rigid. She sets out to do a math problem and starts to get a glimmer that she is making use of the wrong method, but then she doesn't appear able or inclined to back up and consider other approaches. Once she commits to a way of doing something, that's it. It's as if she has no reverse gear, no way to back up and then return to a problem along a new path." The teacher told me that Kendra's mother reported the same pattern of rigidity in her everyday life; she seemed to have an inability to change her mind or her way of doing something. I've met a number of children like this. To address the problem, I try to get an adult to help a child articulate several different approaches prior to doing something (such as a math problem), then opt for what seems to be the best one. If and when that doesn't work, I suggest that the adult review the other options with the child. I also like to teach kids the term "backup strategies," the things you use when your first approach to something isn't working. Having backup strategies is a good way to improve a kid's flexibility.

Resiliency

Some people aren't able to bounce back after setbacks or to overcome the effects of living conditions that promote output failure. On the other hand, some individuals demonstrate extraordinary resiliency— that is, "You can't keep a good person down."

In recent years there has been a great deal of research interest in the notion of resilience. How is it that some people beat all the odds and succeed in life despite enduring more than their share of stress and deprivation? Why is it that so many of the children I encounter who have very serious school problems eventually turn out to be highly productive adults? It's because they are resilient. Very often we find that they are the ones who have had highly supportive adults in their lives, individuals who refused to give up on them, people who encouraged them and advocated for them—true mentors and coaches who may have been within or outside of their immediate family. These are also children who find out how to make good use of their strengths and how to discover a niche in which they can succeed. It is also likely that many such individuals possess some mysterious inborn resiliency.

Several years ago, I evaluated an eleven-year-old boy who was having a terrible time in fifth grade. He was behaving in an aggressive, disruptive manner in the classroom and receiving failing grades. His output was about as low as could be. When he was four, Tony had been adopted from an unbelievably squalid Romanian orphanage—abysmal hygiene, neglect, and possible abuse were in evidence. No wonder Tony was having such a hard time seven years later in school. But then his parents mentioned that they'd also adopted Tony's brother, eighteen months older, from the same orphanage. Joseph was getting all A's in sixth grade and was a perfectly well-behaved kid. How is it that these two boys, sharing the same early experience, reared by the same parents in the same household, attending the same schools, had absolutely opposite outcomes? In some mysterious way, Joseph possessed more potential for resiliency than did Tony.

Control over Social Distractibility and Output-Stifling Peer Pressure

I am frequently reminded of some potential social barriers to output. A teacher recently e-mailed me, "Beth accomplishes almost nothing in class, and I think that's because she can't stop focusing on everybody around her. She is so totally preoccupied, hopelessly obsessed with what everyone else is doing and thinking that it's as if she can't do or think about anything herself! She just can't seem to filter out all those heavy social vibes that go back and forth across a middle school classroom." A distraught mom whose daughter had serious output failure recently commented, "She rushes through her homework, does a basically shoddy job of it all, and just can't wait to get on-line and plug her brain into all that mindless gossipy instant messaging with her friends. She lives for Amy, Sue, and Cindy; nothing else seems to matter much to her at this point." Another stressed-out parent articulated, "I wish I could get Sam to stop arranging his social life long enough to think about his schoolwork. Studying for tests, writing reports, and completing geometry assignments play second fiddle to what he's going to wear to school tomorrow." We witnessed this phenomenon in our stories about Ginny and Scott.

These quotes capture the extent to which some students focus so intently on interpersonal matters that little else reverberates within their minds. Of course, such excessive social distractibility isn't confined to children. Social distractability can obliterate output in adults, but sometimes the grown-up signs and symptoms are more subtle or insidious. I have had employees who seemed so consumed with their relationships with coworkers (some of whom they liked and respected and others of whom they loathed) that their social interactional issues became the overwhelming preoccupation within their chosen occupation.

I have encountered directly and heard about cases where output is compromised because such individuals are too distracted by their own need to build some relationships and perhaps undermine others. Obviously interactions in the workplace are of great importance, but not when they occupy such an elevated priority that they obscure the need to do a job efficiently. I was discussing this matter recently with the head of a large corporation. She identified this phenomenon as a major impediment to productivity. As she put it, "I have executives working for me who seem to exhaust themselves with their backroom gossip, their petty efforts to put down or victimize certain coworkers, their need to conspire against targeted victims, and their adolescent-like yearning to become part of a little gang of cool guys and dolls within the company. In the meantime, these social predators could be accomplishing so much more if they would only concentrate on their own creativity and productivity."

Some students seriously curtail their academic output because they don't want to be perceived as "grinds," "nerds," or "geeks," labels that could stand in the way of acceptance by their peers. They may feel constrained to work secretly or not at all when peer pressures are aimed in nonacademic directions. Children are endowed with different degrees of immunity from these anti-output social influences.

So it is that during school and within a career the ability to filter out excess social "noise" and temptation can facilitate output. I am not suggesting that anyone ought to be oblivious to relationships. Social concerns, however, should not displace the actual content and mission of a job, and it's surprising how often they do. Some kids with output failure suffer from what I call peer addiction. They are intoxicated with and totally dependent upon others of their age group. That addiction becomes their central focus in life, and everything else feels to them like a distraction. Some folks need to have their social filters cleaned.

Parlaying Strengths Rather than Weaknesses

Tenth grader Marcus put forth dangerously low levels of academic output. He was erratic about submitting homework, and what he handed in seldom reflected much sustained effort. His output was skimpy at best. But the boy was a superb artist, a talent that had gone largely unrecognized until a drama teacher at his high school cornered him in the lunchroom and asked him to chair the scenery team for the spring play. Marcus rose to the occasion and thrived in doing so. He designed and executed wildly surrealistic sets that earned rave reviews in the notoriously cynical school newspaper. Upon hearing about his triumph, Marcus's English teacher told him he could write shorter reports for class if he would illustrate them liberally. He did so and started to write some great works that were anything but skimpy. He ended the term with an unprecedented A in English. It's truly extraordinary how an output dike opens up when someone starts using his hidden assets.

Then there was Molly, whose teachers observed that she was a hands-on type of achiever. Because of her expressive-language dysfunction, this sixth grader's oral presentations in class were mostly incoherent. So her social studies teacher told her to construct out of cardboard a typical eighteenth-century American fort and demonstrate it in front of the class. This project earned Molly her first A in that subject. She was allowed to use her strengths in hands-on, artistic assets to facilitate her output, and it worked. Her oral presentation was excellent as she described in words what she had accomplished manually.

In the adult business world it is less likely that your assets will be discovered and brought out by another caring adult, so it is up to you to take the initiative. The onus is on each of us to conduct our own internal treasure hunts, seeking our assets and making sure we are putting them to work along the career track we have selected. I believe that many unhappy people are living through an agonizing mismatching of their personal strengths and the demands of their job. It is possible to hold a position that demands capabilities you don't have. Think about the possible effects on output when a person's passionate interests clash with their inabilities: a surgeon with weak spatial functions, a teacher with expressive-language deficiencies, an auditor with attentional dysfunction. In all such cases, weaknesses rather than strengths are being tapped, and calamitous output failure may result.

Being in the Mood to Work

A perceptive college student once informed me, "I don't have time to work because I'm too busy worrying about my work." Individuals who are chronic worriers may find that their output suffers as a result. In particular, a high level of chronic anxiety may drain all mental energy, making it hard for them to concentrate on output.

Low self-esteem is a common accompaniment of anxiety. Students who have sustained repeated academic failure and endured chronic criticism come to feel terrible about themselves and may entirely give up when it comes to productivity. They may lose all output incentive because they are deeply afraid of encountering more failure and negative feedback. They have lost the mood to work.

It is not unusual for a teenager to become depressed for whatever reason and then show a drastic reduction in output. He may stop studying, fail to turn in homework, and seem to be drained of all motivation. When the depression is treated successfully through appropriate counseling and, possibly, medication, there is often an upsurge in productivity. Sometimes it is difficult to determine whether a person is depressed because of his low output or whether his output is low because he is depressed—or both! In either case, a careful diagnostic evaluation is called for.

Having Education and Career Insights

Metacognition is a term often used nowadays to characterize our ability to think about thinking, to reflect on how we are using our minds. I am convinced that there is something called *expectations metacognition,* a level of insight that some possess and others lack. This form of wisdom allows a person to ferret out what is expected of him on the job or in school. Such an individual takes accurate readings of what it will take to succeed or, even better, excel when it comes to any given job. Ruby, a highly successful eighth grader, knows that Miss Crosby likes students who write highly creative and imaginative social studies reports. She also is aware that Mr. Stone in biology wants you to stick to the hard, cold facts; faithful regurgitation from the textbook is the way to get an honor grade from him. Evelyn has a strong sense of what it will take for her to get into college when she applies three years from now. She is preparing by getting interesting summer jobs, working her way toward being editor in chief of the high school newspaper, and practicing taking multiple-choice tests (currently a serious liability for her). These are kids who are trying to know what it takes so they'll have what it takes! They are astute diagnosticians of expectations. They will then craft their output so that it goes a long way toward meeting these perceived, yet often hidden requirements. If they are really wise, they will find ways of satisfying these requirements while at the same time pursuing a course that fits with their own interests and abilities. They are not merely playing a political game, but they do know how to interpret the unspoken ground rules for school achievement.

Much the same game is played throughout an adult's career. I got off to a woefully slow start as a faculty member in pediatrics at Harvard because during my tender mid-twenties I didn't fully grasp the fact that to please and impress my faculty elders I needed to obtain grants and write articles for peer-reviewed journals. Instead I committed the potentially fatal and unpardonable sin of taking care of lots of patients. I was expected to demonstrate what is called "independence," namely, the ability to generate original ideas and find the money to study them. I also discovered that in a letter of recommendation from Harvard Medical School, the very worst euphemistic put-down was to be described to a potential employer as "solid." So in the likely event that I ever would need such a letter, my track record had to be more than merely solid! Fortunately, before it was too late, I saw the glittering academic floodlight and was able to grind out those papers and become an immodest recipient of outside funding. At last, I had read the expectations accurately. I had become more than solid.

I'm astounded at how many people don't, won't, or perhaps can't seem to undertake a thoughtful analysis of what their bosses, their customers, and their unwritten career "guidelines" mandate in the way of output expectations. They need to be made aware of the need to do so in a very conscious, thoughtful manner. Otherwise their productivity may be chronically inadequate, miscalculated, and misdirected.

The principal internal factors that we've just discussed are captured in Figure 9-3.

THE HIGH STAKES

Our society cannot afford to neglect or remain unaware of output failure. We are paying an exorbitant price for the care of affected individuals as we subsidize their antidepressant medications, chronic unemployment, drug rehabilitation programs, and sometimes even incarceration. That doesn't make sense. Instead let's try to fix the underlying problem. I believe it's never too late.

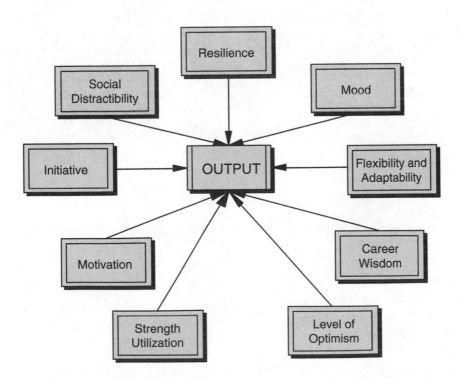

Figure 9-3.   The internal factors that either foster or deter output in children and adults.

In the next two chapters I will discuss the many ways we can cultivate productivity, examining first some methods for helping with writing, childhood's most conspicuous reflector of output, and then by
taking a broader look at output management at home, in school, and
within the adult workplace.

10

THE RIGHTING OF WRITING

No one can know how glad I am to find
On any sheet the least display of mind.
—ROBERT FROST, "A CONSIDERABLE SPECK"

True ease in writing comes from art, not chance,
As those move easiest who have learned to dance.
'Tis not enough no harshness gives offense;
The sound must seem an echo to the sense.
—ALEXANDER POPE, "AN ESSAY ON CRITICISM" (1711)

Clint Walker returned somberly from school one day, his cheeks striated with tearstains. Clint's teacher had the kids in his class correct each other's short stories, an onerous invasion of privacy, in my opinion. As luck would have it, the boy who got to stand in judgment of Clint's work was a very popular outspoken guy and not the kindest soul. When he scanned Clint's attempt at writing, Craig blurted out, as if on the P.A. system, "Oh my God, look at this gross mess. This is retard writing: Clint, are you some kind of retard?" He then exhibited Clint's heavily misspelled and messy production to the kids around him, who willingly joined in on the boisterous denunciation of the panic-stricken youth. The valiant cowboy was deeply wounded and could think of no way to react—so he just stared out the window as if in a trance. When you commit an error in reading, your miscue evaporates into the atmosphere, but when you mess up in writing, you leave behind a permanent document of your inadequacy. That hurts. And it hurt this wonderful little boy, Clint, profoundly—on numerous occasions.

Russell Strinberg took a hammering blow one day when each child was told to write a paragraph summarizing a story the teacher had read aloud. Then some of them were called on to read their summaries so everyone could hear them. When Russell was chosen, he stood up and faltered repeatedly. Poor kid; ordinarily a very strong reader, Russell was unable to decrypt his own handwriting. He felt "useless," he later told me.

When she was in eighth grade, Roberta Chan submitted a science paper on soil erosion. She had worked hard gathering information for her report and she'd meticulously arranged all the information she had compiled. Her teacher accused her of plagiarizing the content from a book or the Internet. She was crushed and humiliated by this accusation, but it was close to accurate. She didn't think there was anything wrong with reproducing text from a book. Besides, it was so hard for her to formulate her own thoughts that copying felt like her only option.

Throughout childhood and adolescence, getting thoughts down on paper easily qualifies as an emotionally supercharged educational requirement. For this reason and others I shall describe, let's look closely at the neurodevelopmental mechanisms that allow written output to take place smoothly and to result in high-quality products. I will also unravel some of the vexing problems with written output and offer some solutions. This chapter has been written mainly with students in mind, but some similar patterns of writing failure afflict many adults, so the approaches described can be modified to apply to any age group. Of course, most grown-ups with writing failure are resourceful enough to steer themselves into jobs that call for little or no need to record ideas on paper. Children can't exercise this convenient face-saving option!

The stories I told earlier in this book allowed me to explore each of the principal ingredients of writing by observing the results when one or more of them are in short supply. Written output is a blend of the following (in no particular order):

• Letting your fingers do the walking (graphomotor function): all the highly complicated motor movements of the fingers during letter formation or keyboarding

• Translating your ideas into a word and sentence code (language production): verbal communication that is generally much more formal and demanding than everyday speech

• Remembering what you need to remember (precise, rapid, and synchronized access to memory): the instantaneous and simultaneous recall of (among other things) spelling, punctuation, capitalization, grammar rules, facts, terminology, and the assignment or topic—plus the ability to hold together ideas and facts in active working memory while writing

• Thinking on paper (rich ideation): the manufacture and use of original thoughts, personal interpretations, problem solutions, insights, concepts, and/or defended opinions

• Paying close attention to the task (focused attention and mental effort): the durable and strong concentration and mental energy needed to accomplish written work

• Applying good judgment (quality assurance): the use of the mind's production controls to plan, pace, make good choices, monitor, and modify the quality of written output

• Curbing your appetites and your social distractibility (resistance to pleasurable diversions): so that insatiability doesn't interfere with productivity

• Getting your act together (organization): the ability to organize and integrate ideas, prioritize and manage the requisite time and materials

WHEN SOMEONE CAN'T WRITE QUITE RIGHT

Cutting accusations of laziness echo throughout the life of a student who fails to write or who imposes on himself a writing embargo. When output failure extends to writing, the resulting pains are felt deeply and widely. The toxic effects may become worse than the writing problem itself. Some seemingly lazy victims who simply hate to write have acquired writing phobias or chronic "writer's block," a paralyzing complication during the school years. Others can write but find that the process causes exhausting mind strain; while they work they feel as if they've torn a brain ligament! For them, writing is downright painful. And for most of them, writing consumes way more than its share of time and drains more mental effort than they feel capable of generating. The writing process simply wears them out—hence, the tide of accusations of laziness. Still others generate written products and are chastised because their writing is devoid of meaningful age-appropriate ideas, far too brief, immature in language use, barely legible, or haplessly disorganized.

There are as many explanations for failed writing as there are reasons for triumphant writing. Each ingredient of written output can fall short and be a cause of writing failure and pseudolaziness. Let's review the impacts of specific missing ingredients:

GRAPHOMOTOR BREAKDOWNS

As we saw in the case of Russell Strinberg (chapter 2), some student writing is sabotaged by one or more forms of graphomotor dysfunction, often very subtle movement glitches that prevent a person's fingers from capturing his stream of ideas and language. For some as yet inexplicable reason, graphomotor impairments are far more prevalent in boys than in girls.

Any one (or more) of the four most common types of graphomotor dysfunction can stack the odds against even the most motivated writer.

Often people with fingers that are not properly wired for writing

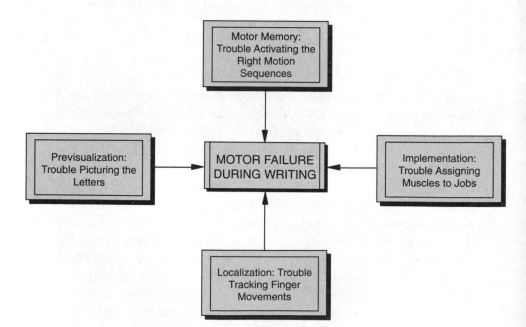

Figure 10-1.   Four of the common mechanisms that cause individuals to have problems with the motor aspects of writing.

have idiosyncratic pencil grasps that aggravate their problems. A variety of contorted grips exists among inefficient writers.

Many students maintain a fistlike pencil grip. If you watch closely, you'll see that they're actually forming letters with their wrists rather than the ends of their fingers. These kids may fail to receive useful feedback from the tips of their fingers while writing. *Finger agnosia* is the technical term for this annoying dysfunction that causes writers to have no idea where the pencil is within a letter, which, of course, makes it hard to signal where it should go next! You'll often notice very young children sitting with their chins squarely down on a desktop watching as they track the pencil point's movement. They are substituting visual feedback for the information that is supposed to be coming from nerves stationed at the ends of their fingers. But visual feedback is way too slow, and it costs too much of your precious attention (which ought to be conserved for spelling, language, and developing impressive ideas). So because their fingers don't report back to the brain regarding their moment-to-moment positions and because their eyes are not great pinch hitters in this game, affected students simply stop employing their fingers for writing. The student's finger joints are literally locked out of the act of writing as she forms a fist or clasps a thumb over her index and middle fingers during letter formation. Then only the wrist muscles can participate in graphomotor work. But these muscles were never designed for extensive writing, so the afflicted student develops a chronic writer's cramp and goes on to write as little as she possibly can get away with (or even less than that). The kid may even earn the distinction of writing the shortest and tersest book reports in her school's entire seventh grade.

Other students have a very hard time assigning specific muscles in their fingers to specific responsibilities during letter formation. You may recall that this was a problem for Russell. This is known as a graphomotor implementation problem. Their indecisive brains just can't decide which finger muscles should do what. Some muscles have to collaborate on vertical movements, others work to achieve rotary motion, others conduct horizontal excursions, and still others stabilize the pencil so it doesn't plummet to the floor in the middle of a thought. Graphomotor chaos ensues when these specific assignments are confused. When they are very young, kids with this problem have a feeble hold on a pencil; it looks as if their unstable hands are made out of latex.

It's as if all of their muscles are tackling the more romantic job of letter formation, and none has volunteered for stabilization duty! Students like this may feel totally inept as they keep dropping the writing implement in the middle of a word. Ultimately some try to compensate and in so doing acquire the opposite condition, a tight and pressured grip, often holding the pencil with great force down near the point and perpendicular to the page. Written work becomes a pain for them (in more ways than one). They often report feeling that the connections between their brain and their fingers are too loose; it is as if they tighten their fingers around a pencil shaft to make up for their poorly connected brain-to-finger circuits. As a boy once confessed to me, "You know how sometimes it will say on your computer screen, 'The computer is not connected to the printer'? That's exactly what happens whenever I try to write. A sign pops up in my mind saying, 'Your brain is not connected to your printer!' "

We need to rescue the many sufferers whose graphomotor engines malfunction. If their problems are severe, they may benefit from the services of an occupational therapist, and all of them require intensive writing practice—whether they like it or not. Often it is important to re-train their pencil grasps so that they adapt to the maximally efficient normal tripod grasp—one in which the pencil is held about three-quarters of an inch from the point and at about a forty-five-degree angle to the page, with the thumb and the middle finger handling most of the movement and the forefinger going along for the ride (but regulating pencil pressure).

That leaves two other common forms of graphomotor dysfunction: problems with visualization and difficulty with motor memory. Kids with reduced visualization have trouble picturing the letters just as they are about to form them. The image of the letter seems to flicker on and off their preview screens—so their messy writing is blemished with crossed-out letters and words, while they may make the same letter three different ways in one paragraph. They may make frequent letter reversals (such as *b* for *d*). Many of them also have a problem picturing whole words, which can lead to some spelling delays as well as illegible letter formations. Some experience difficulty copying from the board because they find it hard to transform the visual symbols into their personal blueprints for the letters.

Those students who experience trouble recalling the motor sequences (the "kinetic melodies" for the letters), on the other hand, usually can spell with accuracy but find letter formation slow and taxing. This was Russell's second obstacle. So the flow of his ideas and language greatly outpaced his finger movements. He and others like him prefer printing to cursive writing, but even their printing may be only marginally legible.

The answer in both of these low-output scenarios, trouble with visualization and undependable graphomotor memory, is fairly straightforward. Before it's too late and writing phobias set in, these kids need consistent heavy-duty drill on letter formation. Each night at bedtime, they should engage in timed trials of letter execution. Their progress can be documented and rewarded generously as they are scored for legibility as well as speed. They may also benefit from practice talking through the movements required for each letter (e.g., "A c is like a circle with a part missing"). Incidentally, many veteran teachers insist that they didn't encounter as many kids with letter-formation and legibility problems in the old days, when far more concerted effort was directed toward the teaching of penmanship in the earliest grades. Apparently that curriculum component has been neglected in recent years—with negative consequences for some students. Should we resurrect the ancient Palmer method? Or should we just start keyboarding early?

WHEN WEAK SPOKEN LANGUAGE LEADS TO WEAK WRITTEN LANGUAGE

If you want to write well, it definitely helps to talk well. Solid oral language ability is essential to lucid writing. Kids who have trouble transforming complex thoughts into words and sentences when they speak are apt to falter when it comes to communicating ideas on paper.

Darnell Mason was a case in point, revealing many of the signs and symptoms we encounter in students whose written language is seriously eroded as a result of their oral language shortcomings. Like him, they need help becoming more fluent and sophisticated speakers. And they ought to get that help both at home and in school.

All students gain from becoming effective speakers. Up and down the grade levels, classrooms should emphasize oral language development. Students should make regular oral presentations and get opportunities to teach and explain things to younger students. They should talk through how they solved a math problem rather than merely coming up with the answer. When called on in class, they should be encouraged to put forth well-elaborated responses rather than using terse utterances like "stuff" and "things" or speaking in incomplete sentences and vague phrases. Kids could also benefit from some formal course work in public speaking. At home, all children should be encouraged to elaborate, to talk in full sentences, to summarize daily experiences, describe TV shows they've watched, form and express opinions about issues, and talk about books that they've read. It is especially important for children to keep elaborating verbally on topics that interest them, their affinities. They should come to see that brushing up their verbal ability is really crucial and that language is like a muscle—it has to be used strenuously to become strong.

THE SPELL CAST BY SPELLING

Who cares whether the manager of a video store, the maître d' at a posh restaurant, or the first tuba in the Vienna Philharmonic is an accurate speller? In most adult occupations skill in spelling doesn't do much to propel careers, particularly in an era of spell-checking technology. But during your school years, spelling may be thought of as a conspicuous marker of your intellectual worth. Put simply, kids who can't spell feel terrible. The adults in their lives may make matters worse by interpreting the problem as a tip-off to a brain's careless laziness. Yet spelling presents a vexing challenge to young writers, as it calls for a unique blend of language ability, memory capacity, understanding of rules (such as "*i* before *e* except after *c*"), and attention control. There are multiple possible breakdown points in the spelling process. In fact, as we saw in chapter 3, the story of Clint, the pattern of spelling errors a student commits may be a dead giveaway to his particular neurodevelopmental glitches. This is explained in the following table.

COMMON SPELLING ERROR PATTERNS:
WHAT THEY MAY REVEAL ABOUT A STUDENT'S
NEURODEVELOPMENTAL PROFILE

Error Pattern	Common Neurodevelopmental Findings
Visually close, phonetically poor approximations (e.g., *barght* for *bought*)	Often found in students with reduced appreciation of language sounds (weak phonological awareness); likely to be accompanied by significant reading decoding problems.
Phonetically close, visually poor approximation (e.g., *bawt* for *bought*)	Seen in students who have deficiencies of long-term visual recall and/or reduced visual-pattern appreciation and storage; often encountered with poorly legible written output.
Accuracy on a spelling test or bee but inaccuracy within sentences, paragraphs	Occurring in students who have trouble spelling while simultaneously generating ideas, encoding thoughts into language, and remembering other aspects of writing (i.e., they show weak simultaneous recall).
Random, inconsistent errors	Frequently present in students with weaknesses of attention controls and/or limitations in active working memory.
Omissions and distortions within words (e.g., *bohght* for *bought*)	Prevalent in students who have trouble with the appreciation, storage, and maintenance of "linear chunks" of data. Often they are accurate in the beginnings and endings of words but not the middles.
Spelling rule and regularity violations (e.g., *bugnt* for *bought*)	Found in students with diminished appreciation of rule governance, regularity, and irregularity. They may use letter combinations that do not exist in English!
Word derivation errors (e.g., *preevyou* for *preview*)	Occurring in students with weak semantic and morphological abilities who fail to use word knowledge to support spelling; often part of broad language dysfunction.
Extreme disparity between spelling recognition and spelling recall	Often detected in students with memory-retrieval weaknesses, who may also be having problems in mathematics and writing; apt to be accurate when facing a multiple-choice format on spelling tests.
Mixed spelling errors	Combinations of the above, likely to be uncovered in students who harbor a significant cluster of neurodevelopmental dysfunctions.

By stepping back and scanning a person's spelling transgressions, we can see recurring patterns of error that may fit with other things we know about that individual. Spelling patterns may reveal a discrete gap in memory, language, attention, or some other neurodevelopmental system. Since some spelling problems seem to be inherited, it should not surprise you that poor spellers in the same family tend to commit the identical kinds of spelling errors.

CLOSE ALLIES: THE THREE *R*'S

Reading and writing are like siblings. But there's no rivalry; they can be intimate collaborators. Active reading helps supply language, ideas, and structures you can use when you write. Reading fosters literacy, and literacy helps to enrich writing. Students who don't, won't, or can't read are less likely to get that reading boost and so are apt to fight writing. Yet I come across plenty of students who read acceptably but nevertheless write poorly. Many of them have been cursed with a double whammy of writing frustration and poor performance in mathematics. That's because arithmetic, like writing, demands sequential ordering, along with rapid retrieval and strong active working memory, even as it puts the attention controls through a heavy workout. If one or more of those capacities is too low, both writing and mathematics seem to self-destruct.

LOCATING THE BREAKDOWN(S)

Sometimes students require testing from a psychologist, special educator, or developmental pediatrician to determine where the breakdown in output is occurring. But very often a reasonably astute parent or teacher can perform some revealing detective work simply by observing a child during the act of writing and closely examining samples of his or her work. Also, don't ever forget to ask a nonwriter why he can't write. That person can provide some of the most telling clues to help solve the low-output mystery. The Writing Troubleshooter in Appendix A of this book may be helpful in prompting a student to uncover his specific breakdowns.

BECOMING AN EASY WRITER

When a child writes, he unknowingly lubricates many of his brain's assembly lines. Written output actually strengthens memory, language, attention to detail, problem solving, and other powerful brain functions, and it forces them to work together. Therefore, we can justify a vigorous campaign aimed at enabling a child to write easily. On the pages that follow, I will describe seven processes that can be cultivated and that have the potential to unlock the writing gears while simultaneously helping kids strengthen neurodevelopmental functions they will be able to use throughout their lives—for more than just writing.

Developing a Project Mentality

A project mentality is the belief (and the experience to support it) that worthwhile and gratifying results are obtained in well-planned steps over an extended period. Ernest Hemingway once said, "Writing is rewriting." All students need to think of their written work as a process of sanding and polishing their thinking and their reporting on their thinking. I find that many kids have been misled to believe that writing is some kind of emergency procedure usually done under the gun of a time limit! On tests or quizzes and while taking notes, students come to associate writing with brain sprints. The act becomes bound in their minds to the admonition "Finish up." As a result, they fail to view written work as workmanship.

Some writing, especially note taking, does need to be fast-paced and efficient, but a sizable proportion of writing should occur in the form of projects, undertakings that are worked out, worked over, and re-worked. In this way writing helps shape habits and practices that will be used over and over in the perfection of any worthy long-term venture, from rebuilding an antique automobile to decorating a bedroom to compiling a grant or a business plan. In all cases, planning and staging are essential. Much important work needs to be performed at a slowish pace—liberally interspersed with pauses for reflection. The Story Developer (Appendix B) and the Report Developer (Appendix C) can be used by students (and adults) from time to time to help them structure their writing activities: to plan a writing project, to implement it in a step-by-step fashion, and to monitor its quality during and after its accomplishment.

Writing needs to unfold in stages that include the following:

1. Strategic planning. A student ought to come up with efficient strategies to facilitate the process. Some of these include answers to the following strategic questions: What's expected of me? How do I figure out what kind of report my teacher wants me to write? How closely do I have to stick to the assignment and how much can I do my own thing?

What kind of writing does this have to be—should it be funny, serious, factual, or interpretive? Are there any strategies I should be using to make the writing a more efficient process? Should I divide my work into steps or try to do it all at once? Do I need to make an outline? What about a rough draft? In what order should I do things? Some students are all-star strategists who instinctively ask themselves, "What's the best way to do this?" Others just do it, and often they do it the hard way because they fail to think in terms of strategies.

2. Compiling a plan and a time line. As a part of their strategic planning, some students set up time lines and deadlines. The time line should be documented in writing and sometimes actually submitted and evaluated before any of the actual writing begins. Kids must get into the habit of extending and accentuating the planning stage of any worthwhile output. So should grown-ups.

3. Brainstorming. Many students benefit from an interval during which they germinate ideas without burdening their minds with spelling, punctuation, good grammar, or other mechanical necessities. Brainstorming ideas may be captured on a tape recorder, or the writer may assemble rough notes or a bulleted list on a computer. Various processes for generating ideas (chapter 7) find their way into the writing act at this point. It is a golden opportunity for freewheeling creativity or laserlike analytic thinking to occupy center stage.

4. Research. Facts are gathered to support and enrich the thinking. Nuggets of truth can be mined from books, articles, the Internet, or friends, relatives, and other reliable consultants.

5. Initial arrangement. Ideas and facts undergo a preliminary shakeout, at which point whatever does not seem good or relevant can be discarded and the best material saved on cards or on a computer-generated bulleted list. This embryonic stage can be developed into an outline or list of likely subheadings.

6. Rough draft. A preliminary version of the written work is created. This crucial first stab can be messy, grotesquely marred with misspellings and grammatical crimes.

7. Revised version. Here we have a more civilized rendition of the writing product. At this point, it is appropriate to seek critical input, hopefully liberally mixed with rich praise, from knowledgeable readers (such as a teacher or a parent, or even an earnest peer).

8. Final product. Now the masterpiece is corrected, completed, and polished for readers to learn from and admire.

9. Product assessment. This is the chance to go back and evaluate the writing achievement—perhaps using a checklist (page 184). This stage can allow for last-minute refinements or a further revised version of the paper.

Employing a stepwise approach to writing, students are not compelled to do very much at once. Thus they avoid feeling as if they are drowning, sucked into the undertow of overwhelming simultaneous demands. The above steps must be appropriately paced and spaced. Ideally, no two stages should ever be attempted on the same day or evening. In this way, the act of writing can help students get into the habit of pacing their output, encouraging the delay of gratification, and discouraging the all too common practice of completing work in a sprint just to get it over with. During the course of a writing project, students should submit their work in progress—proving that they are making use of a stepwise approach.

Writing in stages, such as those outlined above, is especially beneficial when the writer is hampered by memory limitations (Clint's problem). Not having to recall too much at once lessens the strain on memory. All the energy that might be spent trying to remember can then be allocated exclusively to the manufacture of good ideas and language. A staged approach also rescues those who have problems piecing together complex tasks (page 135); they need not do so all at once.

Organizing

Organizing a project is so vital that it merits separate consideration. Writing can be used as a means of getting organized on multiple levels. You may recall that Sharon Taylor couldn't write her reports because she suffered from a cluster of organizational weaknesses. Fortunately, organizational safeguards can be incorporated at the project-planning stage. The organizational tactics include the following:

1. Finding and maintaining the materials needed to get the writing done. Such material-spatial organization (page 138) may involve the well-planned use of folders, note cards, a special bookshelf, and the like. The purpose is to avoid misplacing the "props" that will be needed to complete the assignment. Some students deserve high kudos for getting through an entire long-term assignment without losing anything!

2. Managing time during writing. The time line suggested as part of

the planning stage is critical. Students need practice estimating how long something will take, allocating time, trying not to do everything at the last minute, meeting deadlines or preliminary deadlines, and working back from when something is due to define the timing of the stages leading up to the due date.

3. Organizing thoughts for writing. This part of writing interacts with the later stages of writing production. It requires determining the best order or arrangement in which to present thoughts. It involves the use of certain structural schemes that can give writing cohesion and a logical flow. Some writing needs to take the form of narrative, which is the structure of stories and accounts of personal experience. Expository writing is another common arrangement, one in which facts are presented in a way that is most logical and lucid. In keeping with educational tradition, kids need to be taught how to compose a topic sentence, then various supporting sentences, and finally a concluding statement. They need to understand the architecture of paragraphs. One format to impart this insight is shown in the following table, listing the major types of paragraphs that are important building blocks in expository writing.

PARAGRAPH TYPES

Paragraph Type	Explanation	Example
Description	Provides information about a person or a place	The features of the Sahara Desert
List	A series of items grouped together	The major agricultural products of France
Cause chain	A series of steps, each causing the next one	The people are of different cultures, so they disagree on issues, which makes them angry, which causes them to fight.
Time chain	A series of events in the order they occurred or occur (such as in a story or narrative)	The dog goes outside, then comes in to eat, then naps, then is ready to play.
Argument	One or two views of an issue presented	Pros and cons of using animals to study the effectiveness of drugs
Compare-and-contrast statement	A comparison of two entities	Geese are mainly vegetarians, while hawks prefer meat.
Problem and its solution	An issue and how it gets or might get resolved	The people are malnourished. We need to teach them agricultural methods.

Students should practice writing paragraphs that conform to the structures contained in this table. Such structures help kids come up with the best ways to convey their ideas. Many other kinds of scaffolding have been recommended to support students through the writing process. Writing has the potential to organize thinking, for the act of deciding how to write down your thoughts in an organized manner actually helps you think in an organized manner!

Student writers can often be helped with various scaffolding techniques that provide a framework within which to present their thoughts. Many such methods have become available in recent years. For example, in writing a story, a child can be given written prompts to include: a description of the characters and the setting; the time, events, or actions leading to a problem or conflict; the efforts or events aimed at dealing with the situation; and then its resolution and perhaps the moral of the story. Using this kind of structure, a student can be helped to produce a work of fiction that is coherent and cohesive.

Exercising Quality Control over Writing

Whatever we do, we need to ask ourselves repeatedly one vital question: "How am I doing?" The process of answering this question periodically is sometimes called self-monitoring, and it offers you a chance to regulate what you're doing and get it back on course if it has strayed from your original intentions or needs. Upon completing an action or activity or encounter of some sort, it's not a bad idea to ask yourself, "How did I do?" This might give you some insight into how to improve in the future, or, even better, it could provide an opportunity for generous and well-deserved self-congratulations (assuming your monitoring was honest and accurate). The act of writing offers a great opportunity for students to practice self-monitoring and regulation on multiple levels.

During or soon after writing, a student needs to compare his output to what was originally intended, with queries such as Have I gotten off track? Are my ideas moving away from the original topic? If so, is that good or bad? Additionally, self-monitoring forces kids to identify any careless errors they have committed—mistakes in spelling, poor grammar, punctuation errors, and so on. This is the often needlessly dreaded activity we call proofreading.

The optimal timing of proofreading is essential. No author should be condemned to proofread something immediately after writing it. To do so is tedious and frustrating, and it's an open invitation to reckless skimming. The writing experience needs time to incubate. It is preferable to check something several days later or the night after it came to be. With time, it is much easier to evaluate your own work, to detect and correct its flaws with some objectivity, and to deftly surmount the impasses that felt insurmountable while you were immersed in the act of writing.

On a regular basis, students can also benefit from focusing on the style of their written output, asking questions such as Have I varied my sentence structure or do I keep using the same kinds of sentences over and over again? Do I keep on repeating the same words? Am I making good use of paragraphs? Children benefit from having some system for documenting their self-monitoring. There are many self-monitoring tools. One example, shared with me by Wendy McClain when she was teaching at the Rio Grande School in Santa Fe, is shown in the next table.

Ms. McClain's Writing Rubric

Introduction/ Conclusion	Appropriate to Writing Purpose/Topic	Organization	Mechanics	Sentence Structure	Grammar
Has a strong opening and closing that relate to the topic	Relates to the topic and has a single focus	Key ideas are developed with appropriate and varied details; piece is organized and progresses logically	No errors in mechanics (capitalization, punctuation)	Clearly written, complete sentences; variety of sentence length	No errors in grammar (consistency in tense formation, subject-verb agreement, pronoun usage and agreement, word choice)
Has an opening and closing that relate to the topic	Relates to the topic and has a single focus; some statements drift from the topic	Ideas are developed with some detail and elaboration; piece is organized and progresses logically	Very few errors in mechanics	Most sentences clearly written; simple sentences; some variety of length	Very few errors in grammar

Introduction/ Conclusion	Appropriate to Writing Purpose/Topic	Organization	Mechanics	Sentence Structure	Grammar
Has an opening and/or closing somewhat related to topic	Responses loosely related to topic and focus shifts	Few ideas are developed; little elaboration; no logical progression	Some errors in mechanics that interfere with readability	Some unclear sentences; run-on or fragmented sentences; little variety	Pattern of errors or numerous errors in grammar
Does not have opening and/or closing	Unrelated responses and uncertain focus	Details are general, may be random, inappropriate, or barely apparent	Serious errors in mechanics that interfere with comprehension	Sentences not clear; frequent fragmented sentences; no variety	Serious errors in grammar

Kids also need to monitor the overall quality of their work. In my opinion, whenever a child takes a test or submits an important assignment in school, she should be required to write down in the upper-right-hand corner what grade she thinks she should receive. A student who predicts her grade accurately might be given bonus points for doing so. This gives kids practice in self-monitoring at the same time that it alerts teachers to whose quality control is effective and who is lacking this vital feedback loop.

Children need to feel that it is all right to make mistakes, to acknowledge errors, and to learn from one's miscues. They should always be praised for uncovering and confessing their flubs.

Novice writers can learn a great deal by editing the writing of others, deciding how passages might be improved. This activity should go beyond merely grading a classmate's paper (which, as we have seen, can be injurious and humiliating to many of them). The emphasis should be on discovering specific mistakes and coming up with ways of boosting the quality of the product. In other words, students not only need to have writing experiences; they desperately need to gain practice serving as editors, refining and helping to revise the work of others. This role may be practiced as part of a collaborative writing activity.

Developing Fluent Oral Language
We have commented that excellent writing is language's ultimate feat. But writing also presents an opportunity to perfect language produc-

tion. A back-and-forth relationship can prevail: a student can improve his written language by working on his spoken language and improve his oral language by working on his written language!

To become writers, students need to become proficient at verbal elaboration. This was a serious obstacle for Darnell, whose weak oral language stood in the way of his developing fluent written language. Students like him need plenty of chances to make oral presentations and, especially, to elaborate on topics that genuinely interest them and about which they have some thorough knowledge. Only then can they move toward effectiveness in talking about newly obtained skills, facts, and concepts. At home and in school, kids need to be encouraged to communicate in complete sentences. Responses that use vague words such as *stuff* and *thing* stunt the growth of vocabulary. They should be outlawed in the interest of acquiring richer and more versatile communication abilities.

Thinking on Paper

Writing can help pry open a mind, since getting ideas transcribed on paper, not surprisingly, requires coming up with some. Many of those ideas need to come from within. Brainstorming and problem solving (chapter 7) are powerful mind openers. Some individuals engage in these processes almost instinctively, while others seem to need plenty of prodding.

This should be a time of wild, open-minded, flexible thinking, during which kids can be coaxed to type or write down whatever spontaneously erupts from their liberated minds. They can then move through a phase of deciding what looks most promising, crossing out or deleting ideas that either don't fit with the others or would be hard to develop or research. Next they should take their pared-down list and begin to arrange the items on it in an order that makes the most sense. One possibility would be to create tentative subheadings for the final written product; that way they could approach the act of writing as one of "filling in the blanks."

Children need plenty of practice facing up to the blank page, spawning neat topics, and propagating the ideas that grow out of them. In this way they become novice scriptwriters, producers, orchestrators of personalized thought processing. Such experience will be directly transferable to numerous settings and scenarios as they advance through school and career pathways.

When kids take on a writing assignment, they are actually facing a problem-solving challenge—whether or not they are aware of it. Let's use Roberta Chan as a hypothetical example. Suppose you were working with Roberta to help her become more of an active problem solver during writing.

First of all, let's suppose that Roberta knows that her essay can cover any topic having to do with current events. She asks her mother to choose one for her, a request Mrs. Chan wisely turns down. Instead the girl is coaxed to switch on her brainstorming engines. After some listless deliberation and scanning the Sunday paper, she decides to write about an African country where a ruthless dictator is reported to be slaughtering innocent dissidents and setting fire to the homes of people who resist his totalitarian rule. The newspaper article states that our government is trying to decide whether or not we should send troops in to try to overthrow this dangerous and cruel dictator. When Roberta informs her teacher of her chosen topic, her teacher comments that she can figure out whether or not to invade by writing about the situation. The girl looks more than a little skeptical.

The first step in problem solving is stating clearly the nature of the problem. The scientist Charles Kettering once exclaimed, "A problem well stated is a problem half solved." Writing facilitates the precise and thorough clarification of a problem. Too often problems go unsolved because they have not been adequately defined. It is not sufficient, therefore, for Roberta to state the problem as she did initially: "Should we attack?" Rather, her mom coaches Roberta to represent her quandary in much greater detail: We hate to see all the suffering and bloodshed that is occurring in that country. We may have a moral responsibility to do something about it. As a world leader we can't just stand by and watch all these flagrant human-rights violations. On the other hand, is it really any of our business? Do we have a right to meddle in the politics of another country that poses no risk to us? Is it appropriate for the United States and its allies to assume the role of the world's police force? Is this a good use of our tax money? Do we want our soldiers sacrificing their lives for this? Then again, it's hard to watch all these innocent people suffering without helping out.

The next step in problem solving is called previewing (see also page 84). What would we like things to be like when the problem is finally solved? Roberta's answer to this question was that we would like there to be a good and fair government in place in that country, one that honors human rights and puts an end to the bloodshed and suffering.

The next job is to ask whether the problem can be solved and how hard it will be to solve it. Then we start to consider what are called alternative strategies: Roberta could write that we should attempt to negotiate with the existing government, try a propaganda campaign with the citizens, impose a trade embargo, fly in and bomb the dictator's army outposts and airfield, or simply turn our backs on the crisis and declare that it is tragic but not our problem.

With the aspects of the problem laid out, the time has come to direct the weary but inspired Roberta to do a bit of research on her topic. She might need to read a book chapter or two or perhaps several newspaper or magazine articles, or surf the Internet, and possibly consult directly with a respected authority. Is there historical precedent for this situation? What measures has our country implemented when confronting such dictators in the past?

Hopefully, Roberta's research results (reported on paper) will enable her to argue for the best strategy, which, in this case, might be to negotiate. Then should peace talks fail, she will be able to describe alternative options that might be tried once the first choice has proven futile.

As she develops her ideas, Roberta should be urged to practice the art of self-monitoring. Is this report making sense? Have I written well about the decision-making process? Have I stuck closely to the topic, or did I stray from it? By documenting these steps, kids can create cogent and lively written output while honing their overall problem-solving effectiveness.

Applying Technology

In recent years written output has become increasingly wedded to technology. This marriage can be a boon to all students, but especially to those with output failure. In particular, word processing and the use of graphics, combined with the research potential of the Internet, have made it possible for many more students to savor satisfaction in writing. Word-processing software is especially useful for stymied writers with memory shortcomings (chapter 3). This was enormously beneficial for Clint. The computer's infallible program for letter formation, the rapid visual feedback from a monitor, the spelling and grammar checks, and the opportunities for neat and easy revision can make writing close to pleasurable for those who've long dreaded the activity.

Computers yield a psychological bonus for students whose handwriting is mostly illegible or shamefully messy. Using word-processing software they are able to create physically attractive written documents—what a relief. They no longer need to conceal their work from the smug judgmental gazes of fellow students, and they are shielded from the sharp barbs of their teacher and moral accusations (such as laziness) from their parents, common responses to gross illegibility. This application was a godsend for Russell.

All children with written-output problems, regardless of the underlying mechanism(s), should receive early training and experience in keyboarding. This can start by age seven (even sooner in some cases). At first kids can use one or two fingers to "hunt and peck." But by age ten dedicated campaigns to teach touch-typing should begin. Such instruction can be particularly challenging for students with sequencing problems and for those who struggle with graphomotor implementation (page 26). But it's well worth the effort.

Word processing can also facilitate the process of writing in stages (page 179). On the computer students can brainstorm, arrange ideas in the best order, compose first drafts, and polish revisions with relative ease. They can and should insert tables and graphics to illustrate, dignify, and clarify their expressed thinking.

Some students may need to use voice-activated software for writing. This option has the potential to rescue those who face frustrating graphomotor barriers to writing. However, every effort should be made to enable such individuals to practice their graphomotor function as well. They are likely to need manual writing in the future, at least to fill out forms and attend to other menial inscriptive peculiarities of everyday life.

Computers help students brainstorm. Inspiration software is one example of a program that lets children and adolescents map out or create webs of their thoughts as they think through a potential story or written report before writing it. I recommended this approach for Roberta Chan. See Figure 10-2 for an example of how it works.

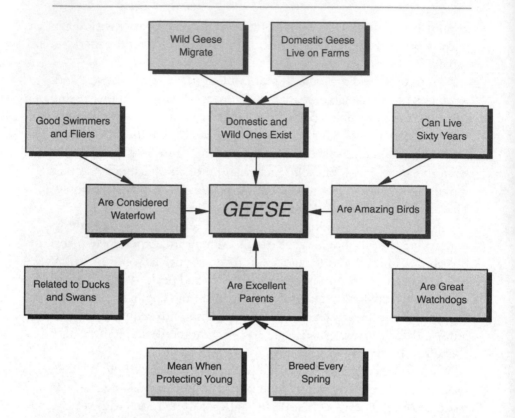

Figure 10-2.   An example of a writing web. A student can use this graphic representation to organize the content of a report on geese for science class.

Exploiting Affinities

Affinities are areas of special interest to a student—often for no obvious reason. Clint loved his cowboy heritage, and animals were his true passions. Affinities like his can flourish through writing, and writing can improve through the exploitation of affinities. Therefore, I encouraged Clint to write cowboy stories, cowboy songs, and cowboy biographies. Affinities can and should evolve into areas of significant expertise for a child. Clint might become the local expert on cowboy lore. Another student might develop a passion for frogs, for drama, for ancient mythology, or for meteorology.

Parents and teachers should always watch for emergent affinities, ready to support and celebrate any spontaneous sparkling of innate interest. Adults should go all out to foster the healthy growth of these interests, which over time can culminate in truly focused expertise. Students need chances to write about the areas that tantalize them, for they often begin to write well by writing about things they know and care about, topics they find romantically alluring in one way or another.

Some children may seem unable to find their personal affinities. They may seem incapable of cultivating a sustained interest and may need a careful search for sparks that can be set off and fueled. Parents, teachers, and clinicians should do what they can to see that a student keeps up one or two consistent interests over time and acquires a solid base of supporting knowledge.

WRITING OVER THE YEARS

Writing ability parallels and in some fascinating ways mirrors a child's development during the school years. At different ages and stages, different components of written output become part of a child's skill repertoire. In fact, a child's writing can serve as a revealing window on overall neurodevelopmental functioning. The next table depicts some general stages of writing growth over time to help you determine whether a child is keeping pace with some key written-output demands.

BECOMING A WRITER:
THE STAGES OF DEVELOPMENT

Writing Stage	New Developments
1. Imitation (preschool to 1st grade)	Fanciful attraction to writing
	Mimicry of actual writing
	Learning number and letter formation
	Use of invented spellings
	Awareness of spacing and lines in writing
	Establishment of hand preference
	Changing pencil grip
2. Visual Emphasis (1st and 2nd grades)	Preoccupation with visual appearance on page
	Discovery of capitalization, punctuation
	Written language simpler than speech
	Early use of complete sentences in writing
	Rapid growth in spelling ability
	Increasingly precise use of end finger muscles
	Growing self-consciousness about written output

(continued)

BECOMING A WRITER:
THE STAGES OF DEVELOPMENT (CONTINUED)

Writing Stage	New Developments
3. Sanding and Polishing (late 2nd to 4th grade)	Use of mechanical details (e.g., punctuation, capitalization) with language
	Start of cursive writing
	Use of conversational language on paper
	Initiation of keyboarding
	Awareness of writing's multiple components
	Initial attempts at creative writing
4. Automatization (4th to 7th grade)	Writing with less expenditure of conscious effort
	Fluent, effortless letter formation or keyboarding
	Ability to write and think simultaneously
	Written language as complex as oral language
	Large increase in volume of written output
	Introduction of planning and draft writing, rewriting
5. Sophistication (7th to 9th grade)	Writing to express and defend a viewpoint
	Written language more literate and sophisticated than oral language
	Problem solving and idea development through writing
	Use of different styles and purposes of writing
	Writing as a means of thinking
	Use in writing of information from multiple sources; research skills
	Incorporation of technical and abstract vocabulary
	Use of subheads, other ways of organizing
	Enhanced word-processing capabilities
	Knowledge transformation
6. Personal Methods and Uses of Writing (9th grade and beyond; for some individuals, a stage that may never be reached)	Development of individual writing styles
	Writing as a way of understanding oneself
	Growing awareness of different readers and their needs
	Accurate and organized note-taking skills
	Greater diversification of language use
	Use of figures of speech, irony, analogies, humor
	Writing as a way of solving problems
	Use of writing as a brainstorming device
	Writing to instruct or persuade others

ADJUSTING WRITING EXPECTATIONS

Writing may become a pleasurable undertaking for many students. But some dread writing and avoid it defiantly. Much can be done to stave off such writing phobias.

First, as I have emphasized repeatedly, kids need time to write. Students too often think of writing as a speed-skating event. Pop quizzes reinforce this perception. In fact, many tests and quizzes discriminate against students whose processing and production of information are slow or laborious. All students need to think of writing as a craft that can be completed over an extended period with plenty of chances for repair and improvement.

The quality and organization of a student's written thinking should be evaluated separately from the mechanics of writing. The latter takes in spelling, punctuation, capitalization, and decipherable letter formation. Teachers should be willing to give students separate grades for the quality of their ideas in writing and for the accuracy of the mechanical details. I feel disheartened whenever I meet a kid who is capable of exploring heady concepts on paper but who becomes dreadfully inhibited because she knows she'll be penalized for her shoddy mechanics. Some students obsess so intently on the mechanics that their ideas run the risk of being "dumbed down." We don't want kids simplifying their ideas because they are afraid to use words that are hard to spell or complex sentences that are confusing to punctuate. Such sacrifices occur when kids are required to focus too much on the mechanics. Students need to learn that the most important part of writing is the reasonably fluent development and clear expression of their thoughts.

Teachers should be flexible with deficient writers. Some students may need extra time on a test, while others, especially those with motor memory weaknesses, should be permitted to print instead of using cursive script. In fact, the form of writing should always be the child's decision. Finally, the use of a laptop or desktop computer for note taking in class should be permitted, and from time to time a student should be allowed to substitute an oral report or a cassette for a written one. These alternate strategies empower all students to keep using language for thinking whether or not they transcribe their ideas on paper.

Writing can be enriched remarkably when students attain a lucid understanding of its component parts, of what it takes to write. Such knowledge is termed "the metacognition of writing." At some level kids need to learn the contents of this chapter. They should have opportunities to ponder and discuss the ways in which different brain processes converge on paper when you write. By understanding these processes and their interactions, they can consciously make use of them while they encode their thoughts on paper. In all academic endeavors, it helps to know what you're doing! Two books I have written for students, *Keeping a Head in School* (for middle and high school kids) and *All Kinds of Minds* (for elementary school students), both published by Educators Publishing Company in Cambridge, Massachusetts, and available through allkindsofminds.org, contain sections that explain the neurodevelopmental functions involved in writing. These resources are meant to foster the metacognition of written output and other academic challenges.

Writing is a prototypical vehicle for intellectual output during the school years, and it presents a powerful opportunity to convene a broad committee of brain functions, inviting them to join forces and assemble a first-rate product. In an intriguing turnabout, the act of writing rewards the very brain functions it taps. Effective functions are required for writing, and if you write sufficiently, those very same functions become even more effective. A positive writing experience can bolster language communication, memory, motor coordination, organization, attentional strength, and high-potency thinking. On the other hand, when kids can't write properly, no such dividends are declared. Instead, especially if they do not receive praise for their work, these individuals are susceptible to output failure's potentially malignant complications, including self-destructive behavior problems, overdependence on social gratification, depression, a loss of motivation, and long-term underachievement.

ADULT CONSIDERATIONS

Many of the output demands in adult careers are the equivalent of writing assignments during the school years and contain mixtures of the ingredients of written output I have discussed. Here are some examples:

- A contractor drawing up an estimate for an addition to someone's house
- A composer writing a new song for an off-Broadway show
- A driver of an eighteen-wheeler charting his route and destina-

tions across the continent and then executing the trip safely in the estimated time

- A teacher planning and implementing a new curriculum on the Middle East for sixth graders
- An automobile mechanic diagnosing and repairing a pickup truck that stalls out at high speeds
- A surgeon preparing for and then performing a coronary-bypass operation
- A politician writing and delivering a campaign speech

Like written output during one's school years, these grown-up examples involve the recruitment of multiple neurodevelopmental functions to plan and accomplish a complex task. In some cases the output is delivered verbally (as with the politician), while in others a motor output delivers the goods (as with the car mechanic). In all of these examples, there is a need for organization, ideation, mental energy, memory, and production control. Could it be that writing throughout school is a great way to prime a mind for any form of high-quality complex adult output? I believe so.

11
CULTIVATING AND RESTORING OUTPUT

It should be noted that most Westinghouse winners seem to have parents who embroil themselves in their children's work, even if they do not quite understand it. . . . Whatever they contribute takes some of the pang of isolation—as unavoidable as it is—out of the projects the youngsters work on. The youngsters get the reassuring sense that their work matters to the people who matter most to them.

—JOSEPH BERGER, *THE YOUNG SCIENTISTS*

The Bartons were justifiably proud of their offspring, Beth, who was ten, and Michael, fourteen. Immensely productive performers in and out of school, they were off to a flying start in life, and they were happy kids. I got to know them when Mrs. Barton was on the school board of a town in which I was involved in training public school teachers. We became friends, and during one of my trips there, she invited me to her home for dinner. She and Mr. Barton made a very deep and lasting impression on me. The kids were consistently earning mixtures of A's and B's on report cards; they were strong students but not at the top of their class rankings. Both loved school and each evening at the dinner table eagerly discussed what they had learned that day. Both had friends they liked, but each equally enjoyed playing alone. They were upbeat, good-natured, motivated, communicative, inquisitive, and productive—in short, great kids. No one will ever accuse either one of being lazy.

I met the Bartons on several subsequent occasions, and at one point, I told Mr. and Mrs. Barton that they ought to write a book on rearing school-age children. They dismissed this suggestion but agreed to share a few key pointers with me. Here's a short list of what they routinely did for and with their daughter and son:

• Each evening the family had extensive discussions of what had gone on in school that day. Mr. Barton regularly asked a wonderful leading question: "What questions did you ask in school today?" That inquiry delivered the message that the kids should be hungry for knowledge.

• Whenever they drove in a car, the radio was turned off (a great help in developing language production).

• There was no TV, instant messaging, surfing the Internet, or listening to music during homework hours, 6:45 to 9:00 P.M. (longer if the work wasn't completed). If the children had no homework, they did other kinds of mind work, such as reading or writing for pleasure.

• While the kids were working, the adults were also reading or writing. No one was exempted (except the three Maine coon cats and two Afghan hounds).

• The children regularly got to visit their parents' workplaces, so they had a model for being productive and a preview of what adult work might be like.

• When the family had guests, the kids stuck around for the first hour or two and learned to converse and exchange ideas with adults.

• The children were helped to organize their "office space" at home and to plan and prioritize the week's tasks and activities in advance.

• The kids were permitted after-school activities only two or three days a week. The rest of the afternoons they were on their own—free to brainstorm, be creative, pursue their personal interests, invent their own games and pastimes.

• The family took many day trips and vacations together. A conscious effort was made to fold a meaningful educational component into these vacations (such as trips to museums, historical sites, or natural phenomena). The family would read about these sites together, before and during their trip. On a number of occasions the trip had a theme, such as understanding rock formations (Michael had a formidable rock collection).

• Both kids knew that their parents not only loved them but respected and admired them.

The Bartons also used other mind-cultivating practices, but suffice it to say that these terrific parents were fostering a life of rich mind intake and output in their two children. They were seeding the self-discipline, providing the role models, and offering the attractive experiences needed so that their children's brains would learn to work and savor satisfaction at the same time. They did not overindulge their kids in mindless entertainment, nor did they overprogram them.

PARENTING THAT CULTIVATES OUTPUT

Kids deprived of mental-work practice at home may never acquire the habits of self-discipline that promote high output throughout life. Practice working makes work a lot easier. Some students feel as if they are under bombardment when they sit their reluctant bodies in front of a desk, in part because they have not learned the kinds of organizational habits and tactics discussed in chapter 8.

When kids generate low levels of work output, they become more susceptible to distractions and diversions that demand little or no mental effort. They gravitate excessively and perhaps obsessively toward television screens, telephones, computer games, and other passive paths of least resistance.

Some children and adolescents with "underemployed minds" may grow to disrespect themselves. I believe that happened to Scott Murray. By the time he entered college, he felt worthless; he had little to show to the world and even less to feel proud of within himself. Down deep, kids, and grown-ups too, feel good about what they've been able to do and bad about what they haven't been able to do. Instead of pride in their work, they experience deeply felt shame over their sparse output. They can react to this inner feeling in many different troublesome ways, at least some of which become downright self-destructive. Adolescents with output failure are excruciatingly susceptible to drug abuse, delinquent behavior, a loss of motivation and ambition, an obsessive preoccupation with their social life, and depression.

What can be done to prevent these hazardous outcomes and instead establish solid working capacities in our kids? The following plan is likely to succeed in most families:

• Provide productive prototypes. One or preferably both parents should set examples in their own lives and careers of the kinds of productivity they expect from a child or teenager. The Bartons were masters of the modeling process. Kids need to see their parents engaged in serious work activities at home and at work. Kids need to discover role models who exemplify constructive output and yet are credibly "cool." When I was thirteen my big brother, Leonard, entered Harvard College. I viewed this event as nothing less than totally awesome. He was always incredibly benevolent toward his borderline spacey-nerdy kid brother, and he invited me and a couple of my friends to spend occasional weekends with him in his dorm. That those academic sojourns inspired me would be understating their impact. I was mesmerized. I saw him and his dormitory peers as strikingly smart and "with it," the kinds of guys I wanted to become. I attended some freshman lectures and became even more enthralled, mentally energized, as if I'd been slipped some intellectual pep pills.

Before my Cambridge pilgrimages, I was a mediocre, borderline-motivated, lowish-output performer in school—not failing anything, just mediocre. But after my exposure to Harvard, my output catapulted, and I earned straight A's from eighth grade onward. I went on to become editor in chief of the school newspaper. Ultimately, I was crushed when I only made the waiting list at Harvard; there was some modest recompense when I managed to graduate from Harvard Medical School. The modeling by my brother had done the trick. My parents were also hard workers; that, too, helped. By the way, kids easily become infatuated with those who are in an age group only one or two notches beyond their own, as I was with my brother and his friends; that's often where we should launch our search for productive prototypes.

• Take an interest. Parents should show a keen curiosity about whatever a daughter or son is working on. They should be willing to learn from and with a child. Whenever possible, they should discuss the work with the kid and help him or her see the relevance and fun in the activity. It is also important for parents to point out how important it is for a person to try hard to enjoy his work. After all, when you grow up, you'll be pretty miserable if your job is no fun.

• Reinforce and praise output. By regularly reinforcing and praising a child's output, parents can help make work seem less like work. Every effort should be made to provide opportunities for kids to display and express abundant pride in the products they are working on, and to use their work as a way of affirming the admiration of their mothers and fathers. Parents should show off the commendable product line to other adults in front of the child. Remember, children usually know that their parents love them. What they wonder about is whether their parents respect them or boast about them to their friends and relatives.

Work output can be used as a source of such praise and parental recognition. A kid can acquire a permanently crippled ego when he comes to feel that he can never please his parents. We must not let that happen.

• Reward productivity, not grades. Parents should reward output rather than scores on tests or marks on a report card. A child or adolescent should receive special recognition for handing in every assignment and/or "logging in" a respectable level of study time. Scores on tests, written assignments, and quizzes are a bit too dependent on luck, test-taking prowess, and work rate, factors that may be beyond the direct control of the student, whereas presumably output, although downright effortful for some kids, is more within the child's direct control. We want to establish rewards for things an individual can actually do something about! So don't say, We'll buy you a new bicycle if you get all B's or better. Instead declare that the coveted prize will be awarded for an agreed-upon level of work output.

• Provide work incentives. Although we would love to see boys and girls become workers for their own personal satisfaction, there is nothing indecent in providing incentives, even material ones. After all, such promised benefits are the generators of a substantial amount of adult productivity! Also, it is vital to inculcate the notion that effort pays. This message provides students with what is called an "internal locus of control," meaning that they come to believe they are in the driver's seat and therefore exercise control over their fate. Kids who believe that they can succeed, of course, are more likely to mobilize effort than those who have come to feel "No matter what I do, I will never make it in school; I'm just stupid, I guess." Such a statement reflects an external locus of control, a deeply held belief that outside forces determine your fate. After all, if you conclude you're not smart, there's not a whole lot you can do about it, and you will consider success and high output beyond your control.

• Undertake collaborative projects. One of the most meaningful experiences for a child occurs when he and one or two parents jointly pursue a common interest or a project. When a kid works with her dad to restore a car, helps his mom plan and plant an herb garden, or jointly organizes a family camping trip, the parents have opportunities to model systematic and stepwise approaches to challenges. These activities also represent powerful forms of attachment and intimacy that can help children feel secure in their family relationships. Kids need to feel that they are making a contribution to family life. Every child should be required to do chores on a routine basis. Despite some zealous protests to the contrary, children sense the profound value of such tasks, which most certainly contribute richly to a young kid's working capacity.

• Design and maintain appropriate office space. In the best of all possible worlds, kids would have well-organized "office space" at home. Most commonly, this site is likely to be in a bedroom. However, some people find it almost impossible to concentrate or study in the room where they sleep. This is especially the case for kids with a sleep-arousal imbalance, which is common among students with attention deficits (remember Ginny in chapter 4). Finding it nearly impossible to remain alert in the same room where they have to focus so fretfully on sleeping, they may spontaneously migrate to the kitchen counter or the living room floor to study. If it is possible, some kind of work site outside of the bedroom is desirable for many kids. The next table contains suggestions for organizing home work space.

SETTING UP AND MAINTAINING A STUDENT'S HOME OFFICE

• Drawers, trays, and boxes should be used to store specific items (e.g., writing utensils, blank paper, paper clips, staples, and diskettes). Each one should be labeled clearly.

• The desk surface and chair should be kept neat at all times—with as few piles as possible. If necessary, a parent should keep the desktop neat for the child—without delivering a sermon on the kid's need to be "independent." Many children need to cultivate a taste for neatness; it's not a natural instinct for them.

• There should be as few visual distractions as possible above the desk.

• There should be at least a small bookcase devoted to storing books—no games, trophies, models, or dolls.

• A student should have a desk calendar for scheduling and working out time lines for long-term activities. Every evening before bedtime, the child should experience the satisfaction of crossing off the day's finished tasks.

• There should be a filing cabinet for important papers. A good filing system should be established and maintained—with color-coded folders, including some for works in progress. All pieces of paper for work and for hobbies should be able to be classified under one of the folder labels.

• A computer should be conveniently located at a good height without taking up all the desk space.

• There should be a comfortable site for reading—other than the bed.

• Arrange for optimal working conditions. Kids need to work in a quiet environment, one that is relatively distraction-free. It's hard for a student to be productive while the rest of her family is howling with laughter over their favorite situation comedy. It's best, in fact, if everyone is engaged in quiet activities while the student strives for high output.

• Conduct output experiments. Some experimenting is called for, since conducive working conditions vary from child to child. Some students insist that they need background music (which may come across to the objective observer as foreground music) in order to work. It's worth a try. Sometimes the music does reinforce a rhythm of output, and sometimes it helps filter out other distractions (ranging from plans for the weekend to the current weather out the window). If a kid listens to music and accomplishes little or nothing, then obviously a new music-free policy needs to be established. Other experiments should also be set up to answer questions regarding whether a child works best after a snack or a meal, whether his work output is related to how much sleep he has gotten, and whether she becomes too distracted in her own bedroom.

• Set up and enforce consistent work times. Consistency is paramount, yet it is not that easy to achieve in our culture. But just as many people are setting aside time each day for physical fitness, kids need to have specific time slots for mental workouts, which may or may not involve only homework. That is, they need time to review subject matter, time to read independently, time to pursue intellectual interests. Such scheduling is most successful when it is fairly regular. As in the Barton family, parents might decide that weeknight evenings, perhaps from 7:00 to 9:00 P.M., will be dedicated to mental work—even if there's no assigned homework. They should never tell their kids that they will be allowed to watch TV or indulge in some other form of intense pleasure when they finish their homework. That is an open invitation to rush through the work and complete it as carelessly, frenetically, and superficially as possible, and thereby be rewarded for speed rather than quality.

It is better to require that a set block of time be dedicated to sustained mental effort.

• Emphasize time management. Some kids have a natural sense of time and how it works, but as we have described with Sharon and Mark Taylor (chapter 8), there are those for whom time plays little or no guiding role. They are all in a proverbial time warp. To varying degrees, all kids can benefit from assistance with time management. At least once a week a parent and child should confer, scheduling activities over the next several days. They should make use of a desk calendar or chart on which they can list specific activities or tasks that will need to be completed, along with estimates of how long each will take. Before going to bed each night, the child should check off what was completed and roughly how long it took to accomplish. It may even be that parents supervising the process will benefit and become perceptibly more efficient themselves. It's never too late to be on time!

• Limit TV viewing and other passive or hedonistic activities. Relaxation is a necessity, and most contemporary kids take advantage of modern telecommunications and other forms of electronic wizardry to rest their weary brains. But high levels of brain-free relaxation are likely to be detrimental to output. Although some television viewing is actually beneficial and culturally revealing for all children and adolescents, it is easy for kids to become mesmerized and far too dependent on the device. They can be harmed by the "no-brainer" experience of laughing only because the canned laughter is laughing, rather than having to discover humor (an important language function).

TV shows that are violent and provide intensely exciting stimuli that demand no heavy thought on the part of the viewer also can do harm to children's minds. Kids need to learn how to delay gratification, but many TV shows resolve everything nearly instantly and effortlessly. Even news programs tend to dole out information in tiny chunks. Plots take time to unravel in a novel or during a theatrical performance. The ability to delay gratification while reading or listening demands sustained attention; strong attention controls are a key ingredient of output. We saw the negative results of weak attention in the cases of Ginny and Scott. When kids watch television they should not overindulge in shows that provide ecstatic levels of excitement with little or no expenditure of mental energy. There are programs that deal with subject matter in some depth, and watching them is to be encouraged.

• Curtail other forms of overstimulation. Kids yearn for fun, and they learn from play. Mindless entertainment is stimulating and relaxing for them, as it is for us grown-ups. Yet too many kids have become too thoroughly saturated with high-intensity instantly gratifying endeavors, an entertainment universe of electronic euphoria and other spellbinding engagements that are geysers of pleasure with little or no mental effort required. I see many kids, especially boys, who are far too busy with incessant movement—on skateboards, surfboards, bikes, or skis. All of these are healthy pursuits in moderation but destructive endeavors when they become obsessions. Parents, doing their jobs as benevolent taskmasters, should closely examine the extent to which their kids are overexposed to overstimulating pastimes that are devoid of output demands. Some limits may need to be set.

• Document time spent and level of output. Maintaining a log of a child's work output can be very helpful, just as airline pilots maintain a record of the hours they spend in the air. Students can maintain accurate records of how much time they spend working and, by doing so, can take pride in the number of brain-work hours they put in during the week. A sample recording system can be seen in the following table.

MY OUTPUT LOG
PRODUCTS I HAVE PRODUCED THIS MONTH
THIS MONTH: <u>MARCH</u> SHEET # <u>1</u>

Date	Product Completed or Worked On	Worked On	Finished	Total Time Taken
3/1	Drawing of dogs		X	2 hours
3/1	Math homework		X	1.5 hours
3/2	Book report	X		3 hours
3/2	Science project	X		30 minutes
3/2	Bike repair		X	45 minutes
3/2	Poster for school party	X		20 minutes
3/3	Oral report for social studies		X	1 hour

This grid was used by a student to keep track of his daily level of output. Such a chart can help a student derive more satisfaction from being productive.

• If you feel like getting especially fancy, even glitzy, it is possible to chart the growth of a student's working stamina or capacity over time (Figure 11-1). Such documentation provides graphic feedback and an authentic sense of accomplishment.

Joe's Output Record for March (in Hours)

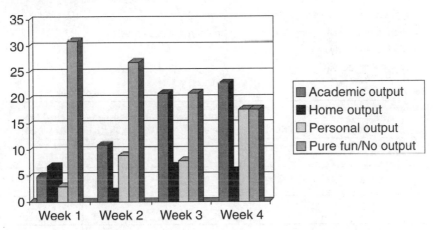

Figure 11-1. This bar graph enables a student to witness his own levels of productive output over a long period. The chart also distinguishes between different forms of activity. Academic output also takes in any independent reading or writing.

- Start early in life. Ideally the measures I have described should be put in place when the oldest child in the family reaches first grade. It is hard, even tumultuous, to establish new home-based work policies for the first time when a rebellious teenager reaches his fourteenth birthday; the sooner, the easier.

- Help with prioritization and multitasking. When a child has trouble setting priorities, a parent can help by sitting down with her once a week to compile a list of all the anticipated activities, both school-related and recreational. Then these can be rated in terms of how important they are, with the expectation that the highest-priority items will be accomplished by the end of the coming week and the lower-priority ones may or may not get completed. A parent and child can also discuss which items deserve the largest allocations of time.

Mrs. Bates made use of such a system to coach Mark in chapter 8 and found it effective. She mentioned to me during a phone conversation that the majority of high school students don't know the meaning of the word *prioritization*. Here is a typical priority chart that can be used by both students and adults.

WEEKLY OUTPUT PRIORITY CHART

Key

1 = Highest-priority activity (only one can be selected)

2 = High-priority activity (including one or more "pure fun" activities)

3 = Moderate-priority activity

4 = Low-priority activity

Beginning of Week   **End of Week**

Activity	Priority	Estimated Time Required	Accomplished (Yes, No, Partly)	Actual Time Required
	1			

This chart can be used to help a child (or an adult) list activities and then rate them in terms of their importance. This process can be especially vital for individuals whose output is hindered by difficulty establishing priorities.

• Foster more than one mode of output. Although formal academic work has been stressed throughout this book, many forms of worthwhile and gratifying productivity are also recreational and can serve the dual purpose of being fun while contributing to a child's working capacities and sense of self-worth. Developing proficiency as an artist or musician is an example. These output channels provide entertainment yet require mental effort, strategic planning, delayed gratification, organization, and self-discipline, which are major ingredients of successful output. Playing organized sports in a disciplined way (e.g., practicing regularly even when you don't feel like it) can also serve as a medium of effective output. Ideally, kids should augment their academic work output with one or more of these alternative modes without overextending themselves so much that they become chronic dabblers with no depth of proficiency or cultivated expertise in any particular domain.

• Serve as a sympathetic and nonjudgmental consultant. Frequently, parents wonder how they should help their children with schoolwork. Homework may become a raging and enraging home battlefield in which a parent and child are in relentless verbal combat. I have found that the most effective parents are those who offer accessible homework consultation without actually doing too much of the work for the child or teenager. Parents should take every precaution not to come across as a child's harshest critic. Never forget that there is no one a child wants to impress more than her parents. Spying on children doing homework may openly expose their weaknesses; that's why some kids become resistant or even hostile at such times. In reality, they feel embarrassed. In particular, if a student has some form of learning difficulty, such as deficient spelling, avoid making too much of an issue of it while offering assistance. Kids are excruciatingly hypersensitive when it comes to the mistakes they make; so are adults. Therefore, the helping parent should be nonjudgmental and as uncritical as possible. A kind and gentle approach prevents kids from becoming rebellious and going on strike with respect to homework. The next table summarizes the ways in which a parent can pull off the fragile responsibility of a benevolent homework consultant.

WAYS PARENTS CAN SERVE AS HOMEWORK CONSULTANTS

• Help the student formulate a schedule or time line for work before starting it.
• Share in brainstorming (such as helping to pick a topic)—without taking it over.
• Get the kid going—provide a jump start (e.g., help write the first sentence).
• Assist in finding and arranging needed materials.
• Make sure the environment is appropriate for brain work (page 201).
• Be accessible to answer specific questions and offer encouragement.

- Devise appropriate breaks from work.
- Assist with self-testing and help with proofreading or quality control.
- Show an interest in the subject matter; let the child try you about what he's working on.
- Isolate weak steps or components. Whenever a child exhibits a specific output breakdown, such as a graphomotor or language gap, that particular step in production needs to be segregated and made into a separate activity or stage. For example, if a child has trouble getting ideas into clear language, he should begin by encoding his thoughts in not very good language. Then perhaps the next night he can go back over his report or oral presentation and polish the language aspects (without having to generate good ideas and legible writing at the same time). In other words, the improvement of a weak component should always be a separate event. If attention to detail is a problem when a student does his math homework, he should do it anyway. Later he can go back and do a "detail check." Parents should be aware that it is really hard to proofread something you have just completed. Ideally a student should put the product away for a while before debugging it.

OUTPUT WITHIN A COMMUNITY AND A CULTURE

To what extent do a child's community and neighborhood nourish constructive output? First, open displays of diligence in school may not be "cool" and may be seen as "nerdy" by a student's peers. Slacking off, on the other hand, may be very cool. To survive on the social scene some kids go into seclusion at times, becoming underground scholars. Others succumb to the pressure to do as little work as possible; this is especially the case when a student anxious for peer acceptance starts out with an underlying tendency toward output failure for one or more of the reasons cited in this book.

Communities must develop activities and programs in which student productivity and creativity are valued and recognized with as much hoopla as the accomplishments of the local football team. Such exhibits of output virtuosity might include: concerts or recitals, kids of different ages engaging in well-attended public debates, a community literary magazine and/or journal of commentaries produced by students and circulated widely, student art exhibitions, student dramatic productions, and community-service activities recognized in the press. Parents should ascertain that every child is engaged actively in some form of intellectual output that is valued and publicly acknowledged by the community. The goal would be to make it cool to be cognitively productive!

Second, our modern culture needs to license kids to become better at brainstorming, one of the essential ingredients of good output. In many communities children have soccer on Monday, kung fu on Tuesday, religious classes two days a week, music lessons on Thursday, Scouts on Friday, and more soccer practice on Wednesday along with dance lessons and math tutoring. While such forays result in admirable output, overdone structure inhibits brainstorming and can snuff out creative flames. Children need their share of downtime, periods when they can engage in imaginary play or other inventive activities, moments when they have to figure out what to do when there's nothing to do.

Having a job after school can be a constructive experience that contributes meaningfully to output capacity and quality. However, some student employment poses a thorny dilemma. Many teenagers work after school and on weekends, and for some, employment is an economic necessity. But such work may exact a costly toll on their intellectual development. Many a job can stunt intellectual growth as well as output. Imagine a sixteen-year-old who spends six hours a day at a supermarket checkout register monotonously bagging or passively passing items over a scanner and thinking hard about her next break. For hours on end, the only verbal output is a garbled "Paper or plastic?" Absolutely no memory, problem-solving skill, creativity, organization, or language facility is required or encouraged. Some teenagers spend as much as thirty-six hours a week (and more during the summer) in such a cognitive vacuum. What effects might this have on a teenager's rapidly developing brain? Injurious ones, I believe, and virtually destructive of output. Also, how seriously can a teenager take education when he is thinking about his job all day and about the car he is saving up for with his income from flipping hamburgers? School is downgraded to a peeving distraction. What can be done about this? We need to put limits on work time. Employers should vary a student's work and provide some opportunities for constructive output, perhaps some form of on-the-job managerial training and experience.

FOSTERING OUTPUT AT SCHOOL

How can schools instill habits of quality output? Our educational institutions need to be arenas that encourage, train for, and reward productivity. At present, this is not always the case. Too often gratifying academic kudos go to clever learners who are the best test takers, and their success may boil down to the fact that they are the best rote memorizers, world-class regurgitators of information. Although tests play a vital role in learning and in the assessment of learning, they should not be embraced as the only ways of showing what you know and what you can do. Kids need to accumulate a track record, a portfolio of tangible accomplishments that should be weighted at least as heavily as praiseworthy test scores.

The well-known educator Grant Wiggins advocates that students build a portfolio in school, on which they are then evaluated. Such a portfolio (e.g., "The Complete Works of Michael Jones") grows over time and vividly demonstrates a student's level and quality of productivity. No doubt this form of assessment is more closely related to later success in life than any multiple-choice test! Schools should be helping kids build their portfolios in various subject areas, but to do so will require some basic changes. As I suggested in the section of this chapter on families, schools should reward high levels of excellent production as much as or more than test scores.

Schools can instill a project mentality (page 179). Kids should always be working on long-range academic enterprises that occur in steps over weeks or even months. Countless adult career activities, from constructing an office building to designing a new line of dress shoes to planning and conducting a marketing campaign, demand this kind of sustained goal-directed activity. Projects in school should often entail collaboration between students, since cooperative endeavors tend to predominate during adulthood.

We should also offer opportunities for highly individual output. Every school year, each student should conduct an independent research project, preferably one that fits comfortably with his or her personal affinities. The result might be a visual display, an oral presentation, a written thesis, or some combination of these final products. In high school, students should engage in independent studies that persist through more than one academic year. Faculty supervisors or designated outside experts might guide them through their research and project development. The community should become a rich source of part-time volunteer faculty members who serve as "thesis advisers" for kids. Such use of local talent can also help forge better relationships and understanding between the school and the town.

I think that all students should be encouraged to cultivate specialties, to find customized niches in which to become uniquely productive. Such specialization can be tied to the independent-study efforts. Every kid should have a zone of steadily deepening expertise, knowing more about insects, racing cars, the Civil War, or clothing design than anybody else in the school (faculty included). Such mastery of content does wonders for intellectual self-esteem while providing the raw material for some powerful output. Being the local expert on computers, cameras, horses, spiders, science fiction, modern art, or rodents is a formative and immensely gratifying position for any kid. But a word of caution: it is important that these well-formed affinities be distinct from pure recreational activities. When I ask a child in my office what interests him and he responds, "Soccer," I have been known to comment, "soccer's a great sport. I'm really glad you enjoy it, and I bet you're becoming excellent. But soccer's a form of entertainment. I'm talking about a topic or subject that interests you a whole lot, that you might even feel passionate about because it gets your mind excited. I think everyone needs both, some fun recreational activities plus some burning brain interests." Too often kids and parents equate recreational pastimes with intellectual interests. Schools should collaborate with parents to foster both of these specialized and individualized pathways.

In an ideal school, opportunities should be available in four respected forms of output. First, every student should have at least one area of outstanding *academic productivity*. Each kid desperately needs the experience of being an honor student in at least one domain, whether it's English, mathematics, history, science, automobile mechanics, or music. Students should generate products to display for their efforts.

In addition to academic output, all kids benefit from negotiating an area of *creative output,* in which they are able to innovate, deploy their imagination, or become entrepreneurial.

Third, every student can benefit from displaying some form of *motor mastery,* through sports, music, art, crafts, or mechanics. Motor accomplishment, like academic and creative performance, should be cumulative; kids need to observe themselves growing in their chosen areas of motor proficiency and productivity. If you are familiar with a child's wiring, you can make some educated guesses with regard to which sport or musical instrument he or she is most likely to master. Some athletic activities are heavily spatial (such as tennis and volleyball), others require fine-tuned muscle control and body-position sense (gymnastics, bowling, swimming, skiing, and golf), and still others demand rapid motor sequencing (basketball and jumping rope). Baseball, for instance, requires substantial attentional strength and delay of gratification, and features significant verbal communication. Obviously it is best to choose an athletic pursuit that sidesteps a child's area(s) of weakness, unless, of course, you want to use the sport to try to strengthen a weak function—possibly worth a try if the child is not humiliated by the experience. As for musical instruments, in general kids with motor dysfunctions do best with the ones that stress the use of large muscles and slower and shorter sequences—thank goodness for the tympani!

Finally, students should either demonstrate accomplishment as *leaders* or should perform important *community service*. Such output shows outreach, the ability to create products that influence others in a positive manner.

Just as parents can acknowledge and honor more than one mode of output, schools should offer diversified high-status output opportunities. Many already do so. However, every effort needs to be made to level the playing field, to make sure, for example, that high school sports are not endowed with too much prestige while the computer club is considered an ill-reputed haven for geeks. The debating team, the literary journal, and the community-service club should each be thought of as a valued venue for accomplishment in the school community. Filling the trophy case in the front lobby with more than just sports memorabilia legitimizes and celebrates the widest possible range of output achievements.

In an ideal school, every class would feature a segment on organization. Within the context of his or her curriculum, each teacher should help kids to estimate how long assignments will take, develop time lines and work schedules for task completion, and mobilize the organizational tactics needed to meet complex challenges in a systematic manner.

Material organization could also be facilitated. Students should be helped to develop a filing system, to make use of folders for computer storage, to utilize assignment pads, and to arrange notebook contents in a logical and accessible manner. In some subjects it may be appropriate to give students a separate grade for organization. Such an evaluation would stress the importance of this enduring ingredient of education and careers.

Schools have to strive to the best of their abilities to minimize the corrosive effects of peer pressure. In many cases friendships have a very positive effect on the development of children and adolescents. However, friends may sometimes prevent friends from blossoming into unique and productive individuals. Peer pressure may lead to conformity and uniformity. Peers may inject mediocritizing venom into one another—all in the name of acceptance and the seductive quest for popularity. Students can benefit from class discussions focusing on the social pressures they face in and out of school—the good effects as well as the downsides. Reading and analyzing case studies about students who have succumbed to their peers and those who have resisted the temptation prompts them to think about ways to develop as individuals and maintain control over their free will and identities while still enjoying the uplifting benefits of friendships. There is a fine line for many kids between out-and-out peer enslavement and well-balanced friendships. Schools as well as parents should help children and adolescents tread this delicate border.

Time may be a serious deterrent to output. Many students would create richer products if only they were granted additional time. I recall one boy, an anguished patient from Charlotte, North Carolina, whose writing was always very shallow but strong in its language and sophistication. Over the years, Teddy improved somewhat, and at the end of high school he was accepted at the University of North Carolina at Chapel Hill. In college his writing was more than passable when he submitted papers (earning mostly B's), but as a history major he ran into difficulty confronting essay tests. He complained that he never had enough time to get his ideas down and organized. To rescue Teddy, I wrote to the head of the history department and asked that on tests he be allowed to submit a bulleted list of points he would have made in an essay if he had had more time. His instructors readily accepted this accommodation, especially since Teddy was meeting his writing demands so consistently with his term papers.

I contend that students are generally given too little time to think, when we should be inculcating in them the need to be reflective rather than impulsive in their thought processes as well as their output. A frenetic curriculum and a stress on short-answer tests may discourage careful productivity. I would impose page limits rather than time limits; a student should take as much time as he needs but perhaps be permitted only four pages to transcribe his thoughts. That model is so much more realistic in preparing students for adult challenges, where there tends to be so much more time latitude. As long as you meet your deadlines, no one cares much how long it took you to write that business plan, book chapter, newspaper feature, or grant proposal, but in all likelihood it can't or shouldn't exceed a certain length.

Some students need to use calculators during math quizzes, print instead of writing in cursive, or use a laptop computer for taking class notes. Whenever possible, kids should do something extra in an area they are good at, in a sense to compensate for the accommodations they are receiving in their area of weakness. We call this transaction "bypass with payback." Russell Strinberg, who was skilled at reading but deficient in written output, was allowed to write a briefer report, but his teacher required him to read and discuss two books instead of just one. Russell was thrilled with this proposition; he declared he'd be willing to read three books in exchange for less writing! Such sensible negotiation preserves a high level of accountability and reinforces the critical notion that everybody needs to be productive but not like a swarm of clones or drones.

MANAGING OUTPUT FAILURE IN CHILDREN

When a kid (or an adult) is licking the wounds inflicted by her output failure, important people in her life should come to the rescue and provide well-informed, sensitive care. But before undertaking any remedy, it is vital to identify the specific neurodevelopmental problem—that is, the weak link or links thwarting output. Knowing, for example, that a child's trouble with writing stems from problems with expressive language (like those of Darnell in chapter 6), the affected child should receive guidance in transforming ideas into words and sentences. A mother or father might review a child's writing and suggest possible ways of upgrading the grammar or finding more precise vocabulary as he battles to communicate on paper. If a student is having a hard time launching a science project on electric eels, the mother or father can help with developing a time line, identifying sources of information, and brainstorming. It should be clear to the reader by now that the best tailor-made assistance to students with output failure must be based on an accurate picture of their neurodevelopmental assets and weaknesses. This can be determined with a thorough evaluation. The assessment should focus on the questions shown in the following table.

KEY QUESTIONS TO GUIDE THE EVALUATION OF A STUDENT
WITH OUTPUT FAILURE

1. Which forms of output appear to be unsuccessful in this child or adolescent? This should include academic output, such as writing and homework, as well as nonacademic channels of output, such as sports and creative activity.

2. How can we describe precisely the specifics of this student's output failure? For example: What pattern of spelling errors do we see? Are there legibility problems? Does she have trouble recalling rules of punctuation and capitalization while writing? Does she work too slowly? Or too frenetically? Is it too hard for her to pick topics or generate ideas for a project?

3. What evidence is there that one or more neurodevelopmental dysfunctions are impeding output? This should be based upon the parents' accounts, examination of work samples, an interview with the student, specific tests, and information from teachers.

4. Can we be specific about which form(s) of neurodevelopmental dysfunction are operating? Is it attention control? Is it memory? Is it language? Is it organization and strategy use? Is it motor function? Is it ideation?

5. How do we relate the identified neurodevelopmental dysfunctions to the phenomena we have documented (in questions 1 to 3 above)?

6. What are this student's strengths and affinities?

7. What sorts of help and support has he or she received in school, and how good is the match between this student and the current educational setting?

8. Are there complicating factors in this child's environment or life circumstances?

9. What kinds of behavioral complications are present?

10. What is the student's own understanding of or insight into his

output failure? Has he decided he's just lazy, or can he pinpoint the breakdowns impeding his productivity?

The Output Inventory in Appendix D provides a systematic way of understanding the particular sources of output failure in children as well as in adults.

A diagnostician making a professional evaluation should not just issue a list of test scores or indulge in simplistic reductionist labeling (e.g., ADD or LD) but instead should identify the student's specific breakdowns as well as strengths and from this analysis derive practical suggestions for his or her educational care.

After reading *The Myth of Laziness* and perhaps making use of the Output Inventory, parents should have some hypotheses of their own about what might be obstructing their kid's output. If a child undergoes testing, parents should be astute evaluators of the evaluation, asking the right questions (e.g., "Excuse me, but how have you ruled out a problem with expressive language that might be blocking output in my son?"). For some, the contents of this book should provide potent ammunition in their campaign to obtain services in school and ensure valid testing.

THE MAGICAL PROCESS OF DEMYSTIFICATION

Most children and adolescents with output failure have no glimmer of understanding when it comes to the reasons for their setbacks in school and in life. Adults may also be thoroughly confused regarding the career-related torment their output problems are inflicting. Many low-output individuals have been tattooed with stigmatizing, mostly unhelpful, simplistic, and pessimistic labels, such as ADD, yet have only a vague sense about which breakdown trips them up when they set out to accomplish work. All too often they write themselves off. They may assume they are afflicted with some form of mental retardation or incurable immorality. Many kids I've known have come to the conclusion that they are just plain lazy. They may feel this way even when no adult has ever even accused them of this sin. These negative self-diagnoses drain motivation and sometimes bring on all sorts of hard-to-fix behavioral complications.

Helping a kid understand and forgive himself through demystification is a significant step in preventing him from plummeting ever deeper into spirals of failure, abysmal self-esteem, and useless suffering. Someone outside the immediate family should do the initial demystifying, although parents can and should reinforce what is said and review it periodically with the child. Here are the demystification steps I go through:

1. *Taking the stigma out of the demystification.* I explain to the child that we are going to discuss his or her strengths and weaknesses and that this is a talk I could have with any kid. There's nothing weird about this information, since every kid has a profile of strengths and weaknesses. Sooner or later everyone will have to deal with his weak areas and decide what to do about them. The sooner the better! Since you're having some problems now, this is an excellent time for you to start thinking about your mind and its characteristics.

2. *Celebrating strengths.* Before discussing someone's weaknesses, it is always best to acknowledge his or her assets. When I do this, I am totally honest; nothing can be more hurtful to a child than false praise. I try to cite specific evidence for the positive things I am saying. Rather than just telling a ten-year-old she has a keen mind for science, I talk about her excellent performance on her biology examinations. Likewise, instead of announcing to an adolescent that he has fantastic carpentry skills, it is better to say that the tree fort he recently built was an awesome accomplishment. Kids also respond best when you compare them to other students. So I might add: "Dennis, there are very, very few kids who have your kind of special genius with tree-fort construction."

3. *Describing and putting borders around weaknesses.* I always use numbers and provide a short numbered list of a child's areas of weaknesses, which I go over with the child: "Here are the things you need to be working on, those little brain gaps that get in the way and sometimes make it seem too hard to get work done. There are three things you need to work on. First, you've always had some trouble with the sounds in language, what we call the phonemes. Your mind doesn't sort them out too well. It's something like a radio with too much static or sound that seems kind of fuzzy. Your sound problem makes it hard for you to read fast enough, and it's affecting your spelling. Second, your fingers don't always cooperate when you try to write. We call that a graphomotor problem. You have an awkward way of holding a pen. It seems as if the tiny muscles down in your fingers have trouble getting the right messages from your brain while you write, so letter formation takes too

much time and effort. That's one reason you hate to write; anyone would. The third and last thing is that you've become sad. You've lost interest in things you're great at, stuff you used to really enjoy. You're probably a little depressed. It may be that school has gotten you down. You'd like so much to be a top student, and you are really discouraged. I can understand that."

Looking at a numbered list of weaknesses, the student sees that the problems are not overwhelming, that she is not totally retarded. We have put limits around the deficits. We have given her the exact words for the things she needs to be working on. Hope is preserved. The plight becomes manageable.

4. *Injecting optimism.* Pessimism about the future stymies many individuals who have output failure. During this part of demystification, I try to instill an upbeat attitude about life and school, and concentrate on the exciting possibilities that lie ahead. Sometimes I explain to a child that lots of people find it easier to be an adult than a kid, saying, "That might really be the case for you." For example, I would describe to a teenager with language delays how her mathematical strengths, her phenomenal social talent, and her natural leadership abilities can bring her fantastic success. We would talk about the career possibilities that would best suit her, helping her see that things can and will get better if she hangs in there and works hard.

5. *Forming an alliance.* This part of demystification affords an opportunity for an adult to express continuing interest in the student's school career. "Patrick, I am really interested in how you do over the next few years. I want you to know that I can be available to you. I am not here to judge you or preach to you. I would like to be on your side. I want to be able to give you whatever advice I think you need, and I am willing to be a sounding board when you have to make tough decisions. Just let me know how I can help." Such statements fill a void for students who desperately need coaches or mentors and advocates as they struggle to overcome the effects of output failure.

I believe that with some modifications the process of demystification can also be of enormous benefit to adults who are in a productivity rut. A good coach can help them find their way by reviewing their strengths and weaknesses and helping them compose an optimistic, attainable view of the future—at any age.

ALTERNATIVE OUTPUT PATHWAYS THAT WORK WELL

Having some sort of laudable product line offers a person a degree of immunity from the complications of output failure. If formal academic productivity fails to materialize, alternative modes can come to the rescue of self-esteem. Here are a few alternative forms of output for kids:

Sports
Musical performance
Collecting
Leadership role in school or community
Apprenticeship
Artistic or craft activity
Caretaking (animals, older people, very young children)
Technology expertise and consultation

It is especially important to provide kids who suffer output failure with high-profile and high-status roles during the school day. Several interesting studies have shown that children who had a hard time in class had as their most positive memories those occasions when they were allowed to perform a service for the school. Such students, who all too often feel they are not first-class citizens in an academic setting, should be given an opportunity to work in the health or guidance office, take charge of the lighting and audio in the auditorium, serve as a computer consultant, assist the track coach, or help teach younger students. These experiences can provide gratification and give their self-esteem its sorely needed boost.

OTHER INTERVENTIONS

Some kids need more targeted help from a professional. Kids with verbal-based output problems may benefit from the help of a trained speech and language professional, who can provide therapy sessions to build up their verbal fluency, elaboration, summarization skills, or sentence construction. Instead of seeing the student directly, sometimes a clinician can provide advice to parents and classroom teachers. Other students need help honing their motor skills (most often from an occupational therapist) or coaching and counseling (from a mental-health specialist) to deal with the emotional toll of output failure. In all instances it is important that parents select professionals who have a clear understanding of the forms of output failure and their impacts on individual lives.

Medication is often considered an alternative treatment for output failure. And sometimes it's helpful. For example, children who have mental-fatigue issues, such as Ginny in chapter 4, or weak production controls, such as Scott in chapter 5, may become more productive after taking a stimulant medication, such as Dexedrine, Adderall, Ritalin, or Concerta. These drugs work on the neurotransmitters, the chemicals that help the brain pass signals from one nerve to another. In some cases concentration and mental effort become stronger, thereby boosting output. When it works, it's great.

But there are definite drawbacks. First, the medication is never the whole answer. Kids need targeted help with their underlying neurodevelopmental dysfunctions; otherwise the medication is likely to provide only temporary relief (if any). Also, beware that the drugs can cover up these underlying problems, like a bandage concealing an infected wound. A child may show some improvement in concentration, leading everyone to say, "See, it was her attention after all." In the meantime a serious problem with language or memory may be festering beneath the surface, only to crop up and cause serious academic famine in the future as the demands intensify. Finally, medication may have side effects, some of which could be long term.

The following are the major points to think about regarding medication use:

- A person should not be put on medication until after a thorough evaluation to determine the underlying reasons for his or her output failure.
- Medication is *never* the whole "cure"; it can and should be part of a multipronged management plan.
- We should try to use as little medication for as short a period as possible and, if at all possible, only one drug at a time.
- Those on medication require careful monitoring over time—with periodic reassessments and physical and neurological examinations.

The same principles apply when using other kinds of medication.

More and more individuals are being diagnosed as being depressed, bipolar (afflicted with wide swings of mood), obsessive-compulsive, or unduly anxious and given antidepressant or antianxiety drugs. These medicines may be beneficial, but I suspect we would need to use much less medication if we worked specifically to help people become productive whose depressed feelings were the direct result of their disappointment with themselves. Personal productivity and the authentic satisfaction that accompanies rich output are powerful elixirs for emotional health.

THE MANAGEMENT OF OUTPUT FAILURE IN ADULTS

It may not be too late. Even grown-ups, seemingly set in their ways, can point to improvement in their output.

The Need for Personal Insight and Good Career Fits

To begin with, we need to obey the ancient adage "Know thyself" and undertake a serious self-inspection. A trained psychologist can help to decipher a person's neurodevelopment profile, his or her current ledger of strengths and weaknesses. Ask yourself, Is there a problem with my attention, communication, organization, ideation, or any of the other patterns described in this book? How well does my profile fit with the current demands of my job? Is my work tapping my weaknesses, or does it play almost exclusively to my assets? If there's a wide disparity between abilities and demands, a change in job or career pathway merits consideration.

Young adults or college students set to launch their careers should be interviewed and/or tested so they can learn more about their own profiles and how they will fit the professions they are pursuing. It is commendable to seek a career that interests you, one you find romantically attractive, but it is just as germane to have a clear picture of the specific tasks that will confront you along the route toward fulfillment. Sharon Taylor knew she had trouble writing but had no idea that being a psychologist would require her to write reports.

A father of a patient of mine was out of work as a car salesman and under treatment for depression when I first met him. It turned out he had significant expressive-language difficulties and some problems with his social cognition—no wonder he didn't sell enough Volvos. That same man had always been good with numbers and small details, hard-working, and entirely reliable. Eventually he got a job as an insurance adjuster. He had found his fit. He thrived; his output became impressive. His Prozac was discontinued. This man might have saved himself wasteful suffering if he had been helped to think more about his professional compatibility before he started selling cars. We do have to worry about people whose interests don't match their abilities. If some people are determined to pursue career avenues for which their profiles are ill suited, they should at the very least comprehend the risks they are taking. And, of course, some of them will beat the odds and succeed; but other mismatched minds will endure failure.

Experimenting

Richard found that carrying a pocket organizer improved his productivity at work by leaps and bounds. He described it as a lifesaver. His buddy Clark got his Palm Pilot at about the same time and kept forgetting to recharge it. After about a month, he lost it and called the gizmo "that totally useless waste of money." Jan discovered at age thirty-five that she does her best work late at night, while her husband found out that he is most productive at dawn. Penny made the discovery that her output grew immeasurably when she worked out every other day. Her sister-in-law Lucille tried the same exercise program and found that the activity distracted her from her work and make her feel tired all the time.

All of this is fairly typical. What works for one individual may well be utterly futile for someone else. Also, as if to complicate our lives, a technique that works initially may not keep working. We have to be willing to keep trying new ways of being productive. I suspect that many productive people do this all the time; they are always seeking better ways to bolster and enhance their output. How, then, do we advise grown-ups on ways to build up their productivity? It's easy; we encourage them to experiment. The following are some grown-up experiments:

• Try doing heavy mind work at different times of the day, and notice when you best handle your most important or demanding work.
• Determine how sleep affects your performance. Consider a well-timed nap or two during the day.
• Try working in different sites to find out where you work best (e.g., in your office, on the porch, at home in your bedroom, or in the bathroom).

• Try different output devices: a really sensuous-feeling pen or mechanical pencil, a microcassette or digital tape recorder, a laptop, a blank pad for important brainstorming.

• Give pocket organizers a try. Try not to lose yours!

• Make use of the kinds of charting of priorities and time-management tactics suggested earlier in this chapter for kids.

• Experiment with the beneficial or negative effects of caffeine or snacks at strategic points during the day.

• Try setting specific weekly output goals and then indicate at the end of each week whether or not you met your goals (using documentation similar to the chart on page 206).

• Find convenient and socially acceptable ways of moving around or fidgeting while working—expending physical energy often stimulates the flow of mental energy.

• Try finding places to work in solitude, especially if you are someone with a high level of social distractibility.

• Try background music as a way of enhancing focus (many teenagers swear by this intervention).

• Practice your weak output link within the context of something you're interested in outside of work. For example, if you have problems expressing yourself but are an ardent sports fan, try elaborating eloquently on last Sunday's football game.

• Determine whether you are spending too much of each day thinking about interpersonal issues (other people you work or compete with) and too little on the real meat of your work. If so, consciously try to put on new social filters; remind yourself when you are drifting into social preoccupation.

• Try regular physical exercise, especially since a sensible diet and moderate exercise are currently recommended as the cure for everything (let's add output failure to the list). It may or may not help.

• Collaborate with a person whose strong output channels differ from your own. Have a frank discussion with him to identify both his and your particular assets. Then set up a project, perhaps as follows: "Joe, you're the hotshot verbalist, so why don't you go ahead and plan the oral presentation; I'll use my great hands and design sense to create the graphics and the scale model. You should give the sales pitch."

• Review the contents of this book. The suggestions pertaining to students can be adapted to enhance output in adults.

Coaching

Some people employ personal trainers to help them exercise and care for their bodies. I believe that many individuals could use the services of personal mind trainers. Dr. Ned Hallowell and his colleagues in the Boston area have been training people to serve as coaches for struggling adults. In a similar vein, a number of universities, including the University of North Carolina, have been coaching college students with a strong emphasis on organizational skills (such as prioritizing and multitasking), handling the workload, and working well with colleagues. I pointed out how this kind of service was implemented for Sharon's son, Mark.

Healing Emotional Scars

Not surprisingly, grown-ups who have suffered decades of output failure are likely to have more than their share of emotional trauma. Many become depressed. I find that their sadness often hides their underlying neurodevelopmental problems. Someone whose communication weaknesses have stood in the way of productivity may reveal the classic signs of depression. I can recall one graduate student in biology who was having a hard time and feeling so despondent that he'd even contemplated taking his own life. He was put on generous doses of antidepressant medication—with some equivocal improvement. But an evaluation revealed that his depression was not the primary problem; his profound sadness was a reaction to the failure of his wiring to meet current expectations. He had sustained significant lifelong problems with his memory and his ability to explain phenomena verbally. He never knew why he always had to struggle in school, but he'd survived with true grit. Now, with an increased workload and the need to give lectures to undergraduates and to present research findings at national meetings, he began to slip precipitously. This was a classic case in which medication couldn't mend the breakdown; it served only to cover it up temporarily.

Facing Family Impacts

When a parent and offspring share an output dysfunction, as we saw in the case of Sharon and Mark, they should work together on it. I remember one nine-year-old girl whose low output resulted from a problem with language production. Her father confessed to me that he too was "a man of few words." And he had endured more than his fair share of academic stress as a child and teenager. He now recognized that his poor grades and low output were attributable to his language short-comings. It was his idea to work together with his daughter to see if they might fix their shared word drought. So they launched extended discussions (using only full sentences) several times a week —mainly in the car, at the dinner table, and at bedtime. The girl's mother, who seemed to manifest the opposite trait (verbal flooding), decided that she needed to do more listening and less talking at meals. These communication special events became a family project. The father later reported to me that he had seen some clear benefit for him and his daughter, and that their joint output campaign had had the unanticipated effect of bringing them closer as a family.

WORK ETHICS AND ACCOUNTABILITY

In downplaying the notion of laziness, do we run the risk of some-how excusing low output in a student or adult? Are we implying that since the problem is not willful, the individual should be exempted from the acceptance of responsibility for productivity? Should a child be encouraged to announce to his teacher, "Look, I can't do that project you assigned because I have problems with time management. Sorry, I was born that way; it's not my fault"? I would not have written *The Myth of Laziness* if I felt that its ideas would justify such cop-outs.

I believe that once an individual understands the sources of her output failure, she can be held more accountable, not less so. Her teacher might say to the child with a time management problem, "I'm really sorry about your trouble getting organized with time, but please tell me what you're doing about it. Also, let me know how I can help." But she still can be expected to complete that project. Most children and adults want to feel accountable and prefer not to be treated like invalids. They possess a work ethic, one that keeps reminding them that they must find their ways of producing. To live in a society is to contribute to it, to do one's share at any age. And that's accomplished through good work and good works—whether or not you are plagued with output failure!

THE HOPE

Laziness is a myth. No one really wants to close down his or her assembly line. All children and every adult can savor the special joy, the many dividends, the satisfaction that come with productivity, but only when and if they find the output channels that work for their kinds of minds. Benefiting from understanding and compassionate guidance, every individual can be a producer of worthy and gratifying products. Periodically, children and adults ought to take stock and determine whether the nature and quantity of their current output call for rethinking. As our lives unfold, each chapter reflects both our accumulated output and our work in progress. We have it in us to enrich the content of these chapters in ourselves and in those we care about.

EPILOGUE
OUTPUT'S OUTCOMES

So we beat on, boats against the current, borne back ceaselessly into the past.
—F. SCOTT FITZGERALD, *THE GREAT GATSBY*

At last he rose, and twitch'd his mantle blue;
Tomorrow to fresh woods, and pastures new.
—JOHN MILTON, "LYCIDAS"

If I should labor through daylight and dark,
Consecrate, valorous, serious, true,
Then on the world I may blazon my mark;
And what if I don't, and what if I do?
—DOROTHY PARKER

You cannot be a seasoned pediatrician without regularly wondering what became of a former patient as an adult. Aside from plain old curiosity, knowing the later chapters of the life stories of kids you once cared for (and about) helps you help the succeeding generations. All that precious follow-up information yields revealing hindsight into what worked and what didn't.

So I wonder which victims of juvenile output failure turned things around (possibly with my help), overcame their barriers to productivity, and claimed their share of gratifying kudos? And I wonder about those who failed to make the grade, the ones who could not handle the output demands of grown-up life? Are there some whose output failure didn't go away, who somehow failed to overcome or outgrow that low flow? I feel fortunate that I have heard from scores of my former patients who are now well into adult life, including many who exhibited output failure when I knew them as kids. I've learned that I can never have much certainty about how a mind will turn out and what that mind will turn out to do. Yet there are patterns that seem to recur.

A constant tension plays between what a person was like as a child and what she or he turns into (and turns out) as an adult. So many of our traits and so many of the problems they posed for us early in life seem to keep intruding, returning periodically as we age. At the same time, though, we mature and acquire new abilities, possibilities, interests, and life circumstances.

Taking all these different factors into account, I want to sketch some likely later-life scenarios for the patients I described earlier in this book.

RUSSELL

Russell, the sometime-depressed boy with gross motor and graphomotor dysfunctions, along with some troubling body image setbacks, had plenty of strengths to deploy as he grew up. Despite his writing difficulties he was an impressive learner and could more than keep pace with school's reading demands. The boy had many assets: he was creative and insightful, and he had no trouble retaining facts and most skills. Russell, like his dad before him, wanted to pursue a career in medicine. There's every reason to believe he would have succeeded in doing so. His illegible handwriting might even be construed as a qualification for membership in the healing profession!

Russell might have met with some problems during his various surgical rotations in medical school, those courses in which your hands need to obey verbal orders and your mind is called upon to store your personal repertoire of complex motor plans, the ones needed for tying surgical knots, sewing lacerations, and implementing all sorts of therapeutic procedures. But he would have performed well in such courses as pediatrics, internal medicine, family medicine, and psychiatry; and it's more than likely that he opted for a career in one of those latter relatively motor-sparing specialties. When I was in medical school, I was impressed with how many athletes pursued surgical careers. Maybe that's why I became a pediatrician! It's also conceivable that Russell sought an alternative performance arena that could accommodate his interest in people, his good communication abilities, and his mathematical competency. Plenty of options exist for using his strengths and for others with profiles similar to his.

I have noticed that in many cases grown-ups who were like Russell and had trouble competing in sports try to find careers that are not overtly competitive. They've suffered too many ego wounds striking out in the bottom of the ninth inning or failing to return volleyball serves to take competitive risks as adults. That may be a reason for some to shy away from the business world or from trying to work their way up a steep and highly competitive corporate ladder.

I believe that through demystification I have helped Russell and others like him to weather the inevitable storms, to cope, and to forgive themselves when their dysfunctions temporarily get in the way of success. Russell entirely understood his specific motor breakdowns after I explained them to him. He could then anticipate their impacts, and instead of feeling utterly hapless, he regarded his inabilities as gaps that exist outside his mind's specialties, that is, problems he has doing things he probably wasn't wired to be doing in the first place. That realization fortifies self-esteem, especially if he thinks about all that he can do commendably within his strong areas.

In all likelihood an individual like Russell had to keep on contending with his body image issues. Having endured the shame of obesity, enuresis (bed-wetting), illegible handwriting, and athletic ineptitude, he was left with a profound sense of bodily defectiveness. There are many adults like Russell who make a concerted effort to lose weight, to exercise conscientiously, and even to discover an activity through which to affirm some form of motor efficacy (perhaps a musical instrument, artistic medium, or individual sport). I can't help believing that, if they are to make a healthy life adjustment, all individuals with serious body image preoccupations need to prove to themselves that they are not defective beings.

As for the writing process, we can bet that Russell's writing is at least faster and more efficient than it once was, albeit not that much more aesthetically appealing. Concerted intervention to improve the motor components of writing should have served him well in college and beyond. There's a good chance he is the owner of a dictation machine and a well-worn laptop computer. Adulthood commonly permits the use of a much more extensive toolbox for bypassing your weak spots than what was available and permissible in school.

CLINT

I see many kids like Clint, the irrepressible cowboy who revered and adored animals and who yearned to become a veterinarian despite the substantial memory dysfunctions that were taxing his output exorbitantly. In my opinion, if we can preserve and respect their lofty aspirations and their zealous motivation, the outlook for kids like Clint should be bright. For one thing, the good news is that few careers demand the constant loading and unloading of rote memory, those ritual memorization operations that take place multiple times per day in school and are so frustrating for kids with good understanding but poor memory. Lucky for them, when you go for a job interview, your prospective bosses are unlikely to inquire about the state of your rote memory. Employers understandably are more interested in thinking skills, interpersonal relationships, and track record. In fact, when schools place a heavy emphasis on memory, I wonder just what it is they are trying to prepare students for in adult life.

I feel very uneasy about a young person whose career preparation requirements fail to coincide with his strengths. So often it's not the actual profession that will defeat him but instead the rigid academic path he will have to follow to gain entry to that career. Such was the case with Clint, an outdoorsman, a hands-on learner who aspired to go to veterinary school, where he would need to memorize large amounts of factual material from texts. A memory overload could precipitate his academic downfall. I've seen some students with memory shortfalls survive their years in medical school, law school, or other fact-heavy curricula; miraculously, their tenacity prevails. But others drop out.

I had spent a great deal of time helping Clint understand the manifestations of his memory difficulties and providing him with strategies to enhance the filing of information in his mind. These insights and techniques seemed to benefit Clint in school, but we could not be certain they would continue to operate well as the memory load intensified in a graduate program. Nor could I know whether Clint would ripen as a user of increasingly sophisticated memory strategies to meet the heavier burden.

Since I try never to dampen ambition, I hope kids like Clint will pursue their passions and then accommodate to reality over time if need be. After all, Clint could have satisfied his thirst for animal work by managing a ranch, becoming a veterinary assistant, or selling farm equipment. Another stellar feature of adulthood is that there is more than one way to fulfill an interest. I would expect that when the educational memory burdens were lifted, we would have witnessed a dramatic upsurge in Clint's output. I've been told of this exhilarating rebound effect in a number of my former patients.

GINNY

Ginny was that insatiable and entirely delightful girl who had trouble turning on and maintaining sufficient mental energy to accomplish tasks in school. She also was socially distractible, and she had problems with active working memory (difficulty holding several things in her mind at once while using them). Kids like her are often seen as scatterbrained, restless, lazy (of course), and far too preoccupied with their friends. Adults like her remain vulnerable to persistent output failure, but at the same time they may transform some of their previously crippling traits into beneficial characteristics. Numerous individuals describe themselves as "night people" and will tell you they have been denizens of the wee hours all of their lives. Ginny and other nocturnal creatures might have displayed much higher levels of output during childhood if they could have attended night school! Instead, they were forced to follow the academic routines and rhythms of the day kids. They frequently endure agonizing frustration trying to fall and/or stay asleep and are at their best during the late evening hours. As adults, they may well use those periods to accomplish weighty tasks, to work the night shift, to write compelling novels or screenplays. That's why I kept reassuring Ginny that her attentional problems in no way meant that she had some kind of brain damage or disorder. To the contrary, they represented a different way to be wired, a way that was causing glitches in school but also a way that might work well for her someday. Such a realization might have prevented Ginny from giving up on herself.

Ginny's insatiability made it hard for her to finish work in school when that work was not particularly exciting or amusing; she routinely felt bored and restless within an academic environment. I have seen such insatiability cause many an undergraduate to drop out of college after having managed to eke out a high school diploma. It's my impression, in fact, that insatiability is a common cause of both college and career failure. Almost as soon as such an individual settles into a routine, he may start thinking of all the exciting things he'd much rather be doing. Insatiable adults may also be prone to excessive risk taking and substance abuse, including alcoholism. However, insatiability can mutate over time into drive and ambition; if you decide you want things badly enough you may well get most of them. That is, if all goes well, insatiability can fuel an intense craving for success, thereby turning on the faucets of motivation. Many highly productive adults have had a history of insatiability. The puzzling and common paradoxical trait can jet-propel you to success or failure. I like to think that kids who are understood and supported by adults and kids who have the firmest grasp on their own insatiability are most likely to convert this seeming deficit into a major strength. On the other hand, those who grow up hearing nothing but criticism of their ways are more likely to write themselves off and give in to immediate gratification in life. I made sure Ginny was knowledgeable regarding the pros and cons of her insatiability. Her parents helped reinforce this thinking.

I recall vividly a girl much like Ginny who seemed to be taking decades to pass through college. She, too, was a night person, a highly insatiable girl who was easily distracted by her friends. Like Ginny, she had a creative spark waiting to be ignited. Ultimately, she became a high school drama teacher and received many awards for her spectacular productions of the standard repertoire. She also wrote and produced several hilarious musical comedies. Her adolescent students idolized her and seemed to respond to her frenzied pace. She loved working with the many socially obsessed teenagers. Her lifelong social distractibility had instilled in her a deep understanding of people and their innermost feelings. She had profound empathy for the students with whom she worked and she helped many of them who were not succeeding in other parts of the high school curriculum. Members of the community were impressed when they drove past the school late at night and observed the lights in the auditorium, where this teacher was designing costumes and scenery for the next school play. Recall that Ginny had to deal with gaps in her active working memory. So did this girl, but they never impeded her effectiveness as a drama teacher. Wherever she went she carried with her a clipboard (her portable active working memory) and compulsively made use of checklists, writing down every task and decisively crossing off each on completion. Output failure was a thing of her past.

SCOTT

Scott was another insatiable student, a boy engaged in a never-ending quest for ecstatic pleasure. His insatiability earned him costly speeding summonses, contributed to his drug problem, and made it nearly impossible for him to function as a productive student. His family's wealth seemed to aggravate Scott's insatiability. An overdose of monumentally entertaining life experiences plus a surplus of enviable material possessions were like lighter fluid fueling his flaming appetites. The more he got, the less satisfied he felt.

Scott's production control problems complicated his insatiability, leading him to become a highly impulsive, reckless kind of guy, one who did too many things too fast without enough forethought. But Scott had his allocation of redeeming strengths, including his world-class interpersonal style and highly effective communication skills. Which ultimately would win out, his strengths or his deficits?

Knowing many kids like Scott, I would guess that he would have accumulated a rather disastrous record in college if he elected to enroll (which he probably would do because of his family tradition of doing so). As an undergraduate, he would experience far too much freedom and not know what to do with it. He would find it impossible to filter out all the work-contaminating social temptations that can grab unwary undergraduates like the suction cups on the arms of an octopus. He would most likely devote himself mainly to being ultracool and rising to the summits of peer adulation and popularity; he might consider his academic work a low priority. Moreover, believing that he could never come close to matching the accomplishments of his parents and his older brother, Scott might have elected not to try, concluding that it looks and feels better to do little or nothing than to make an effort and come up short. So Scott's output failure may well have lingered beyond high school.

During my meetings with Scott, I tried repeatedly to warn him of the future dangers I saw. I think he could hear what I was saying, but I am not sure he could internalize any of it. Sometimes guys like him need to hit rock bottom; they have to personally experience some calamitous consequences before they can see where they're headed. Nevertheless, we have to keep trying to warn them.

Scott and other kids with production control problems desperately need to find a groove in which they can generate some good output. They must discover an area within which, for some seemingly magical reason, their minds are able to decelerate, exercise good judgment, and produce high-quality output. I have worked with Scott and others like him to launch them on the search for output channels that will work.

I remember a boy much like Scott whose output surged when he went to work for a hotel chain. He had always loved to travel and he was endlessly sociable. Working around the world in hotels, he became highly productive and was promoted regularly in his chosen field, the hospitality industry. Never could there have been a better fit. The last I heard of him he was a partner in a successful restaurant where he insisted on being the maître d'.

I believe that Scott might have been helped immeasurably with more encouragement and approval from his father and his older brother. They might have demonstrated greater respect for this boy and helped him seek ways he could have offered something meaningful and unique to their various businesses—if Scott wanted to. My guess is that Scott would have risen to the occasion if given an opportunity. People have trouble believing in themselves when those closest to them don't believe in them.

DARNELL

Students like Darnell, plagued with expressive language problems, have much to overcome if they are to become productive. Some find careers that entail working alone and focusing on activities that don't call for much literate language production. Fortunately, countless adult pursuits demand far less heavy-duty verbal output than is required in most classrooms. But language production woes may carry with them some serious troubles anyway. As I have pointed out, numerous studies have linked expressive language dysfunctions to destructive aggression, including violent crime. Darnell was already manifesting this disturbing behavior pattern when his mother first told me about him. This boy's vulnerability only amplified growing up in a violent neighborhood and lacking positive and approving male role models. Fortunately, Darnell had the unswerving confidence and love of his mother and his sisters. They were his loyal fan club. Everyone needs one.

I know of an individual much like Darnell who eventually pursued a career as a social worker so he could help kids similar to him overcome their disadvantaged beginnings. He, like Darnell, had effective social English despite his literate language shortcomings. He could use his strong social language ability to communicate masterfully with adolescents. Over time he even improved in his literate language performance and became an avid reader of historical novels. This man exhibited the very special phenomenon we call resiliency, a potentially potent internal force described earlier. We don't really know what it is that makes some individuals more resilient than others, why and how they pull themselves up by their bootstraps and emerge from poverty or overcome serious dysfunctions or both, while others facing similar life obstacles plummet deeper and deeper into spirals of failure. No doubt, getting help makes a difference. So does believing in yourself and preserving a sense of optimism regarding your future possibilities.

ROBERTA

Roberta was highly focused, and her kind of mind resonated with the precision of biochemistry. That was her area of concentration in college and beyond. She was likely to remain committed to a career as a scientist. Recall that in high school, Roberta was found lacking in independent thinking, the generation of original ideas. Would this be a handicap in the laboratory? Or might it turn out to be an asset? It could be argued that her tendency to focus intently on the facts at hand could make her a razor-sharp analyst of research data, a role that might not call for creative thinking. Not every scientist needs to be a tremendous innovator.

Some of my friends and professional colleagues engage in scientific research. I have observed the differences that exist between them. Some, as I described Roberta (page 114), can be thought of as predominantly bottom-up in their thought processes. That is, they are entirely rigorous and narrowly focused at gathering and interpreting scientific data. However, their work tends to be based very closely on other people's work or on refinements of their own previous output. They are not great intellectual risk takers, but they nevertheless can make vital contributions to our knowledge, a little bit at a time. They have been described as inchworms rather than grasshoppers. Then there are the top-down thinkers (including, for better or for worse, this author), those who keep seeking paradigm shifts, we intellectual grasshoppers whose instincts are to infuse our own original ideas, scouting new ways to interpret information and novel experiments to launch, trying to change the state of the art by leaps and bounds. Our work may not be tied to the previous efforts of others or even necessarily to our own earlier endeavors. We call such thinkers "top-down" because much of what they produce derives more from brainstorms in their heads than from analyzing details on a page. Top-down thinkers are at their happiest synthesizing ideas that are out of the box; they love going out on a limb, taking intellectual risks. And they tend to prefer the career road less traveled.

I suspect that most people fall in neither of these two categories; they are able to blend top-down with bottom-up processes. But both extremes can prosper in the sciences (and in many other fields). In fact, top-down and bottom-up individuals can become highly productive partners. So we might hope that Roberta would team up with someone who seeks opportunities to engage in some intellectual leaps. She would then provide the intellectual sobriety, the precise methodology. She would search the background literature and carefully generate the experimental data needed to advance or refute the ideas of her divergent partner. Highly disciplined scientists like her savor the rigor of their work; they find their results and those of their fellow bottom-up peers to be elegant. Many of them believe that it is sloppy and perhaps irresponsible to be too broadly focused and to seek to advance knowledge by leaps and bounds.

I suspect that even Roberta, as she became increasingly comfortable with her subject matter, might come up with some fertile ideas for study, although it is unlikely they would be all that radical. In the long run, what counts is the harmony between your particular style of synthesizing useful output and your own sense of fulfillment and gratification. We must be able to look back at our accomplishments and find them attractive. Such productivity becomes habit-forming.

SHARON AND MARK

Organizational problems may last a lifetime. We can all get more "together," but ugly remnants of disorganization may keep on reappearing, depositing land mines along the pathways of productivity. We might suspect, therefore, that Sharon and Mark continued to wage battles with their deficiencies in time and material management and their difficulties in prioritizing and managing complex tasks. They may have been susceptible to lifelong output failure. But both were highly intelligent and motivated individuals. Through sheer competency and the mobilization of their many strengths, they might have been able to override their chaotic life and work styles. Even the most absentminded professors can be highly productive.

Ultimately, while working with Sharon I harbored the suspicion that she was getting burned out. I think such burnout eventually cripples

many highly disorganized adults. They seem predisposed to tumultuous midlife crises. To deal with this gradual deterioration, Sharon may
have sought a new career, applying her extraordinary understanding
and love of people to a dramatically new venue. She could be out front
in an art gallery, a restaurant, an employment agency, or a boutique but
only with the close collaboration of a skilled manager capable of tying
together Sharon's loose ends. I knew one very astute social worker who
started to feel overwhelmed and overworked as a clinician, so she became a real estate agent. She later told me that she used her social work
diagnostic skill to figure out what kind of house people were likely to
buy and what she needed to say to convince them to purchase one that
was a bit more expensive than what they had in mind! By the way, this
social worker who, like Sharon, had trouble writing timely reports, told
me she appreciated an occupation in which she filled out forms. The
forms provided the framework she had always needed. She also worked
with two partners who were meticulously organized. One of them, her
sister-in-law, actually arranged her desk for her several times a month!

I bet Mark had a hard time in college. The demands of undergraduate
life can inflict cruel and unusual punishment on a disorganized kid.
Others and I worked with Mark to enhance his organizational tactics.
This seemed to help him negotiate high school. But it is not unusual for
a student to enter college and make believe he has never had any output problems. Denial takes control, and the student spurns any offers of
assistance, interprets adult advice as a put-down, and exhibits steadily
declining output. While I knew him as a teenager, Mark showed consistent improvement, but the very heavy workload is one of the major
challenges of college life. Also, students often find they have far more
time to use up in college than they ever enjoyed in high school. Having
excessive time is hazardous to your academic health if you are a person
who has never been able to organize time. Kids like Mark may notice
that there is nothing due in October, so they are apt to do nothing in
October!

Often the most accomplished college students are those who deploy effective tactics that allow them to plan their work, orchestrate
their time, take good notes, study systematically for examinations, and
achieve an optimal mix of work and debauchery. I call such students
methodologists; they have conscious ways of doing things rather than
just doing them. These methodology tools might not be found in
Mark's academic kit.

I have discovered that many students like Mark enter college and then have to leave. In my experience most of these students ultimately graduate but seldom from the school they entered and almost never in four years. Their undergraduate experience is a roller-coaster ride for them and for their parents, but over time, with determination, they seem able to tame the workload. On the other hand, there are under-graduates who come into their own when they find an area of concen-tration that feels right for them and when they are able to relate closely to one or more members of the faculty. Students like Mark are most likely to succeed if they get some kind of coaching to help them sur-mount the organizational challenges in college.

I recall a number of my disorganized patients who have had to reckon with their disorganization in selecting a career. Often their choices reflect unconscious ways of coping with their inefficiencies. Several such kids I knew enlisted in the military, believing that some-how the routine, the discipline, and the predictability of a military ca-reer would enable them "to get their act together." This may work, although I remember one young woman who was asked to leave the Air Force because, despite repeated stern warnings, she never got any-where or finished anything on time.

I also have had several patients who felt so overwrought when faced with workloads that they sought out less-complicated lives. I know of one man who fled his suburban middle-class milieu and values and dropped out of college at age twenty to join a commune. His parents were crushed and did not see or hear from him for years. This intellec-tually profound person became a potato farmer on that commune and committed himself to a religious doctrine that stressed the simple life. In this setting he was able to rid himself of the oppressive sense of being too often too far behind, unable ever to catch up and accomplish what needed to be accomplished, a highly unsettling feeling that was suffo-cating throughout his school days. Also, this young man fully believed that he had been a bitter disappointment to his parents and that he could never begin to live up to their expectations. In a previous chapter, I mentioned the flight of Fran (page 155). She kept running away from home and chose a life of rebellion at least in part because she felt the need to sidestep competition and its risks. This maneuver is a time bomb, one that often becomes self-defeating. It is often fueled by a dis-torted notion: If you believe there's no way you can please your parents, why not just disgrace or punish them? It makes little sense, but that way of thinking predominates all too often.

I wonder how many people who seek such alternative lifestyles are doing so at least in part because they lack the strategies needed to deal with complex demands. In some worst-case scenarios, disorganized kids strategically retreat into drugs, alcohol, and other self-destructive tactics as a means of escaping and trying to simplify their lives. They are almost always encouraged to self-destruct by a loyal cohort of peers, who themselves have suffered the pain and futility of misunderstood output failure. In every community, such individuals find each other. They congregate and they actually often complicate rather than simplify their existences. We need to help them taste the flavors of productivity, output that garners praise, before they feel compelled to stray into such hazardous trails through life. All kids can experience the pleasures of high-quality high output. Some need our concerted assistance in finding and encouraging their unique ways of being productive.

SOME LESSONS TO BE LEARNED

I have learned so much about human aspirations and their realization or frustration just by following the progress of my patients over time. The people described in this book (composites of those I have worked with) offer us a host of valuable lessons about growing up with output failure. Here are some highlights of these lessons:

A FEW LESSONS LEARNED ABOUT OUTPUT AND OUTPUT FAILURE OVER TIME

- Underlying neurodevelopmental sources of output failure may linger into adult life, but with the right kind of insight and help, their effects on productivity can be minimized.
- Some individuals reveal a remarkable degree of resiliency and surmount their output failure—having supportive parents and teachers— adults who demonstrate that they admire and respect you—can only help in the long run.
- If we are able to preserve their self-esteem, their optimism about the future, and their motivation, children with output failure can grow up to become tremendously productive people.

- Many adults generate commendable output by working closely with individuals who have very different neurodevelopmental profiles from their own.

- Some individuals with long-standing output difficulty become slow and sometimes inefficient producers. The quality of their work ultimately may be commendable, but they seem to require inordinate time to get their jobs done. Such people need time lines (indicating what part of a task needs to be done by when) as if they are lifelines. They have to concentrate on staging and pacing their output at a reasonable rhythm or else shape their careers in such a way that they are not constantly holding up the work of those who depend upon them.

- There is a hidden brain process called the "speed-quality trade-off" that enables a productive person to achieve the optimal balance between the quality of a job and the rate at which it is accomplished. Productive children and adults virtually intuitively know how to achieve this balance, sometimes even modifying their perfectionist ways to complete something in a timely manner. Others work too frenetically, wanting just to get the task over with; such high-speed workers sometimes may need to decelerate and strive for higher quality. We all face the challenge of attaining the delicate balance between speed and quality when undertaking significant output challenges.

- What appear to be dysfunctions during childhood may transform themselves into assets as individuals mature. There are ways to make such transformations likely.

- People with output failure may become exceptionally productive when they grow up and discover a brain-compatible niche, that special specialty that seems to resonate with their kind of mind. They may need help discovering their productive pathway, and they are likely to need encouragement to stick with it.

- Students with output failure should understand clearly their own strengths and weaknesses, especially so that they do not overrate their shortcomings, thinking of themselves as hopelessly incompetent.

- When students have clear insights into their mind's wiring, they are more likely to devise and apply personal tactics to facilitate high-quality output.

- A career offers far more flexibility than does education; there are all kinds of ways of making a living out of an interest in cars, animals, design, technology, or any other affinity. Kids need to be made aware of the diversity of opportunities.

- Biographies contain chapters; it is possible to pursue different forms of productivity at different times of life. Starting a new chapter at any point in life may uncover and revive a host of underutilized capacities, and that boosts output.

- At its best, work is fun. When you enjoy your work, productivity can become child's play. I often tell kids that when I drive to work in the morning, it never feels as if I am going to work. That's the truth, and that helps me be productive.

- Laziness is in the mind of the accuser; hopefully the target of an accusation of laziness will not respond by resigning himself to a low-output existence, thus fulfilling this accusation. When you say someone is lazy, you admit that you don't understand him!

A SISYPHUS REPRISE

I started this book by referring to the Greek king Sisyphus, who was condemned to use his head and his hands incessantly to roll a massive boulder up a mountain. The French author and philosopher Albert Camus, one of my personal heroes, believed that something of Sisyphus infects the lives of all of us. It may seem unjust and senseless at times, but we are all condemned to struggle. We all at times contend with demands that elude and frustrate us. We all know what it feels like to feel overwhelmed.

Some of our goals recede to the horizon as we pursue them. We may shoulder the blame or decide to blame ourselves for our failures to produce what is expected of us or what we expect from ourselves. But somehow, like Sisyphus, using our heads and our hands, we manage to keep on rolling boulders up mountains. Albert Camus concluded *The Myth of Sisyphus* with the provocative mandate, *"Il faut imaginer Sisyphe heureux"* ("We must imagine Sisyphus happy"). I will conclude *The Myth of Laziness* with a modified version of this thought: "We must imagine Sisyphus happy—and productive."

APPENDIX A
THE WRITING TROUBLESHOOTER

PART ONE

The following statements about writing were made about kids like you in school. Please read each of these and check off how true each sentence is for you. Keep in mind, this is *not a test, so there are no right or wrong answers to any of these statements.* Just think hard about what it's like when you write, and be honest. Thank you.

STATEMENTS				
Finger Movements While Writing	**0**	**1**	**2**	**3**
1. Kids sometimes complain that their hand gets very tired when they have to write a lot.				
2. Some students have an unusual way of holding a pencil or pen.				
3. There are kids who think they write too slowly on tests and homework.				
4. Some people can print much better than they can use cursive.				
5. Lots of students say forming letters is not as easy for them as it is for other kids.				
Putting Your Ideas into Words	**0**	**1**	**2**	**3**
6. There are students who find it hard to get their ideas into words when they speak in school.				
7. Some kids make too many grammar mistakes when they write.				
8. While they write, some students have to think too long about how to say their ideas on paper.				

(continued)

Statements (continued)				
Putting Your Ideas into Words (continued)	0	1	2	3
9. When some people write, they have trouble using good vocabulary; they use only easy words.				
10. A lot of students put simple ideas down because they have trouble figuring out how to say complicated ideas when they write.				
Thinking Up Ideas to Write About	0	1	2	3
11. Some students find it very hard to think up topics or decide what they want to write.				
12. There are kids who would hate to have to write a story.				
13. It can be very difficult to know what to write or include in a report.				
14. A lot of kids says it's not easy for them to come up with their own original ideas about things when they write.				
15. Some people say it's really hard to write about their opinions or what they think about things.				
Remembering While You Write	0	1	2	3
16. It is confusing to remember so many things at once (like spelling, punctuation, vocabulary, etc.) while writing.				
17. Some kids have much neater handwriting when they copy from the board than when they write a paragraph.				
18. When writing a report or story it's hard for some kids to remember the ideas they have while they are writing.				
19. Some kids have said that they have much better ideas when they speak than when they write.				
20. Problems with spelling make writing especially hard for some people.				

STATEMENTS (CONTINUED)				
Organizing	**0**	**1**	**2**	**3**
21. It is extremely hard to do all the different things you have to do while you are writing.				
22. When they write, some students have trouble getting their thoughts down in the right order.				
23. Some students don't think much in advance about what they are going to write; they just start writing.				
24. There are students who have trouble getting together the books, paper, and other tools they need to write things.				
25. It is hard to know how long it will take to write a report or a story.				
Concentrating	**0**	**1**	**2**	**3**
26. It can be really hard to get started with a writing assignment.				
27. Many kids have trouble handling all the little details in writing.				
28. Some kids feel bored and tired whenever they try to do much writing.				
29. A student may race through a writing assignment without much thinking or planning.				
30. Some kids never or hardly ever proofread anything they write.				

PART ONE

1. Is there any kind of writing that you enjoy doing? If so, what is it?

2. What's the hardest part about writing for you? What's the easiest?

3. Is there anything you've learned to do that makes writing easier for you?

4. Do you feel embarrassed when other kids look at things you've written?

5. If you were having trouble writing a report, what could you do?

6. Have you used a computer for writing? Has this made writing easier for you? Do you have any problems with using a keyboard?

7. You need muscle coordination for writing, for playing sports, and for doing art or fixing things. Which of these things do your muscles work well for and which are especially difficult for your muscles?

8. Do you have any other comments about your writing?

APPENDIX B
THE STORY DEVELOPER

Student's Name _____ Date _____

Class _____ Due Date _____

Assignment or Topic _____

Probable Length _____ (pages or words)

Reader(s):   Teacher   Classmates   Parent(s)

Other(s) _____

A. STAGING AND SCHEDULING: TIME LINE

Writing Stage	Estimated Time Needed for Stage	Estimated Date and Time of Completion	Actual Date Completed
Brainstorming			
Outlining or Listing			
Rough Draft			
Refining Ideas and Language			
Second Draft			
Sanding and Polishing			
Final Version			

B. Preliminary or Working Title

_____

_____

C. Major Characters

Character	Brief Description
1.	
2.	
3.	
4.	
5.	

D. Background

Setting _____ Place _____ Time _____

E. Events and/or Conflicts

1. _____

2. _____

3. _____

4. _____

5. _____

6. _____

F. ORDER OF EVENTS

1. _____

2. _____

3. _____

4. _____

5. _____

6. _____

_____

G. PREVIEW OF THE ENDING

_____

_____

Preliminary last line of story _____

_____

H. OTHER INTERESTING OR ENTERTAINING DETAILS

1. _____

2. _____

3 _____

4. _____

5. _____

6. _____

I. FINAL TITLE

J. SATISFACTION WITH RESULTS
(TO BE FILLED OUT BY WRITER UPON COMPLETION)

Very Pleased _____ *Good Enough* _____ *Disappointing* _____
How Difficult It Was (1 = Very Hard; 2 = Hard; 3 = Not Hard)

Writing Step	How Hard It Was
Writing or Keyboard Speed	
Writing or Typing Neatness	
Using Punctuation	
Using Good Grammar	
Spelling Accurately	
Using Story Developer	
Choosing Title	
Thinking Up Story	
Getting Events in Order	
Writing Enough	
Concentrating on Work	
Proofreading and Revising	

Was this fun to write? Very much _____ *Some* _____ *Not at all* _____

Other comments: _____

APPENDIX C
THE REPORT DEVELOPER

Writer _____ Date _____

Subject or Topic _____ Deadline _____

Assigned by _____

Probable Length _____ (pages or words)

A. STAGING AND SCHEDULING: TIME LINE

Writing Stage	Estimated Time Needed for Stage	Estimated Date and Time of Completion	Actual Date Completed
Brainstorming			
Research			
Outlining or Listing Points			
Rough Draft			
Refining Ideas and Language			
Outside Review(s)			
Second Draft			
Sanding and Polishing			
Final Version			

B. TOPIC REFINEMENT

Narrowing and Focusing of Subject:

_____

_____

_____

_____

_____

C. FRAMING OF QUESTION(S) TO BE ANSWERED IN REPORT

1. _____

2. _____

3. _____

4. _____

5. _____

6. _____

D. INFORMATION RESOURCES

Kind of Information	Anticipated Sources of Information	Used
1.		
2.		
3.		
4.		
5.		
6.		
7.		
8.		

E. KNOWLEDGE SYNOPSIS
(PERSONAL STATEMENT AND SUMMARY OF THE STATE OF WHAT'S KNOWN)

F. REPORT WRITER'S VIEWS AND OPINIONS

G. Practical or Personal Implications and Ideas

_____

_____

_____

_____

H. Satisfaction with Results
(to be filled out by writer upon completion)

_Excellent _____ Good _____ Fair _____ Disappointing _____
How Difficult It Was (1 = Very Hard; 2 = Hard; 3 = Not Hard)

Writing Step	How Hard It Was
Writing Fast Enough	
Writing or Typing Neatly	
Using Punctuation	
Using Vocabulary	
Using Good Grammar	
Spelling Accurately	
Using Report Developer	
Choosing and Refining Topic	
Doing Research	
Summarizing	
Forming Opinions	
Writing Enough	
Concentrating on Work	
Proofreading and Revising	

Was this report interesting to write?

_Definitely _____ Somewhat _____ Not at all _____

APPENDIX D
AN OUTPUT INVENTORY

An Output Inventory is intended to help pinpoint possible trouble spots that might be causing a child or a grown-up to put forth disappointing levels of output or "products" of poor quality. Such specific identification of one or more areas of weakness can aid in helping you understand yourself and suggest ways of improving the amount and the quality of your output.

This inventory pertains only to output at work. Many individuals with output problems show remarkable output when it comes to activities they find particularly entertaining or gratifying, such as sports, music, electronic games, or various hobbies. While these forms of productivity are highly valuable and rewarding, they are not the subjects of this inventory. Nor does the inventory take into consideration such important issues as motivation, self-esteem, work ethic, emotional health, and the quality of opportunities, all of which may exert some influence on output.

A teacher, a supervisor, a parent, or the individual child or adult in question may complete the inventory. In fact, it may be useful to compare the observations of several persons. The form on the next page is divided into areas, such as motor function and language. Each item should be scored by placing an X in the appropriate box on the right. Then add the scores of the five items listed to come up with a total score for that area. Use the key to interpret the scores for each area.

TOTALS KEY
12–15: Unlikely to be an area of concern
8–11: Most likely a source of output problems
Less than 8: Definitely a source of output problems

The final portion of the grid should be used to insert any additional current strengths or weaknesses that could have a bearing on this person's output.

Person Described _____ *Date* _____

Area	Function *(How is this* *person at . . . ?)*	Very Good	Pretty Good	Not So Good	Very Poor	*Totals*
		3	2	1	0	
Motor Function	Forming letters and words legibly					
	Forming letters and words fast enough					
	Keyboarding effortlessly and accurately					
	Holding pen or pencil in a "normal way"					
	Using hands for nonwriting jobs					
					Total Motor =	
Language	Expressing complicated ideas					
	Finding the right words					
	Speaking grammatically					
	Elaborating on and ex- plaining things to others					
	Using written language well					
					Total Language =	
Memory	Remembering several things at once					
	Recalling rules, details, and facts while writing					
	Spelling accurately while writing					
	Recalling facts					
	Remembering how to do things (processes)					
					Total Memory =	

Area	Function *(How is this person at . . . ?)*	Very Good	Pretty Good	Not So Good	Very Poor	*Totals*
		3	**2**	**1**	**0**	
Mental- Energy Control	Sleeping at night					
	Maintaining alertness while working					
	Finishing things					
	Performing in a consistent way					
	Getting started with a task					
					Total Energy =	
Production Control	Working at an ideal rate (not too fast or slow)					
	Planning before doing something					
	Detecting own errors (monitoring)					
	Learning from experience					
	Thinking about the best way to do something					
					Total Production =	
Ideation	Coming up with original ideas					
	Making good use of concepts					
	Pulling together ideas or thoughts					
	Creating sophisticated products					
	Solving work-related problems					
					Total Ideation =	

(continued)

Area	Function (How is this person at . . . ?)	Very Good	Pretty Good	Not So Good	Very Poor	Totals
		3	2	1	0	
Timing and Sequencing	Meeting deadlines					
	Allocating adequate time to tasks					
	Organizing ideas in the best order					
	Doing tasks one step at a time					
	Knowing how long something should take					
					Total Timing =	
Handling Materials	Keeping track of possessions					
	Knowing where and how to find things					
	Organizing paperwork					
	Maintaining an organized work space					
	Remembering needed materials					
					Total Materials =	
Additional Work Functions (Strong and/or Weak)						

General comments:

INDEX